TAOISM: THE ROAD TO IMMORTALITY

Taoism
The Road to Immortality

JOHN BLOFELD

Shambhala
Boston 2000

SHAMBHALA PUBLICATIONS, INC.
Horticultural Hall
300 Massachusetts Avenue
Boston, Massachusetts 02115
www.shambhala.com

ISBN 978-1-57062-589-3

Published by arrangement with
George Allen & Unwin Ltd. London

LCC 77-90882
Printed in the United States of America
⊗ This edition is printed on acid-free paper that meets the American National Standards Institute Z39.48 Standard.
Distributed in the United States by Random House, Inc.,
and in Canada by Random House of Canada Ltd

The cover art is a detail from "The Transformations of Lao-chun," a handscroll in ink and color on silk painted in the 12th century by Wang Li-yung. The photograph is reproduced courtesy of the Nelson-Atkins Museum of Art, Kansas City, Missouri (Nelson Trust).

Contents

List of Illustrations

To Huang Chung-liang (Al Huang)
of the Living Tao Foundation
and to my daughter Hsüeh-Ch'an (Susan),
also called Snow Beauty

Foreword

Taoism – ancient, mysterious, charmingly poetic – born amidst the shining mists that shroud civilisation's earliest beginnings, is a living manifestation of an antique way of life almost vanished from the world. Now that the red tide has engulfed its homeland, who knows its further destiny or whether even tiny remnants of it will survive? For people who recognise the holiness of nature and desire that spirit should triumph over the black onrush of materialism, it is a treasure-house wherein, amidst curiously wrought jewels of but slight intrinsic value, are strewn precious pearls and rare, translucent jades. Folklore, occult sciences, cosmology, yoga, meditation, poetry, quietist philosophy, exalted mysticism – it has them all. These are the gifts accumulated by the children of the Yellow Emperor during no less than five millenia. The least of them are rainbow-hued and the very stuff of myth and poetry; the most precious is a shining fulfilment of man's spiritual destiny, a teaching whereby humans can ascend from mortal to immortal state and dwell *beyond* the gods!

How strange that, with the single exception of the philosophy of those delightful sages, Lao and Chuang, so little of this has hitherto been touched upon in Western languages! Of Lao-tzû's *Tao Tê Ching* there are over fifty(!) translations and Chuang-tzû's work has begun to receive a modicum of the attention it deserves, but what of all the rest of Taoism? It seems that, by an ironic twist of fate, Taoists are still paying for their temerity in laughing at the humour-less rectitude of the Confucian establishment that was itself swept away at the beginning of this century. Smiling individualists who, like the young people of the world today, mocked rigidity and pomposity in all its forms, they were smeared by the ruling hierarchy as people lost in superstition fit only for illiterate peasants; and the fiction that Taoism has no more to offer than picturesque but worth-less superstitions has somehow stuck until today – just as, until very recently, Tibetan Buddhism was held to be Buddhism in its most degraded form! Ha ha ha ha ha! Curiously, though both Chinese and Western scholars have scornfully echoed the Confucian strictures on Taoism as a system utterly debased, I have rarely met anyone who, prior to the coming of the red flood, actually visited Taoist hermitages for more than a day or so to discover for themselves what went on there. As for me, I did quite often visit those remote and delightfully situated places and I arrived at the conclusion that, though the obloquy hurled at Taoism is occasionally justified, it is flagrantly false in most cases.

My first surprise was to discover that, despite a widespread supposition, Lao and Chuang were not the actual founders of Taoism, but notable blossoms on a tree hoary with age even in their day – around two and a half millenia ago! Indeed, Chuang-tzû himself makes frequent, if ironic, mention of its traditional founder, Huang Ti, the Yellow Emperor. Whether or not that excellent monarch ever existed as a *person* is beside the point. The dates of his reign (2697–2597 BC) place him in an epoch so remote and allow him to have reigned so long that it seems fair enough to regard him as a largely if not wholly mythical figure. But then? Supposing there never was such a person, the poetic legends surrounding him have endowed him with reality, and why should he not be accepted as an apt symbolic representative of the shadowy founders of Taoism long lost to sight in the darkness of prehistory? His followers speak of him poetically as a person. Would it hurt us to go along with them as we have gone along with the Romans in according a place in our history books to Romulus and Remus? The Taoists themselves like to refer to their system of belief as 'Huang Lao', thus honouring both Huang Ti (the Yellow Emperor) *and* Lao-tsû as their founders. This makes a lot more sense than saying that Taoism has degenerated from what it never was in the first place.

As I have said, by no means all Huang Lao beliefs and practices are of great worth. Some are too bizarre to call for more than a smile, which is scarcely surprising when one considers their enormous antiquity; yet, embedded in much charming moonshine is a precious core of wisdom and exalted spiritual aspiration so striking as to make me almost ready to believe that an 'Ancient Wisdom' was once dispersed throughout the world of which scattered fragments still remain. Huang Lao Taoism may be thought of as a kingdom wherein peasant-like naivety prevails throughout the far-flung provinces; in the central area lies a smiling parkland embellished with hills and streams where poets and lovers of nature's mysteries roam; and, in the midst of this, stands a citadel of wisdom so sublime as to lead beyond the world of mortals to the secret heart of Being. Strangers entering that kingdom without credentials are not likely to penetrate to the citadel without some effort (and courtesy!) on their part.

Even those Huang Lao beliefs that strike us as pure moonshine are touched with the magic of poetry and have long been a rich source of inspiration to painters, calligraphers and carvers of ivory and jade. They are rarely without charm and almost never ugly.

My earlier book of Taoism, *The Secret and Sublime*, was in most respects very different from this one; for when I wrote it I had little more to draw upon than recollections of my visits to hermitages tucked deep among the mountains and imperfectly remembered conversations with the lovable recluses dwelling there. I could speak only in very general terms about Taoist yoga and other matters pertaining to the spiritual path known as cultivation of the Way, for my primary interest in Buddhism had led me to neglect some unique opportunities of studying living Taoism thoroughly. This defect has since been repaired thanks to an invaluable gift sent to me by one of my former Chinese students – a book published by the Chung Hwa Book Company, Taipei, Taiwan, Republic of China, entitled *Tao-Chia Yü Shên-Hsien (Taoist Philosophers and Immortals)* by Chou Shao-hsien. The *Tao Tsang* or Taoist Canon, consisting of 5,485 volumes, is so vast that an Englishman with an imperfect knowledge of Chinese like myself could be excused for not even dreaming of plumbing its mysteries. Mr Chou Shao-hsien, however, has obviously spent many decades on that task, for his book contains the quintessence of what is to be found there. For various reasons it is not suitable for translation, unless for a very select English-reading public with a thorough knowledge of Chinese history and much else besides, but as source material it is invaluable, the more so as it contains carefully documented quotations from all the great Taoist masters through the ages. With that and some other works to fall back on and my own memories to lend colour to the scene, I have been able to write much more authentically of Taoism than before. To the best of my knowledge, the present work is the first attempt ever made to give a comprehensive sketch in English of Huang Lao Taoism as a whole.

The cream of my researches, of which the principal source is Mr Chou's work, will be found in the eighth and ninth chapters. The precious eight-stage Yoga of Immortality detailed in Chapter 8 can be practised to perfection only with the guidance of a gifted teacher; certain omissions have been inevitable, for the yoga is a secret one and some of its essentials can never have been committed to writing. Alas, Taoist teachers these days are almost as rare as horns on a rabbit or dugs on a serpent; even so, the written instructions are far from useless; even though they do not reveal all secrets, they can lead to a state of spiritual exaltation, whether the yoga is practised on its own as originally intended or as a support to some other meditative or yogic practice (Taoist, Buddhist or otherwise) of the yogin's own choosing. It is not impossible that this yoga, if carried out with unwavering determination by one who has truly mastered the art of stillness, will lead to the glorious spiritual apotheosis set forth in Chapter 9, that of expanding the yogin's being to include the entire universe – the most dazzling prospect ever held up to man!

I am immensely grateful to that devoted scholar, Chou Shao-hsien, whose book may do much to assist Taoism to survive these days of peril. To him I owe not only most of the yogic knowledge just mentioned, but also many of the quotations from the Taoist Canon scattered throughout this book, some of the details embodied in my text (such as the description of the Shantung coast opposite the Isles of the Immortals), and all the poems in my chapter on the Poetry of Stillness. I also offer my warmest thanks to Burton Watson from whose translation of Chuang-tzû I have, as on a previous occasion, borrowed extensively. Both these men richly deserve the honorary title of Immortal and who knows but that they will attain true immortality by virtue of their learning and wisdom? I greatly appreciate the kindness of the Chung Hwa Book Company and the Columbia University Press in permitting me to make use of Mr Chou's and Dr Watson's works respectively.

Among English works I have consulted, the following may be of interest to readers who would like to know more of various aspects of Taoism:

Yoga
Taoist Yoga by Lu K'uan-yu (Allen & Unwin); *Sexual Life in Ancient China* by Robert Van Gulik (Brill, Leyden).

Philosophy
Truth and Nature, a particularly enlightening translation of the *Tao Tê Ching* by Chêng Lin (Wan Kuo Shu Tien, Hong Kong); *Lao Tzû: Tao Te Ching* by D. C. Lau (Penguin); *Chuang-Tzû* by Burton Watson (Columbia).

Folklore
The Eight Immortals by T. C. Lai (Swindon, Hong Kong).

Magic
Tao Magic by Lazzlo Legezzo (Panther) – a most excellent book!

Art
Creativity and Taoism by Chang Chung-yuan (Harper Row).

General
Taoism by Holmes Welch (Beacon Press); *The Secret and Sublime* by John Blofeld (Allen & Unwin and also Dutton).

The list is short, but could not be greatly lengthened, except under the heading 'Philosophy', for that is the only aspect of Taoism on which many works are available in English and even these are largely confined to just one subject, the *Tao Tê Ching*. Much remains to be written on the subjects of Taoist yoga and mysticism especially. Taoist magic and Taoist art are other fruitful fields. If some Taoist beliefs strike us as naive, that naivety is more than redeemed by poetic charm. Going further, one may taste the cool tranquility of philosophers and poets enraptured by nature's mysteries, glean yogic knowledge of true worth and, in the end, learn how to mount upon a dragon, soar above the clouds to the palaces of immortals and, having supped with them on wind and dew or powdered moonbeams, penetrate to the very source of Being – the immaculate, undifferentiated Tao! *This can be done!*

JOHN BLOFELD, who once received a cherished title he would wish to revive – the 'Ox-Head Recluse'

The Garden of Immortals
Mid-Autumn Festival
4673rd Year since the
Accession of the Yellow
Emperor (1976)

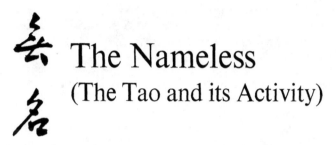

Chapter 1

The Nameless
(The Tao and its Activity)

(Readers who find this chapter rather heavy or too vague may enjoy it more if they read it after instead of before the lighter chapters that follow.)

'From the Tao all the myriad objects derive their being, their illusory separateness being wrought by the interplay of *yin* and *yang*.'

This perception of existence as a vast and timeless ocean of spotless purity upon which, through the interplay of dark and light, a myriad illusions play like ever-changing cloud formations or restless waves, is of such immense antiquity that none can say whence it first arose. Perhaps more ancient even than whatever can properly be called Taoism, it was a belief seldom questioned by Chinese no matter what religion they espoused; embodied at an early date in the archaic folk religion, it became the very core of Taoist teaching, was accepted as a matter of course by the Confucians – for all that they differed from the Taoists on so much else – and was even woven into the fabric of Buddhism when it arrived in China from beyond the western frontiers. In our own times there are some who allege that Mao Tsê-tung and Chou Ên-lai owed their phenomenal success to a closely guarded secret – mastery of the science of *yin* and *yang*! Though no one is likely to discover whether there is truth in it, such a curious allegation serves to illustrate that the ancient Chinese concept has retained some of its all-pervading influence right up to today.

In East Asia generally, the notion of a Supreme Being, so essential to Western religions, is replaced by that of a *Supreme State of Being*, an impersonal perfection from which beings including man are separated only by delusion. Gods, though they are widely believed to exist, are allowed no ultimate significance; like demons, animals or fish, they are a separate order of beings as closely bound as man by the inexorable law of impermanence. Even so, if exalted spiritual aspiration is taken as the hallmark, then Taoism stands very high among religions; for the true Taoist adepts, though serenely indifferent to the uncountable divinities inherited by their more simple brethren from the popular folk religion, were far from indifferent to divinity itself; by cultivation of the Way, they aimed to become *much more than gods*! I wonder if Christian missionaries, when they spoke to such men of God, realised that they might just as well have been discussing some kind of bird or ghost, a part of the background scenery, not negligible, but of little concern to humans.

Ah, the Taoist concept of the Ultimate is an exalted one, in which profound philosophy, spiritual aspiration, the poetry of nature and reverence for the holiness of every being and object mingle, but it is a concept so alien to the Judaeo-Christian tradition that it needs explanation, the more so as it forms the basis on which all Taoist notions and practices from the most naive to the unquestionably sublime are founded; yet it seems a little unkind to expect the reader to wrestle with it before being offered more amusing fare by way of an *hors d'œuvre*, especially in a book intended to be more light than heavy, since heaviness and Taoism scarcely go together. Well, there seems no help for it, no alternative to asking him to leap forthwith upon a dragon – there is always one obligingly within call –, gather his robes for a journey beyond sun and moon, and soar straight to the heart of infinity.

The Tao

The Tao is unknowable, vast, eternal. As undifferentiated void, pure spirit, it is the mother of the cosmos; as non-void, it is the container, the sustainer and, in a sense, the being of the myriad objects, permeating all. As the goal of existence, it is the Way of Heaven, of Earth, of Man. No being, it is the source of Being. It is not conscious of activity, has no purpose, seeks no rewards or praise, yet performs all things to perfection. Like water, it wins its way by softness. Like a deep ravine, it is shadowy rather than brilliant. As Lao-tzû taught, it is always best to leave things to the Tao, letting it take its natural course without interference; for, 'the weakest thing in heaven and earth, it overcomes the strongest; proceeding from no place, it enters where there is no crack. Thus do I know the value of non-activity. Few are they who recognise the worth of the teaching without words and of non-activity.'

Lao-tzû tells us that 'Tao' (Way) is just a convenient term for what had best be called the Nameless. Nothing can be said of it that does not detract from its fullness. To say that it exists is to exclude what does not exist, although void is the very nature of the Tao. To say that it does not exist is to exclude the Tao-permeated plenum. Away with dualistic categories. Words limit. The Tao is limitless. It is T'ai Hsü (the Great Void), free from characteristics, self-existent, undifferentiated, vast beyond conception, yet present in full in a tiny seed. It is also T'ai Chi (the Ultimate Cause, the Mainspring of the Cosmos). It is also T'ai I (the Great Changer), for its changes and convolutions never cease. Seen by man with his limited vision, it is also T'ien (Heaven), the source of governance and orderliness. It is the Mother of Heaven and Earth, without whose nourishment nothing could exist.

Manifestly this conception of the Tao makes it much greater than God, since theists hold that God and the creatures of his creation are forever separate. Christian man, though he aspires to live in God's presence, does not dream that creatures can be *one* with God! Therefore God is less than infinite, excluding what is not God. To a Taoist, nothing is separate from the Tao. Mystery upon mystery, as Lao-tzû says of it.

Elsewhere in the *Tao Tê Ching*, we find: 'The universe had a prior cause, which may be called the Mother. Know the Mother that you may know the Child; know the Child that you may grasp the Mother.' In other words, the world of form is not to be understood unless the void is grasped, nor the void to be penetrated without understanding the world of form. These two are aspects of One.

Again, 'I do not know its name, so I call it Tao. If you insist on a description, I may call it vast, active, moving in great cycles. . . . "Nothingness" is the name for it prior to the universe's birth.

"Being" is the name for it as the Mother of the Myriad Objects. Therefore, when you seek to comprehend its mystery, it is seen as unending void; when you seek to behold its content, you see that it is being.'

Such then is the concept of the Ultimate inherited by Taoists from the ancients.

Yin and Yang

From ideas inherant in the *Book of Change*, it seems possible that centuries before the birth of Lao-tzû the Tao had been conceived of as operating through the interaction of *yin* and *yang*, the one negative, passive, female; the other positive, active, male. Speaking of this, he said: 'The Tao gave birth to One, the One to Two, the Two to Three, the Three to all the myriad objects which carry the *yin* and embrace the *yang* harmoniously intermingled.' This seems to mean that the Tao, in giving birth to the potentiality of forms, produced the One; that the One's passive and active principles, *yin* and *yang*, are the Two; that these two in combination produced 'three treasures',[1] the Three; and that from these are born all the myriad objects in the universe. Everything being imbued with the wholeness of the One, there are at the ultimate level no you and I, no this and that, whereas at the level of relative truth there are innumerable seemingly separate objects. That the One can simultaneously be one and many points to two levels of apprehension, the ultimate and the relative.

This book on Huang Lao Taoism opens with so many quotations from Lao-tzû, a comparative latecomer on the scene, not because he originated these ideas, but only because there is no earlier work *now in existence* which sets them forth, despite plenty of evidence to show that the *yin* and *yang* doctrine is of very much earlier date. For example, it forms the basis of the *Book of Change* (*I Ching*) which was written centuries before Lao-tzû's time. Subsequently, that doctrine was to be further developed and there came into existence a school of *yin* and *yang* philosophers who held that a meticulous study of the *yin* and *yang* components of processes, substances and objects engenders such insight into the workings of nature that one may learn to anticipate the unfolding of events as easily as the varying lengths of night and day or the cycle of the seasons. Hence

[1] Soon to be explained.

the ubiquity of the *yin–yang* symbol in Chinese art and in much that is not specifically Taoist, though it remains the special symbol of Taoism like the cross of Christianity, the swastika of Buddhism. It will be noticed that each of the two principals is depicted as containing the seed of its own opposite (an insight rediscovered in modern times by, of all un-Taoistically inclined people, Karl Marx!); for it is believed that, under ordinary circumstances, pure *yin* or pure *yang* is not to be found in the world except in a cosmic form yet to be described. Sometimes pure *yang* is spoken of as pertaining to heaven and pure *yin* to earth; but these two, the void and non-void, interpenetrate in a very intricate manner.

Cyclic Change
The Tao in its differentiated non-void aspect is seen as unending flux, everything being subject to unceasing change from moment to moment. Nevertheless, the changes proceed in orderly cycles, the outlines of each pattern being endlessly repeated. Whereas fallen autumn leaves never produce identical patterns on the earth, the comings and goings of autumn itself vary only within narrow limits. Such cycles are foreseeable, as for example the alternation of day and night and of the four seasons. Taoist adepts learn both to contemplate and investigate the various sequences of change; contemplation engenders the tranquillity that arises when loss, decay and death are recognised as being no less essential to the whole than gain, growth, life; investigation permits one to foresee, within certain limits, what will inevitably occur. That ancient work, *The Book of Change*, which is revered by Taoists and Confucians alike and prized to this day as an unfailing resource in divination, derives from observation of nature's cyclic patterns and their interpretation in terms of the interaction of *yin* and *yang*.

Wu Hsing (The Five Activities or 'Elements')
The last two paragraphs involved a descent from the pure sublimity of the Tao back to terrestial regions. Dismissing our dragon-steeds, we may resume an atmosphere mortals find easier to breathe. The *wu hsing* doctrine, possibly not quite as ancient as that of *yin* and *yang*, is sometimes known in English as the 'science of the five elements', doubtless because of a seeming analogy with the ancient Greek belief that everything in the universe is reducible to four

elements. In fact, the five *hsing* are not elements so much as *activities*, this being the true meaning of the ideogram *hsing*. The sages who devised the science recognised five main types of natural process whose interactions bear a certain resemblance to the interactions of wood, fire, earth, metal and water, the affinity being more allegorical than actual. They understood that nature's workings depend upon a system of fine balances among processes that may assist, hinder or block one another according to the relative strength of each in a given situation. Having devoted much of their time to tranquil contemplation of nature, they had watched these sometimes conflicting forces at work and learnt to predict the outcome of such conflicts, or even to manipulate that outcome within certain narrow limits, as when one drives a serpent from a frog or diverts the water in a stream. Mastery of the *wu hsing* science conferred a degree of foresight that amounted to divination and the power to divert the course of nature in ways that must often have seemed spectacular to the uninitiated. Accordingly, this science came to play an important part in the development of *popular* Taoism and certain individuals won much credit from their ability to divine the future and forestall events on behalf of their clients. However, serious Taoist adepts bent on spiritual transformation by various means collectively known as 'cultivation of the Way', though they enjoyed studying nature's processes, had not the least desire to divine or to manipulate anything whatsoever. Content to contemplate in silence the majestic progress of the seasons and the planets, they were serenely averse to interference whether with nature or the activities of man. Seeing everything in true perspective, they found that all of it is 'good' – for ups there must be downs, for light there must be dark, for in there must be out, and for life there must be death. Why, then, interfere? For men of this calibre, the *wu hsing* science was of interest solely for the light it shed upon nature's mysterious workings, thus adding to their reverence for such wonders.

Not all Taoists shared this lofty frame of mind or were capable of seeing things in a perspective that left them totally unconcerned about the outcome of this event or that. In what may be called institutionalised Taoism, the *wu hsing* science acquired such importance that it would be improper to dismiss it with no more than a single paragraph. On the other hand, since my main concern is with the progress (and mistakes) made by serious cultivators of the Way,

I have placed elaboration of the subject in an appendix, believing that it will be of special interest to users of the *I Ching*, in that it affords additional insight into the significance of each hexagram.

Dragon Veins

Since pure *yang*, also known as cosmic *yang*, pertains to heaven and pure or cosmic *yin* to earth, there has to be a means for them to comingle. It is taught that, at certain places, there are 'dragon veins', that is to say invisible lines running down from the sky into the mountains and along the earth, whose function is rather similar to that of the psychic channels within the human body which play such an important part in acupuncture and in yoga, whether Chinese, Indian or Tibetan. Into these dragon veins pours down *yang ch'i* (cosmic vitality) to mingle with the *yin ch'i* (vitality of earth). Invisible to the ordinary eye, these veins can be detected by men learned in the science of *yin* and *yang*. This concept is clearly reflected in Chinese landscape painting, in which the veins are delineated as great sweeping curves marked at their source by the contours of the clouds, then by the undulations of mountains and hills, and finally by the meanderings of rivers or some other landscape features. Gazing at these paintings or at actual views in the more scenic parts of the globe, one can almost *feel* the power streaming downwards and impregnating the surroundings with vibrant energy.

There are other ways in which paintings convey Taoist concepts more directly than verbal description, especially the idea that the entire cosmos is formed of spirit. The voidness of the non-void is hinted at by vague expanses of ocean, snow, cloud and mist, and by solid objects which seem just on the point of emerging from or melting into the void. Man's triviality in relation to heaven's vastness is suggested by rolling landscapes in which mortals and their dwellings appear insignificant against the grandeur of their surroundings. Mountains appear cloud-like; clouds resemble mountains; rocks and tree trunks seem strangely animated, as though peering at the viewer or smiling; or the contours of men and animals are so united with those of natural objects that they appear to be of a single substance. Apparently trivial objects – say, a dragon-fly perching on a twig – arouse a sudden intuition that each tiny creature is a particularisation of a vast and holy universality, an embodiment of the inconceivable immensity of the Tao. Everything seems imbued with a portentous mystery on the very point of being unveiled; an eerie feeling is aroused that everything in nature is vibrantly alive. From all of this one is led to understand that the cosmic vitality sweeping down through the dragon veins spreads out and interfuses the entire creation.

The Taoist artist deliberately leaves his work unfinished, that the viewer may complete it from his own intuition. Just as, in Ch'an (Zen), an apparently nonsensical set of words or sudden action may bring about an extraordinary communication from mind to mind, so do paintings of this kind sometimes cause an illuminating blaze of intuition to leap into the beholder's mind and he is conscious of being touched by the flow of cosmic energy communicated by the painting.

From the notion of dragon veins has grown up a science known as *fêng-shui* (the wind and water science, or geomancy). The siting of new dwellings and of graves is determined in accordance with this science, so as to take maximum advantage of the inflow of cosmic vitality and ensure a correct balance of *yin* and *yang* (two to three being the ideal proportion). Professors of this science are guided in their choice of site by the relative positions of mountains, hills, valleys, depressions, streams and expanses of still water. Whatever degree of credence, if any, one may attach to this curious science, it has had some admirable results, being largely responsible for the exquisite siting of hermitages and monasteries. In mountainous areas it is seldom hard to find lovely spots, but *perfect* spots with a delicate balance between rugged and smooth contours, the positions of hills and streams, the alternation of precipices rearing up from where one stands and splendidly open views, with just the right proportions and positioning of rocks and trees – such spots would be hard to determine without the help of *fêng-shui* professors skilled in maintaining a harmonious balance between *yin* and *yang*. Thanks to their discernment, there are few places in all the wide-flung realm of China which, meeting these strict requirements and being reasonably accessible, lack a delightful Taoist or Buddhist edifice to add perfection to perfection. Nor can one help feeling when staying in such places that blend of vibrant well-being and holy awe that would naturally arise if one were indeed standing in the path of a great down-sweep of cosmic vitality.

The Three Treasures

Three substances or energies of immense importance in Taoist yoga and therefore known collectively as the Three Treasures are: *ching* (essence), *ch'i* (vitality) and *shên* (spirit). Though chiefly of interest in a yogic context, they must be mentioned here in the context of Taoist cosmology because they are believed to be active at all levels of being from the tiniest organism up to the vast macrocosm itself. Whereas in their pure, cosmic form they are too subtle to be easily recognisable except by the transmutations they occasion, they are also present in the human body in a coarse form that makes them easier to identify. 'Nourished' (that is to say conserved and strengthened), 'augmented' and 'transmuted', they assist in the attainment of the immense physical and spiritual benefits which Taoist yogins pursue throughout their lives. The refinement and transmutation of *ching*, *ch'i* and *shên* in order to increase the vigour and the lifespan of the adept, as well as to augment and purify his natural stock of spirit, constitute the very core of Taoist yogic and spiritual endeavour – a secret process that was mistaken by the uninitiated for something very different, hence the common supposition in the old days that Taoist yogins were no more than alchemists seeking to transmute base metals into gold! The misunderstanding arose from the esoteric language of the Taoist yogic manuals, the effect of which was that, among Taoists themselves, there were not a few who failed to recognise the true spiritual purport of the texts. As a result, the goals pursued by genuine and would-be adepts varied from the amusingly naive to the spiritually exalted. All are touched upon in the following chapters, preparation for the high yogic goal being dealt with in the chapter called 'The Yellow and the White'.

Wu Wei (No Action out of Harmony with Nature's Laws)

It is taught that there is a Tao (Way) of Heaven, a Tao of Earth and a Tao of Man. This last is the way ordained by nature from which it is always unwise and often perilous to depart. Nevertheless, human society began to depart from it at a very early date, as can be gathered from the plea of such ancient sages as Lao-tzû and Chuang-tzû that men return to it. As to the present time, the gulf between nature's way for man and man's way for himself is now widening so rapidly that our very environment is threatened with destruction! The time has come when it would be well for the teaching of Lao and Chuang to be given precedence over every other subject! But can one even imagine that happening within our lifetime, or the lifetime of our children's children? Now even the Chinese have finally turned their backs on their greatest source of wisdom. Communists and Confucians, though their ways of thought are so greatly opposed, are alike in several respects, two of them being devotion to a monolithic state and hatred of the individualism that is the hallmark of Taoism.

A dedicated Taoist is one who seeks to live as closely in accord as possible with nature. From the outset, this involves contemplation of nature's ways, recognition of their fitness, and perception that all of them are 'good' in the sense of being essential to the pattern as a whole. Depart from them and chaos and destruction loom! To go along with nature effortlessly, as does a fish or a master artisan, is to swim with the current, to let one's knife slip along with the grain. When nature is taken as a guide, a friend, living becomes almost effortless, tranquil, joyous even. Care departs; serenity takes over. *Wu wei*, a cardinal principle of Taoists, literally means 'no action', but not in the sense of sitting all day like a dead tree stump or a block of stone; rather it means avoiding action that is not spontaneous, acting fully and skilfully by all means but only in accordance with present need, being lively when required but never over-strenuous and certainly not strained, eschewing artfully calculated action and every activity stemming from a profit motive. A plant in need of sunlight bends towards the sun instinctively, effortlessly, its movement economical and wholly without calculation but none the less effective. So should it be with man. Free from greed, free from strain, a stranger to anxiety and fear, the sage takes whatever action may be needed, stopping the very moment his objective is attained and, far from congratulating himself on its success, puts it out of mind as soon as it is done. A modern analogy that pleases me is that of a skilful driver; such a man never fails to do with brake and clutch exactly what should be done, but always in response to immediate need, never with calculation or any tendency to keep the action in mind when the need for it has passed. *Wu wei* was undoubtedly one of the main factors responsible for the success of Taoist adepts in retaining their powers of mind and body to an advanced age and living long. Where there is no anxiety, no calculation, there is little wear and tear!

Stillness

'The recluse's heart is a placid lake unruffled by the winds of circumstance.' I remember seeing these words inscribed above the doorway of one of the first Taoist hermitages I visited. Later I was to encounter words to the same effect carved upon rock, brushed on wall-scrolls, spoken by Taoist masters and included in almost every book connected directly or indirectly with cultivation of the Way. If any one word is pre-eminent among Taoists, it is 'stillness'. One had only to inquire about the Way to be sure of some such answer as: 'To return to your original state of being, you must become a master of stillness. Activity for health's sake, never carried to the point of strain, must alternate with perfect stillness. Sitting motionless as a rock, turn next to stillness of mind. Close the gates of the senses. Fix your mind upon one object or, even better, enter a state of objectless awareness. Turn the mind in upon itself and contemplate the inner radiance.' Should one reasonably object that this is very difficult indeed, the answer would be: 'It is easy if you know the way. You must learn to live frugally, unstirred by longings for wealth and fame. When passion or desire arises, see it as your enemy, the disturber of your serenity, and quietly abandon it. Take things as they come. Be a stranger to care, to anxiety about what you think is going to happen and, above all, to regret for anything that has already happened. Grief and disappointment come from outside yourself. Lock your door on them. Be rid of them. Having done this, you will find that stillness comes easily and of itself. No effort is needed to fix a mind that has turned away from all sources of disturbance. Do not think your life will be empty then. Quite on the contrary, you will find that the greatest joy of all is just *to be!*'

Yet in all things Taoists are moderate. Their method is never to repress passion but quietly to transcend it. It is deemed that peaceful contemplation of the ugliness and wreckage wrought on every hand by greed and passion is enough to make a wise man wish to turn away from them. This turning away leads to stillness and, in the meanwhile, daily cultivation of stillness, even if only for a few minutes morning and evening, helps in the process of turning away. It was from this experience that I came to understand why Tao was chosen as a convenient name for the Nameless. Tao means Way, the significance of which is that the goal and the way to it are one and the same; thus, one turns away from passion to achieve the goal of stillness and makes oneself still in order to be able to turn away! Paradoxical perhaps, but that is exactly how the method works. As with passion, so with longings. Remembrance of the agonies of longings unfulfilled coupled with reflection on the tawdry nature of their objects and on the transcience of such satisfactions as they sometimes bring is a most effective remedy, causing longings to melt away as soon as they arise. In Taoist hermitages, a cup or two of wine with dinner is not forbidden and if the younger recluses find sexual continence unbearable they are free to return to 'the world of dust' for a time and then come back to pursue their cultivation untroubled by desire. Excess is the real enemy of stillness; to be puritanical, no less than being licentious, is to stray from the Tao. Nothing really worth while can be done in a hurry. As cultivation of the Way proceeds, passions and longings diminish of themselves without the least need for repression; imperceptibly, the young recluse's happiness comes to depend less and less upon external objects, more and more upon the joy that comes from within. Stillness brings an ever-increasing joy in stillness.

Goals
The stream of Taoism, flowing down through the ages, has sometimes meandered into strange valleys. The teachings are too lofty, too subtle to be understood by men of mean intelligence or lacking in intuition. Illiteracy in itself does not matter, as knowledge or the lack of it has little to do with wisdom, but illiteracy coupled with absence of spiritual insight has sometimes produced curious results. Whereas well-educated men, if not gifted with intuition, might not get very far with cultivating the Way, they would at least not be disappointed to find that their teachers could not teach them to soar about in the heavens like birds! Would-be adepts from illiterate peasant families who went into the mountains in search of masters were not rarely driven forward by genuine spiritual thirst; these flourished and sometimes became great masters in their turn, as I was occasionally to see for myself; but many such people came athirst for supernatural powers and some fell into the hands of charlatans or found teachers who, believing themselves to have both knowledge and wisdom, had aims as impracticable as their own. Moreover, there were serious adepts who, to guard their secret yogas from misuse by the profane, liked it to be thought they were intent upon

compounding the elixir of life or transmuting base metals into gold. The resulting misunderstandings were compounded by the esoteric language of the yogic manuals into which many bizarre meanings can be read, to say nothing of texts which, in the absence of an initiate able to supply the oral key, convey no intelligible meaning at all. Even figurative passages describing the bliss of meditation and the powers of the spirit, such as 'mounting a dragon, he soars above the world, drops in at the cloud palaces of the immortals, wings his way beyond the fiery sun and enters the courts of heaven', have sometimes been taken literally by the ingenuous. Besides, there have been Taoist adepts of intellect and learning who honestly believed that, since identical laws of nature operate at all levels, the processes laid down for spiritual refinement must be equally applicable to physical substances. Such an attitude would, after all, have been quite acceptable to their Western contemporaries (say, from one to two thousand years ago). Indeed, to this very day, His Holiness the Pope and the Archbishop of Canterbury – both of them men of learning – solemnly affirm as an article of faith the *bodily* resurrection of the dead! In theory at least, one cannot be a faithful member of the Catholic Church or Church of England without fully adhering to a creed containing the words: 'I believe in the resurrection of the body', which only goes to show the pitfalls of using words to describe mysteries beyond human understanding. Seen in this light, the *popular* Taoist belief in flesh and blood transmogrification does not seem so utterly absurd.

The terms 'golden elixir' and 'transmutation' properly refer to the physio-spiritual yogic processes described in Chapter 8, but they have been widely misunderstood, sometimes with the connivance of yogins who wished to guard their secrets from the uninitiated. For centuries it was widely believed that Taoist alchemists could in fact transmute base metals into gold and compound a drug that would ensure perpetual youth and immortality. According to that belief, a successful yogin's body would be transmogrified into a weightless, jade-like substance impervious to fire and ice, sustained by sups of wind and sips of dew, and able to endure forever. Known thenceforth as immortals, such beings were thought to dwell in the inaccessible mountains of Central Asia, on the faery isles of P'êng Lai in the Eastern Sea, or in cloud palaces of pink and coral, in the glittering ice palace on the moon, and in sumptuous edifices presided over by the Jade Emperor in the courts of heaven.

Considerably less naive was the belief that, either by the use of medicinal drugs or by yogic practice, youthful vigour could be restored and enormous longevity attained. Full restoration of youthful loveliness or a lifespan measurable in centuries is surely impossible, but I have certainly encountered elderly and even aged recluses strikingly young and vigorous for their years, as well as two or three ancients alleged to be well into their second century. I had no doubt of it, having actually met a Turk aged over 130 at Cambridge and feeling quite certain that my Taoist friends were not at all the kind of people to lie for the sake of winning a little spurious fame.

Much more difficult for me personally to accept was the belief that a yogin can create a 'spirit-body' able to leave and return to his mortal body at will; but one does hear of people who have undergone the experience of looking down on their own bodies lying in bed beneath them, or who have sent forth their consciousness while lying in a state of trance. My Tibetan teachers are convinced that this is possible and scientific opinion seems to vary; I can no longer exclude such feats as being utterly impossible.

When Taoists speak of creating a 'spirit-body' in which to enter at death, the term 'body' may or may not be used figuratively, but in any case this is a characteristically Chinese conception. Most people hold either that death is final or that immortality is thrust upon us willy-nilly, whereas the Chinese believe that it must be won. Taoists, who are inclined to accept the traditional belief that man has two souls – the *p'o* that lingers near the corpse sharing its disintegration and the *hun* which enjoys a longer but not limitless existence in the upper regions – hold immortality to be a dazzling prize demanding unremitting effort. In any case, speaking of the creation of a spirit-body is often another way of stating their belief that the adept must undergo a process of refinement if he is to enjoy the full reward of cultivating the Way.

We now come to what I like to call the *real* goal of Taoist mystics, shorn of hyperbole and simply stated. It involves two stages, present and ultimate. For the present, the adept seeks to live in harmony with nature, enjoying happiness in the here and now, serenely indifferent to what may follow since, to one who lives wisely, everything happens for the best, whether death come sooner or later. Meanwhile, the dross of ego-born delusion is refined away until nought remains save pure spirit but slightly hampered by a fleshly envelope which, whenever death comes, will be discarded. For the future, the aim is to return to the Source by undergoing an apotheosis that can at best be hinted at in words. The illusory ego falls away, yet nothing real is lost. Spirit, freed from its bonds, returns to Spirit, not as a dew-drop destined to form an insignificant particle of a vast ocean, but as the boundless returning to the boundless. The liberated consciousness expands to contain – to *be* – the entire universe! Could there ever, ever be a more glorious endeavour?

Immortals
'Immortality' is the term by which Taoists at every level of understanding designate their goal; hence the picturesque title 'immortal' conferred alike on Taoist sages, masters of yoga and even on elderly recluses who, on account of their wisdom and bearing, are politely deemed to have achieved their goal. Whether the curious notion of flesh-and-blood immortality preceded the sublime concept of immortality in a mystical sense, or whether, from the very first, transcendent immortality was the true goal and bodily transmogrification a fiction put out to guard the secret knowledge of the wise, is arguable. Personally, I am convinced that transcendent immortality was always the true aim, even though the actual title *hsien-jên* (immortal) came into use much later, when it became necessary to distinguish the idea of a perfected sage in the Taoist sense from the Confucian equivalent; for, during the centuries that followed immediately upon the passing of Lao-tzû and Confucius, such titles as the Princely Man, the True Man, the Holy Man were used by followers of all creeds.

For me, the word 'immortal' is fragrant with a thousand memories. It is delightful to toy with the idea of meeting in some dell or cavern a bearded sage who has flown thither on a scarlet-feathered crane, a dragon with shimmering scales of green and gold, or a blue-tailed unicorn; and, in the mountains of China, there are places so magical that one would not be immeasurably astonished to encounter such a being.

Nevertheless, for the sake of understanding the real nature of the Taoist quest, it is necessary to set forth the meaning of 'immortality' in the sense it has for mystics and yogins fully initiated into the mysteries of cultivating the Way:

An immortal is one who, by employing to the full all his endowments of body and mind, by shedding passion and eradicating all but the simplest and most harmless desires, has attained to free, spontaneous existence – a being so nearly perfect that his body is but a husk or receptacle of pure spirit. He has undergone a spiritual rebirth, broken free from the shackles of illusory selfhood and come face to face with his 'true self', aware that it is not his personal possession, being no other than the sublime undifferentiated Tao! With the vanishing of his seeming ego, he sees himself no longer as an individual, but as the unchanging Tao embodied in a transient cloud-like form. Death, when it comes, will be for him no more than the casting off of a worn out robe. He has won to eternal life and is ready to plunge back into the limitless ocean of pure being!

The Central Teaching

All these matters, baldly stated, lack the miraculous poetic quality which made it such a joy for me to converse about them amidst archaic scenes redolent of the mysteries of this beautiful faith. So that its tenets may come alive, I shall recapitulate them briefly in the kind of language that was used in giving instruction, having first sketched in a suitable setting.

It is an afternoon in late summer. On the humid Szechuan plain far below us, the people must be vigorously plying their fans; but at this height a cool breeze plays among the branches of the trees shading this ancient courtyard and the sunshine is no more than pleasantly warm. The hermitage stands on a natural platform with steep slopes rising on three sides; the fourth overlooks the course of a stream that tumbles precipitously down towards a vista of green foothills rising from the unseen plain beyond. Just now we have our backs to the low monastic buildings with their heavy roofs and fantastically upward-tilted eaves; we are looking towards a low creeper-covered wall with an ornamental coping of dark green porcelain tiles, for the brickwork is pierced at intervals by openings fancifully shaped liked leaves, each framing a vignette of the view beyond so that it looks like a painted landscape. Presently a bearded Taoist, clad in an ample sky-blue robe and wearing a gauze hat through the top of which protrudes his topknot of jet-black hair, seats himself on a low stool facing us; though usually the most relaxed of men, he now sits cross-legged, hands folded in his lap, body held straight, for it is proper for him to assume on such an occasion the hierarchical posture of a teacher of the Way. To either side of him are ranged porcelain tubs of chrysanthemums with petals of deep bronze; these just happen to belong there at this season, but do not fail to add to the dignity of a sage engaged in making an important pronouncement. His discourse lasts for an hour or so. Reduced to its essentials, it runs:

Tao	The Tao is a softly lucent ocean of pure void, a pearly mist, boundless, immaculate. Born of this ocean, two
yin and yang	dragons sport entwined – the male, bright as the sun with fiery golden scales, master of activity; the female, radiant as the moon with shining silver scales, adept at passivity. Their intercourse brings forth the
cyclic change	rhythms of cyclic change – the movements of the planets, the progression of the seasons, the alternation of day and night. From their sport proceed five shining
wu hsing	vapours – blue, red and yellow, white and black – which, swirling, overshadowing, contending, intermingling, give to heaven its roundness, to earth its squareness, to the myriad objects their transitory
the three treasures	shapes. From heaven pour forth like rain three cloud-like essences of *yang*; from earth arise like mist three essences of *yin*; these meet and intermingle. Thus has it been since heaven and earth were formed. Such is the original perfection.

Blind to perfection, men live darkly. Lost to all knowledge of the Tao, they pursue unworthy goals. Piling gold upon gold, jade upon jade, they contend for wealth, rank, power and fame. Opening the gates of the six senses, they steep themselves in extravagant luxury and foolish ostentation. Yet some there are who know how to value the teaching without words, to

wu wei   cultivate the art of leaving well alone. Eschewing the high pinnacles of fame, the manacles of wealth, they take their ease and wander through lonely vales far

from the haunts of men, or sit rapt in contemplation
of the interplay of shining vapours. Free from passion
stillness   and inordinate desire, in stillness they absorb the
cloud-like cosmic essences, blend them with the secret
the secret   treasures of their bodies and attend to the light within.
alchemy   Attuned to nature's rhythms, they perceive the Tao's
perfection. Such are the men who win to immortality.
immortals   Rightly are they called immortals; for, when the time
is ripe, they leap upon the backs of dragons and, rising
from the earth, enter but do not loiter at the gates of
heaven, that they may swiftly attain the Source. Thus
they return, winging ecstatically to the softly lucent
ocean. Themselves now limitless, eternal, they plunge
into the Void.'

Chapter 2

黄 Huang Lao,
老 the Yellow and
志 the Ancient
(A Historical Survey)

Huang Lao means Taoists, in the sense of followers of both Huang Ti (the Yellow Emperor) and Lao-tzû (the Ancient Sage). The majestic figure of the Yellow Emperor looms through the swirling mists of time, for he was one of the Five Emperor-Sages belonging to China's Golden Age (2852–2255 BC) who presided over the birth of the Empire, endowing it with such precious skills as the use of fire, of ploughs, of silk-looms. He personally is credited with having discovered and transmitted the secret of immortality. Legend has it that he spent most of his life engaged in a quest for the secret of eternal life, but what precisely he sought is not clear since Taoists, holding everything in existence to consist of spirit, seldom distinguished in their early writings between spiritual and material. What is said about his researches may be taken figuratively or literally. His interest in the cure of disease, nourishing vitality and lengthening the normal lifespan led him, if accounts set down some two thousand years later are to be believed, to experiment with transmuting the combined essence of male and female couples in order to attain a spirit-body. The details are related in several manuals written in the form of dialogues between the Son of Heaven and a succession of divine teachers, including T'ien Lao (the Heavenly Ancient), Su Nü (the Plain Girl, a minor goddess of fertility and music) and Ts'ai Nü (the Elected Girl or Girl of Multi-hued Apparel).

Later, he undertook alchemical experiments and is said to have succeeded in distilling a golden elixir. Having partaken of this drug, he was transmogrified and, after transmitting the recipe (to persons careless enough to lose it!), he 'mounted a dragon and winged his way to the realm of immortals'. The biographies of many an ancient Taoist sage end in the same way, leaving the reader to choose between literal and hyperbolic interpretation.

In speaking of the Yellow Emperor, what is really meant is that the ideas and activities credited to him have come down to us from a source so ancient that no one knows whence they originated. As the Chinese script had not so much as come into existence in his day, it was said that the works relating his exploits were first written in the 'script of heaven', a pleasant fiction that has probably seldom been taken seriously. Nevertheless, Huang Ti's memory has stayed green, for the works are deemed to have merit regardless of their authorship. His name was often on the lips of Taoists one met in the 1930s and 1940s. That he is formally regarded as the original founder of Taoism implies that there is much in Taoist esoteric law that is centuries older than Lao-tzû.

The Golden Age
The age to which the Yellow Emperor belonged, placed by the Chinese as commencing almost five thousand years ago, is too remote to come within the proper purview of history. The many similarities between not only myths but also profound mystical doctrines of ancient origin have given rise to a theory that there was indeed a Golden Age throughout the world, the culmination perhaps of a great and widespread civilisation or else an epoch in which gods and men were closer to each other than they have been at any time thereafter. Some associate the Golden Age with the epoch prior to the disappearance of a great continent, Atlantis. I know nothing of this matter; but, if there is any truth in it, then during one of those cataclysms wherewith nature maintains balance between progress and return, that civilisation must have perished in a manner more sudden, complete and final than the dismal end of the Romans, leaving but few scattered remnants in the form of buried ruins and confused memories of the wisdom of its sages. Though all of this is hard to believe, it is pleasant to fancy that Taoism preserves a little of that vanished wisdom. At least such speculations allow man a nobler

origin than the one propounded by Charles Darwin. It is better to be half god, half beast, as Elizabeth Browning suggested, than to be wholly ape!

That there is much in popular Taoism that strikes us as not being of a high spiritual order does not invalidate the possibility that its essential teaching derives from a Golden Age when, according to legend, men and gods were kin; for it is scarcely possible to find an old religion that has not been diluted with a great deal of nonsense. It is not rare for the spiritual progeny of sages to pile autumn leaves upon their heritage of yellow gold!

The Fang Shih (*Prescriptioners*)

According to tradition, in the era of the Five Emperor-Sages men dwelt in harmonious accord with nature's laws, knowing well how to remedy sickness and attain to ripe old age. Intercourse between heaven and earth was close. Virtuous sages sitting rapt in stillness and tranquillity communed with that which is formless, undifferentiated, eternal. Cultivating the Way, they drew upon the very source of divine wisdom, the gods delighting to hold converse with mortals so worthy of their high regard. The precious knowledge thus received was transmitted to posterity, clothed in a language that would guard its secrets from the profane.

The Golden Age, alas, was succeeded by an era of decline, as mortals by and large departed from the Way. Instead of valuing wisdom, the princes of the Empire gave themselves up to gratifying voluptuous desires. The Way became shrouded from the sight of man; gods and goddesses responded less readily to human importuning. Though there were sages who clung to the wisdom of the ancients, many of their disciples embarked upon a quest for more tangible rewards. In those early days, there was no talk of Taoists, for all literate Chinese were heirs to the one divine tradition; a need to differentiate arose only in the fifth century BC with the emergence of Confucians who stressed social values such as loyalty to rulers and filial piety instead of seeking stillness and mystical communion with the Way. The first cultivators of the Way to be distinguished by a special name were the *fang shih* (prescriptioners) who achieved fame as physicians and as men able to retain youthful vigour and live long. Some *fang shih*, it was whispered, knew the secret of immortality, whatever that might mean.

Lao Chün (Lao-tzû)

In the eyes of Taoists, the sage Confucius has always been over-shadowed by his senior contemporary, Lao-tzû, whom they respect-fully call Lao Chün (Lao, the Venerable Lord). He, by virtue of his stillness, attained communion with the Way and, though he was not one who cared for sticking out his head, felt obliged like Confucius to attempt the instruction of the feudal princes and their ministers, so that 'all below heaven' might be delivered from the reigning anarchy. Indeed, though Confucians have always denied it, Taoists assert that it was Lao-tzû who instructed Master Confucius in the rites and it is recorded that the latter was so overwhelmed by the elder sage's wisdom that he compared him to a dragon ascending to heaven on wind and clouds. Unfortunately, Lao-tzû's royal pupils preferred feasting and hunting to imbibing the cool wisdom of a sage. Giving up a hopeless task, the old man rode off on a buffalo into the solitudes beyond the Empire's confines. At the frontier, the Keeper of the Pass besought him to leave behind some record of his wisdom for future generations, and in this the sage obliged by brushing the five thousand characters destined to become known as *The Scripture of the Way and its Virtue (Tao Tê Ching)*. Then he rode on. There are varying accounts of his end. Some say he lived to be 160 years old, others that he lived to be over 200, and yet others affirm that he achieved fleshly immortality. There is a popular belief that, soon after his arrival in the courts of heaven, he was promoted to high rank among their divine inhabitants, a legend that proved convenient when Taoist recluses found they were expected to take on certain religious functions in return for financial support from people dwel-ling in the neighbourhood of their hermitages.

The teachings of Lao-tzû and of his posthumous disciple Chuang-tzû were destined to play such a tremendous role in the development of Taoism that it has been necessary to give them a chapter to them-selves, Chapter 3.

The Wandering Philosophers

Lao-tzû and Confucius were but two of some hundreds of wandering sages eager to instruct the feudal princes of those days. The Chou Empire had declined so much that the territorial princes and dukes had virtually royal status which they sadly abused, governing oppres-sively, making war upon one another and doing nothing to improve the lot of their miserable subjects. Though differing radically from one another, these sages all desired to ensure good government in accordance with 'the laws of heaven' which each interpreted in his own way. It was not until five centuries later that, from among all the conflicting doctrines, that of Confucius was adopted by the central authorities of the newly unified Empire; it was destined to become the fount of morality and main substance of Chinese learning for the next two thousand years, maintaining its absolute control up to the beginning of the twentieth century. Meanwhile, the rival philosophers each put forward his own concept of the Perfect Man and ideal ruler. The Confucians saw this being as a sage of lofty principle using his powers to foster a happy paternalistic society in which juniors would give unquestioning obedience to seniors and be repaid by benevolence in a spirit of loving reciprocity. The Taoist ideal was very different.

The Taoists could not imagine that a man of true wisdom and holiness would involve himself in the mundane affairs with which politicians and civil servants have to deal; for, as Lao-tzû said, 'Minute and subtle is the mystery to which [the Sage] attains, its profundity too deep for recognition.' Chuang-tzû's definition was: 'The Spiritual Man [*Shên-jên*] is one who attains to the Way of Heaven and Earth.' Even Mencius, though a Confucianist, shared this exalted conception, saying: 'He who is called a Spiritual Man is one so holy that none can know [his holiness].' Ch'êng-tzû, another Taoist sage, declared: 'The most marvellous quality of holiness is that it cannot be perceived; this is a truth to which [ordinary] men cannot penetrate.'

The Perfect Sage or True Immortal
Writing centuries later, the great Taoist master Ko Hung remarked that the Sage or Holy Man must possess six qualities, namely: lofty virtue, deep sincerity, love of stillness unmarred by the stirring of desire, wide learning, devotion to a teacher worthy of his veneration, and clear understanding that true holiness develops from a heaven-implanted human instinct, the way of the sage and the way of humanity being inseparable. A characteristically Taoist description of the ideal man runs: 'The most exalted Spiritual Man is one who rides on light, forgetful of forms. This is known as shining, as attaining to [the principle of] life [itself], all [sensuous] feeling vanquished. Sharing

the joy of heaven and earth, he forgets that he was ever ensnared by the myriad objects.' These are the words of a true mystic who perceives that wisdom and virtue arise not from a mastery of externals, but by turning the mind inwards to contemplate the light. Another delightful definition runs: 'Thus the True Man [lives] in heaven above while remaining on earth below. He has "left" the world and yet remains within it. . . . Wherever he goes, he never comes to a place that fails to fulfil his utmost wishes.' In other words, the Sage neither separates himself from humanity nor indulges in worldly pleasures. Lowly in appearance, exalted in spirit, he is so blissfully independent of environment that there is nowhere in heaven or earth where he does not feel entirely happy and at ease. Thanks to his inner tranquillity, he is invulnerable to fate's arrows, but this in no way interferes with his usefulness and helpfulness to those around him.

Mao Mêng

Some of these definitions have carried us away in time, though not in spirit, from the age of wandering philosophers to which we must now return. Of Chuang-tzû (fourth century BC?), whose teaching is discussed in the next chapter, of Yang Chu and Lieh-tzû (dates unknown) there are no biographical details. An early Taoist sage of whom some biographical details are known is Mao Mêng (third century BC). He and the long line of Taoist masters who followed him are described as seeking immortality by various means, some of which it would be hard for us to take seriously, whereas some are known to be conducive to the attainment of powerful yogic results, assisting as they do in promoting radiant health, vigour and longevity. They include: rigorous dieting; bathing at prescribed times and in accordance with meticulously detailed rituals; distilling concoctions that included not a few dangerous ingredients such as cinnabar, mercury and lead; having ritual intercourse with their wives in accordance with the instructions received by the Yellow Emperor from the Plain Girl regarding timing, posture, rhythm, etc.; various yogic exercises and breathing techniques; meditation during which light is seen by the meditator to stream from certain centres in his body; and the use of charms and mantras. Some of these practices have long ago been discarded; others are still employed as aids to attaining the mystical intuition upon which success in cultivating the Way depends.

Mao Mêng and those who followed him were far from being innovators, for these practices date back to the time of the Yellow Emperor, that is to say they are of such antiquity that none can say when they first began. Mao owes his fame to a fortunate accident; had not the great Emperor Ch'in Shih Huang been inspired by his mystical poems to visit Mount T'ai in the hope of encountering some of the immortals said to dwell there, Mao might have shared the oblivion that has overtaken so many other ancient sages. Such men, having withdrawn from the world of dust to seek solitude amidst the mountains, were shy of public notice and shunned it, for which reason many a remarkable sage must have escaped the notice of historians. Mao Mêng was by no means delighted to have been singled out for attention by the Emperor; as he said, 'life passes swiftly as a flash of lightning' and there were better things to do with it than be travel guide to a cruel and ambitious emperor. His biography ends characteristically with the words: 'Having obtained a recipe for immortality from Master Kuei Ku, he secluded himself on Mount Hua, there to cultivate the Way and study the physician's art.... Mounting a dragon, he ascended to heaven in broad daylight.' In the coastal province of Kiangsu there is to this day a mountain called Mao Shan which takes its name from Mao Mêng and two other sages of the same surname, Mao Ying and Mao Sêng; it remained an important centre of Taoist learning right up to the middle of this century when the forces of yet another Mao drove the recluses back into the world of dust to labour for their living. The farmhouse where Mao Tsê-tung was born has now become a national shrine; it would be well if Mount Mao had been similarly treated in honour of the first members of the Mao clan to have their names and works recorded for the instruction of posterity!

P'êng Lai Shan, an Island Realm of Immortals
The Emperor Ch'in Shih Huang (246–209 BC) was but one of several emperors who, beguiled by the esoteric language of Taoist sacred writings, hoped to attain flesh-and-blood immortality! For the great Lieh-tzû had declared that, upon a certain mountain, dwelt immortals 'feeding upon the wind and sipping dew, but eschewing the five grains. Their minds are like springs welling from deep gullies, and they have the appearance of young girls [i.e. their skin is soft and smooth and delicately tinted]. Strangers to fear and love, they com-

mand spirits to attend them.' Moreover, another sage, Kung-sun Ch'ing, had clearly stated that, although coming face to face with immortals is so difficult that years of searching may be required, unless one does encounter them, one can scarcely hope to obtain the elixir that confers immortality. Naturally Ch'in Shih Huang was all agog to meet these beings, as was another great Emperor, Han Wu Ti (140–88 BC), in his turn; no doubt many of the Western monarchs of two thousand years ago would have been similarly beguiled if they had come upon such writings.

Both of the emperors mentioned were eager to behold P'êng Lai Shan, an abode of immortals lying somewhere in the Eastern Sea off the coast of Shantung. Lieh-tzû had written that a singularly fortunate mortal might behold it as often as several times in the course of a single year, but that it was more often hidden from the eyes of men for years together. The allurement of this mountainous island is easy to understand, for in all China there is no place so pregnant with magic as the coast of the Shantung peninsula. From towering peaks, says Chou Shao-hsien, himself a native of that region, one gazes upon an island-dotted sea of tremendous depth and often so rough that gigantic waves rear up like mountains before hurling themselves furiously upon the rocky coast. At sunrise the sky blazes red and gold and at sunset one sees pink and coral clouds fantastically shaped. In a strong wind when the waves crash upon the cliffs, their spray resembles a profusion of silvery pearls being scattered upon the rocks by heavenly nymphs. At other times, mists sweeping in from the sea take the form of demons. So rapid are the transformations wrought by sun and cloud that it is easy to believe the place enchanted. There are moments when the sunlit peaks of mountainous islands are seen rising from a sea of silver mist that veils from sight the ocean; and it used to be said that, in summer when the weather is propitious, a mortal worthy of stupendous gifts from fortune can see in the far distance the peaks of P'êng Lai Shan, Island of Immortals! Despite the great distance, he is permitted a fleeting glimpse of its forests and mountains dotted with the enchanting pavilions wherein the immortals dwell. Even their many-splendoured city may be seen upon occasion with noblemen galloping in and out of its fantastic gateways. Then suddenly the scene is blotted out and all is as before — a vista of limitless ocean stretching to the horizon.

P'êng Lai Shan, though occasionally glimpsed, has never been visited by mortals. Ships sailing towards it are driven back upon the coast by contrary winds. Ch'in Shih Huang, on learning that the vessel he had sent there had been destroyed by a tempest in mid-ocean, accepted the sad truth that he had no hope of ever setting foot there; but he remained convinced that what had occasionally been glimpsed was altogether too splendid and the details reported of it too precise for one to accept them as mere illusion.

Shantung province has long been associated with Taoism. The centre of the *yin-yang* philosophers and diviners, it never lost its hold on the imagination of poets and mystics, to say nothing of the wizards and witches who flourished there throughout the centuries. Less than a century ago, it was the scene of a terrible holocaust; hundreds of Taoist recluses of both sexes, having barricaded themselves in a castle, chose to burn themselves to death sooner than surrender to the Confucian authorities, busybodies who, mistaking dual cultivation (sexual yoga) for immorality, intended to punish them and stamp out their religious practices.

Heavenly Teacher Chang
In the Later Han dynasty (AD 25–167) there emerged an immortal whose spiritual descendents were destined to enjoy the status of 'Taoist Pope' for close on two thousand years, the last of them being evicted by the communists in 1949. The seat of these spiritual sovereigns was Dragon-Tiger Mountain which is situated in Kiangsi province. I shall always regret having had no opportunity to visit an establishment where the way of life had remained essentially intact for nearly two millenia! One of the special attractions of Taoism prior to the coming of the red flood was that living links with remote antiquity had survived to an extent probably unequalled elsewhere in the world.

The first in the line of Heavenly Teachers or T'ien Shih was Chang Tao-ling, who is popularly believed to have perpetuated himself by reincarnation, rather in the manner of the Dalai Lama, except that he was invariably reincarnated in the offspring of his own loins. 'T'ien Shih', a title of his own choosing for himself and his successors, remained a courtesy title for some centuries, until the T'ang Emperor Hsüan Tsung (AD 713–56) bestowed it formally on the Founder of the Line. Subsequently the Mongol Emperor Khubilai issued a decree confirming it in perpetuity on his successors.

Born during the second century of our era, Chang at one time had a secretarial post in the army. His unit being decimated by a fearful epidemic, he attributed his own escape to the potency of a charm he carried for subjugating demons. This led to a decision to spend the rest of his life cultivating the Way; so, in AD 177, he retired to Shu (the present Szechuan province), where he lived on Snow Goose Mountain. There his interest soon rose above demonology and presently he was writing books on hygiene and healing. The country being in a state of anarchy, he emerged from retirement and organised the local people to govern themselves and protect their own livelihood, as well as to embrace a form of Taoism he expounded which was notable for supernatural and moralistic elements. Numbers of well-educated men respected him as their spiritual teacher and his remarkable cures aroused so much attention that two emperors in turn summoned him to court. Rejecting these summonses in true Taoist fashion, he retired to the mountains where, in course of time, 'having compounded a nine-times refined elixir, he attained immortal state'. In his 123rd year, he 'mounted a dragon and ascended to the realm of immortals'.

Chang's grandson, Chang Lu, is memorable for fanaticism, uncharacteristic of Taoism, that led to his followers being known as 'demon warriors'! A contemporary physician, also surnamed Chang, carried fanaticism even further. Should a patient's illness be diagnosed as the fruit of adulterous behaviour, the poor fellow's sins would be recorded on three slips of paper and ceremoniously announced to 'heaven, earth and water' in turn! After that, he would be prayed over by Demon Ministers and made to pay a doctor's fee of five pecks of rice! All this may seem too trivial to be worth mentioning in the context of cultivation of the Way, but it illustrates how, at an early date, some Taoist leaders came under the domination of the ancient folk religion with its innumerable gods and demons. This trend unfortunately continued and much of the obloquy directed at Taoism results from it.

Sects

The mystics and yogins whose practices figure largely in this book mostly belonged to one of two main schools, each with numerous branches known as sects. The Northern or Perfect Realisation School, which for centuries had its headquarters at Peking's White

Cloud Monastery, recognises Wang Chung-yang as its founder; whereas the Southern School, known by various names and in fact an offshoot of the former, recognises Liu Hai-ch'an as its Original Master. Some confusion arises from the fact that Heavenly Teacher Chang's Orthodox Unity School is often popularly referred to as the Southern School, though it differs from the other two to an extent that makes them barely comparable; for it is the school of popular, highly institutionalised Taoism more concerned with magic than with yoga and chiefly responsible for the derogatory criticism often levelled at Taoism by educated Chinese. Even so, the Mongol Emperor Khubilai was so taken with it that he gave the Changs jurisdiction over all Taoist temples in South China; though they never actually came to wield that much power, the school flourished mightily and the remnants of Taoism to be found among Chinese communities in south-east Asia are mostly of that persuasion. Many of its devotees are fascinating people and their practices delightfully colourful; but it is a pity that their very colourfulness has led to so much publicity as to put the – to me – more admirable schools somewhat in the shade and cause Taoists to be confounded with magicians.

The Yin and Yang Professors
Though the doctrine of *yin* and *yang* derives from the Golden Age of the Five Emperors, it was not until the first century of our era that a school of 'philosopher-scientists' devoted wholly to the workings of *yin* and *yang* came into being. Whether they can properly be called Taoists is a matter of opinion but, like the priests of the folk religion, they have been popularly regarded as such, probably because the word 'Taoist' has for centuries been misused as a convenient label to include everything to do with philosophy and religion that is not specifically Confucian or Buddhist. In any case, Taoists have always accorded a very important position to the *yin* and *yang* doctrine. The difference between ordinary Taoists and these new professors was that the latter employed their knowledge of *yin* and *yang* interaction for the purpose of divination and for manipulating future events, which proved to be a profitable enterprise. The researches of these *yin* and *yang* philosophers, together with those of another group who specialised in the science of *wu hsing* (the five activities or 'elements') became incorporated into the main body of Taoist teaching.

Wei Po-yang

A deeply revered Taoist master is Wei Po-yang (second century AD) who, besides incorporating the *wu hsing* science and a much more ancient science based on the trigrams of the *Book of Change* into the corpus of Taoist studies more explicitly than had been done before, wrote an extraordinary book which was destined to be of the greatest importance to the development of Taoism. This was the *Ts'an T'ung Ch'i*, a title impossible to translate, although it has sometimes been rendered 'The Union of Three'. It is an esoteric manual setting forth the practice of the internal and external alchemies which were to form the very heart and centre of Taoist cultivation at many different levels. So enigmatic is its wording that there are passages which can be applied to such widely different pursuits as transmuting base metals into gold, compounding the golden elixir, practising an internal yogic alchemy, attaining to mystical union with the Way, creating an immortal foetus by means of bedroom arts, and even military strategy and the art of government – a miscellany made possible by the conviction that, since the same natural laws apply at all levels, there is nothing that cannot be accomplished by making use of them in an identical sequence though in widely different contexts. What one can never be sure about is whether Wei Po-yang and the authors of similar manuals really believed in the possibility of transmuting base metals into gold and compounding a universal panacea, or whether this interpretation of their works was a blind to guard more exalted purposes from the profane.

Yü Chi

Another Han dynasty sage was Yü Chi, who first achieved fame as a maker of 'charm waters', medicines made by burning slips of red paper inscribed with magic words and mixing the ashes with pure water for the patient to drink. Some of these medicines were believed to confer invulnerability against weapons and disease, so a huge demand for them arose. Later he seems to have become a mystic with real knowledge of the Way, as may be judged from his extant work; but of course the popular demand for magic charms was to persist for centuries and it may be that his fame long continued to rest on his magical rather than yogic or mystical abilities.

Ko Hung

A century or so after the beginning of our era, the greatest Taoist master of all time was born. His real name was Ko Hung, though he has been much more widely known by an affectionate nickname, Pao P'u-tzû (He Who Embraces Things in the Rough), meaning something like 'a plain and natural man' or 'a man without frills'. (Elsewhere I have translated '*p'u*' as 'the Uncarved Block', following D. C. Lau's rendering, but it would not fit quite well in this context.) In his day, conditions in the warrior-ravaged Empire were still chaotic. Coming from a family of Confucian scholar-officials and having from very early years been fond of study, Ko Hung acquired a fund of learning for which he was universally respected, not least of all by his Confucian peers. His interests included philosophy, moral principles, medicine, all kinds of religious beliefs and the manners and customs of his age. Planning to enter the civil service and climb to high rank like his forebears, he mastered the Four Books and Five Classics so thoroughly that the Confucians venerated him as an adept in their own branch of learning; yet, from the first, he was drawn towards Taoist mysticism and he became an adept in that field above all. During the reign of the Emperor Hui Ti (AD 290–307), he was ordered to lead the imperial troops to suppress a rebellion – it being the civilised practice of the Chinese authorities to bestow such tasks on men of literary attainments much better qualified than soldiers to pacify areas recovering from a revolt, since they would be likely to display both intelligence and sympathy. Indeed there is a Chinese proverb which runs: 'Good iron is not used for making nails, nor good men for making soldiers.' The campaign was a great success, but it left Ko Hung with a distaste for public life and he decided to seek refuge from the world of dust in rural seclusion. After wandering for some years, he settled on Lo Fu Mountain and became absorbed in cultivation of the Way. Passing away at the age of 81, he was found sitting cross-legged like one who has fallen asleep during meditation; and it was remarked that his complexion was still youthful, his body as supple as a youth's – sure signs of progress along the Way.

By that time, no less than 116 volumes had flowed from his brush! His erstwhile Confucian admirers can hardly have been pleased with his dictum that 'to be an expert in Confucian studies and yet not believe in the Way of Immortals is not just laughable, but a perversion of true knowledge'! His writings on philosophy reveal a spirit akin to Chuang-tzû's. One passage runs:

> The myriad objects of the universe – hard is it for humans to comprehend them fully. The Way of Immortals – this is not something that ordinary people can hope to understand. The Emperors Ch'in Shih Huang and Han Wu Ti, though they loved to be called Taoists, were no true followers of the Way. As for those *fang shih* (prescriptioners), how can people with a desire for profit deserve to be called Taoists? Ordinary people fettered by their surroundings can never free themselves from common things; how can such people hope to practise the Way?

He insisted that a good teacher is essential to making progress with Taoist studies, that what is written down can never be fully satisfactory. To awaken to spiritual truths, one must have faith and great subtlety of perception, 'for things that are invisible are not for that reason no-things'; Then again:

> ordinary people who long for fame and riches cannot hope to practise the Way, for which the utmost determination is required. Winning longevity or immortality is not a matter of performing rites, reciting charms or taking magical potions; the prime necessity is to be virtuous and firmly abstain from evil. Taoists who think only of nourishing their bodies by yogic practice are bound fail. Without a good teacher they will never learn what is meant by 'compounding the elixir'. Just relying on writings, since these cannot be of real importance, is a waste of time.

It may be that Ko Hung arrived at the opinions just stated rather late in life, for some of his earlier works deal with more mundane matters. He left instructions for compounding various medicines, one of which would make it safe to sleep side by side with invalids suffering from contageous diseases. Also he set much store by breathing yogas, both as a means of keeping free from illness and for winning the supernormal powers which successful yogins usually acquired. Among the recipes he left were 149 secret formulas attributed to Lao-tzû for dealing with the hazards peculiar to solitary mountain dwellers such as 'demons, spirits, tigers, wolves and venomous reptiles'. It may be, of course, that he never lost his faith in such things, but wished to make a distinction between certain useful arts on the one hand and true cultivation of the Way on the other. That part of his works known as 'the esoteric writings' deals with a puzzling medley of subjects. The most interesting of those volumes concern such abstruse matters as the mysterious laws of the universe, the Way of Immortals and transmutation seen as a spiritual rather than merely physical process; but there are others containing instructions for drawing magical diagrams and for the conjuration and subjugation of gods and spirits. Nevertheless, he firmly insists that the subject of attaining immortality is altogether misunderstood by many so-called Taoists, that immortality is a spiritual state to be won only by the spiritually perceptive. In short, he was an enigmatic sage. It is a mistake (into which I sometimes fall myself) to judge such men by twentieth-century standards regarding what is or is not possible; for, though we are less inclined than our fathers and grandfathers to pooh-pooh the possibilities of yogas directed at spiritual aims, most of us still draw the line at what strikes us as magical or spiritist. The point is that when we find writers of old sharing the superstitions current in their age we ought not to deduce from that that they were spiritually or intellectually ungifted and therefore unworthy of respect. One does not, fortunately, condemn Socrates as an ignorant man unworthy of our respect merely because, a few moments before his death, he remembered that he had promised to sacrifice a cock to the God of Healing. I suspect that the wise men of our own day accept many contemporary beliefs that will be laughed at in the future and yet are none the less worthy of honour.

With the passing of Ko Hung the development of Taoism ended, its form having become stabilised for all time. During later dynasties, various students of his works came to the fore, and a few high dignitaries and even emperors evinced enthusiasm for Taoism, although the authorities in general, since most of them were Confucian literati, remained unalterably opposed to a system that placed spiritual cultivation above the cultivation of such virtues as loyalty to the ruler, parents and elders. As for the ordinary people, they could perceive no conflict of ideals; with a tolerance unequalled elsewhere in the world, they embraced Confucianism, Taoism, Buddhism, the cult of ancestors and the folk religion as pertaining to various parts of a supernatural order in which distinctions are superfluous.

T'ao Hung-ching

An ardent follower of Ko Hung who achieved prominence in the latter part of the fifth century was T'ao Hung-ching. While still a child of ten, he procured a copy of Ko Hung's teachings and studied it from morning to night, deriving therefrom a firm determination to nourish his body according to yogic rules so as to be sure of attaining a ripe old age. As a youth he attracted the attention of the reigning emperor by his skill in music and chess, but preferred the solitude of a recluse's life to being a court favourite. It is recorded that his love for the music of wind in the pines was so intense that the sound of it would fill his heart with joy. Sometimes he would been seen bathing in a rocky spring-fed pool and, with the charming and youthful appearance he retained while well on his way to old age, he was several times mistaken for the genie of the pool! An expert in the *yin yang* and *wu hsing* sciences, as well as astrology, compounding herbal medicines and *fêng-shui* (geomancy or the wind and water science), he made such accurate forecasts of events of importance to the national welfare that the reigning emperor is said by one authority to have paid him the unheard of honour of going to visit him in his retreat! Whether or not this improbable story has some truth in it, it indicates that even a Son of Heaven might find it difficult to ensure a Taoists recluse's obedience to a summons from the palace. At the age of 85 T'ao Hung-ching so closely resembled a youth that people were amazed and he was implored to reveal the secret of imperishable youthfulness, but this he staunchly hid from all but a few chosen disciples. Well versed in the Confucian classics and Buddhist sutras as well as Taoist works, he wrote a number of important essays which were long revered, especially on Mao Mountain, the headquarters of a more exalted form of Taoism than the neighbouring Dragon-Tiger Mountain where dwelt the Heavenly Teacher.

The Emperor Hsüan Tsung

Since this chapter has turned out to be a kind of history in which fact and legend are mingled, it would be a pity to omit a T'ang dynasty legend which is highly characteristic of the stories that used to circulate about Taoists. It concerns Hsüan Tsung, the Bright Emperor, who was the very monarch to confer posthumously upon the descendents of Chang Tao-ling the title 'Heavenly Teacher'. Close to the end of his glorious reign, during which poetry, painting, dancing and music flourished as never before, his favourite concubine, the Lady Yang, hanged herself to appease mutinous troops and save her husband's throne. Overcome with grief, the bereaved Emperor abdicated, having lost all desire to live unless some means could be found to communicate with the spirit of his beloved. At last an aged Taoist priest came forward and, having agreed to carry a message to the spirit of the dead lady, sat cross-legged as for meditation and seemed to fall asleep. Returning to consciousness after midnight, he informed the ex-Emperor that, after visiting in spirit numerous realms of immortals, he had at last come upon the Lady Yang in a lovely palace on P'êng Lai Shan in the Eastern Sea. She had been moved by the tidings that His Majesty mourned for her with single-minded grief, so deeply moved, indeed, that she had promised they should be reunited in another life and, as an earnest of the truth of this, had handed to the messenger half of a jade comb with which the Emperor had once presented her. On seeing this ornament, the hitherto unhappy lover was filled with joy, for the existence of this comb of which each of them possessed a half was unknown to any third person.

This story has a weakness. One does not know what the Lady Yang had done to deserve a palace on, of all places, P'êng Lai Shan, unless beauty in itself is a passport to entry among the immortals. However, it is the theme of one of the loveliest and saddest poems in the Chinese language and, for that reason, is remembered.

The Growth of Taoist Influence
With the decline of the T'ang dynasty (AD 618–907) came the end of any hopes there may have been that Taoist influence at court might lead to the replacement of Confucianism by Taoism as the national religion. In the Sung (960–1279) and Ming (1368–1644) dynasties (between which came the brief Mongol dynasty which encouraged all religions, but especially Buddhism), Confucianism underwent a strong revival. As to Taoism, almost the whole of its higher level teachings and practices, except the practice of the internal alchemy (a yoga aimed at the attainment of spiritual immortality), were gradually absorbed into Ch'an (Zen) Buddhism, leaving the huge Heavenly Teacher Sect as the rather inadequate representative of Taoism, since it was in some ways closer to the ancient folk religion than to the teachings of Lao and Chuang or Wei Po-yang and Ko

Hung. Opinions differ as to the extent to which Taoist mystics continued to flourish.

In the Ming dynasty, however, Taoism exercised a notable influence on Confucianism. The Sung scholar Chu Hsi and his Ming successor Wang Yang-ming in turn attempted to give Confucian philosophy a more profound metaphysical basis by incorporating both Taoist and Buddhist concepts. Wang Yang-ming, in particular, having had a warm affection for Taoism in his younger days and at one time been almost on the brink of becoming a recluse, endowed the Confucian notion of the Princely Man or Perfected Sage with some of the qualities to be looked for in a Taoist immortal. Thenceforward, such typically Taoist terms as Tao, *wu* (nothingness), *pei t'i* (pure being), T'ai Chi (the Ultimate) and T'ai Hsü (the Great Void) entered the vocabulary of Confucian writers, and much importance was attached to *ch'i* (vitality) which came to be used somewhat in the sense of pneuma. Confucians took to sitting in meditation and accepted the Taoist doctrines of man's essential unity with all manifestations of nature. Whereas the Confucians of an earlier epoch had envisaged the Perfected Sage as one with a lofty concern with the well-being of society, to that ideal was now added the profounder Taoist notion of attaining perfection by unifying all the energies of body and mind and seeking to come face to face with man's true self. Thus, though organised Taoism declined, the best of Taoism came to be perpetuated first in Ch'an Buddhism and later in neo-Confucianism.

During the Ch'ing dynasty (1644–1911) Taoism made no great headway, yet Taoist philosphers and yogins continued to exist, quite apart from the popular Taoism-cum-folk religion of the Heavenly Teacher Sect, for some of the communities I visited as late as the 1930s and 1940s had unbroken histories going back several centuries. The republican government of the Christian Generalissimo Chiang Kai-shek was inimicable towards both Buddhists and Taoists. Though these religions suffered a decline, they did not die out until monks and recluses were driven forth into the world of dust in the 1950s, there being no place for spiritual cultivation under communism.

Taoism has also had a powerful influence on China's poets and painters throughout the ages, for it inspired a truly religious veneration of nature. Many of the loveliest Chinese works of art owe their haunting beauty to insight into the holiness of all creatures and all objects. Poets such as Li T'ai-po and Po Chu-i were in a real sense Taoist adepts, so deep was their affinity with nature and so loving their appreciation of its workings. The theistic notion of God as a being forever separate from his creation allocates to nature the role of a mere mechanism and the Western world has been blighted by Newton's development of this notion. Taoists exalt nature and living beings, perceiving in them the holiness conferred by their underlying unity with the creative Tao. They recognise that, by allowing itself to be borne along on the tide of creative activity, a creature rids itself of obstacles to direct communion with the Source of life. The sage, according with nature's rhythms, lives tranquilly in the knowledge that there is neither conflict nor division between himself, the universe and the Source which is also the Being and the Goal. For him attainment means relinquishing the thought of anything to be attained. He is satisfied *to be*!

The End
With the coming of the red tide, the recluses were driven from their hermitages back into the world of dust to earn their living as best they could. Rather than describe what little I know from hearsay of this tragic dispersal of the Yellow Emperor's progeny after wellnigh five thousand years, I shall relate a curious little story which reveals that, for two of them, the end was happy. It was told me by a young lady in Singapore who had returned there from her university in China at a time when the communists were completing their take-over of the southern provinces.

The university, as you know, lies at no great distance from some hills where there are many temples. While on a sightseeing trip there, I fell under the spell of a very old Taoist and often used to visit him at weekends. The red cadres who descended on the province just before I left made no secret of what was in store for hermits and for Buddhist monks and nuns.

'What will you do, Master?' I asked, weeping a little at the thought of that poor old man being driven from where he had lived happily almost half his life.

'You are sorry for me, Yi,' he answered. 'Why? Wouldn't it be laughable if a lifelong disciple of Lord Lao were to be afraid of change? I am too old to be put to work and these people care too much for the *look* of things to let me starve in a neighbourhood where so many poor folk have come to love me.'

'How will you *live*, Master?'

'Stop weeping, little girl, and I will tell you. At my age, I can see into the future much better than I can recall the past. When they drive away the others, they will let us old and useless ones stay on, living as best we can on what we manage to grow in our vegetable garden. From kindness? Not exactly. This place is too poor and too remote for them to be in a hurry to use it for some other purpose; and, as three or four of us are so very old, they will look to death to relieve them of the problem of our disposal – rightly so. The Vasty Gate Recluse and I propose to leave this world together on the evening of the Mid-Autumn Festival next year. No, no! Be calm, little Yi. Do you suppose we shall hang ourselves or swallow a *liang* or two of opium? Preposterous! With wine, incense and other things we intend to hide away, we shall perform the festal rites as usual, walk up to the terrace to admire the autumn moon and there sit down. Passing in meditation to the very source of *yin* and *yang*, we shall plunge together into the ocean of the void.'

Though he laughed so merrily, I burst out weeping again. Then suddenly he said: 'Little Yi, are there herons in Singapore?'

'Herons, Master? I – I – no, no, there are not.'

'Good. Rather than have you sad for us, we shall gladly postpone eternal bliss for an hour or so. Be sure to remember what I am going to say. Next year, at the hour of the boar on the night of the festival, go to a high place and watch the sky just above the ocean that surrounds your island. I have a great desire to see the sea by moonlight, never having seen it in all my years. There we shall meet and bid each other a joyous farewell.'

Thinking he was trying to comfort me, I nodded, but did not take the words seriously. Then we said goodbye.

The following year when the festival came round, my father took me to dine with my fiancé's family in a flat overlooking the sea. Although wishing in a sentimental way to do as the old man had asked, I easily allowed myself to be dissuaded by my father's 'You cannot just walk out of a dinner party and go off into the night by yourself. Whatever would the Huangs think of a girl who behaved like that ?'

The meal started late and was a noisy, long-drawn-out affair. We were still at table when the clock struck ten [mid-point of the hour of the boar]. Suddenly I felt strangely dizzy and was advised to go out on to the balcony of the flat, which faced directly on to the sea-shore. It was a lovely clear night with a brilliant moon shining down upon small foam-capped waves. Presently two of these foam-caps rose strangely into the air and sailed rapidly towards me. I put this down to my giddiness until, all of a sudden, I realised that what I had taken for foam-caps were two large white *herons*! Flying very low, they came almost up to where I was sitting and flew round and round uttering what I can only call very happy-sounding cries, long-sustained and beautiful. While this was happening, a sensation of extraordinary bliss made me tingle from head to toe. Instantly I knew that my Taoist friend had not only kept his promise, but had even touched me with something of the ecstasy that would be his for ever in his union with the void!

Chapter 3

为
朴 The Uncarved Block
(The Lao-Chuang Influence)

Attainment of immortality means successful cultivation of the Way. Cultivation of the Way is a lifelong process of refinement of the adept's consciousness. Bringing to bear his fully integrated powers of body and mind, he gradually discovers his real self – which in a sense is no-self. Or, to put it another way, he succeeds in freeing his real self of the gross encumbrances masking its perfection. By no means all Taoists have penetrated to the hidden meaning of their sacred writings; but, no matter at what level of understanding one takes them, those writings carry him high above the dismal preoccupations of worldly life. A mind fed on words such as heaven, earth, dew, essence, cinnabar, moonlight, stillness, jade, pearl, cedar, and winter-plum is likely to have a serenity not to be found in minds ringing with the vocabulary of the present age – computer, tractor, jumbo jet, speedball, pop, dollar, liquidation, napalm, overkill! Who would thrill at the prospect of rocketing to the moon in a billion-dollar spacecraft if he knew how to summon a shimmering gold and scarlet dragon at any time of the day or night and soar among the stars? And how full of wisdom is a philosophy that draws man away from the rat-race, from the tooth-and-claw struggle for status, wealth, power or fame, to live frugally and contentedly in harmony with nature, reaching effortlessly for the tranquillity that flowers in a heart nurtured in stillness!

In touching upon the development of Taoism from the Yellow Emperor down to Ko Hung, Embracer of Things in the Rough, by whom the colourful tapestry was completed, we have passed over the humorous yet sublime philosophy of Lao and Chuang which lends its subtle tones to every part. This we shall now return to; but, as Lao-Chuang philosophy has so often been erroneously put forward as the whole of Taoism in its pristine form, from which the rest has been seen as a falling away, it is best to begin by stepping back to contemplate the tapestry as a whole. Wrought of cunningly interwoven strands, rich but subdued in colour except for flashes of crimson, coral pink and gold here and there – the strands emerging and re-emerging to portray a host of varied and delectable scenes – the whole possesses a unity that can be appreciated only if one perceives that the many divergent aims and practices of Taoists are based on conviction that natural laws like that governing the interaction of *yin* and *yang* are of universal application, so that whether one's purpose is sublime or trivial, pure or corrupt, the way to set about it and the sequence of processes for pursuing it are much the same.

Forming the warp and weft of this tapestry is the ancient concept of Tao, the Way, with its majestic cycles of change motivated by the ceaseless play of the *yin* and the *yang* and the everlasting dance of *wu hsing* (the five activities). Thereon the spiritual progeny of the Yellow Emperor wove the theme of immortality, the idea that individuals enmeshed in desire-born delusions, by according with nature's laws and entering into stillness, cast off those toils and return to the Source of being; the idea of distilling within the body a golden elixir – pure spirit purged of dross so as to be once more identical in substance with the cosmic spirit from which it originally derived. This concept of self-purification was enriched by two parallel streams of thought – the mysticism of Lao and Chuang and their followers, and the secret alchemy of the yogins. Finally, from the marriage of Taoism at the popular level with the ancient folk religion were derived the figures of gods and demons which, though perhaps too fanciful to match the elegance of a tapestry whereon hitherto the only anthropomorphic likenesses had been those of bearded sages and perpetually youthful immortals enraptured by the joys of sky-soaring freedom, nevertheless have their own colourful if occasionally grotesque charm.

I have never quite known how it happened that, in the West, Lao and Chuang came long ago to be regarded as the founders of Taoism, and all its other manifestations to be dismissed as degeneration –

pollution even – of their lofty thought. There is ample evidence in the writings of those sages to indicate that their ideas were derived from a source so old as to have seemed ancient even as far back as the fifth or sixth century BC. The *Book of Change* (*I Ching*), itself a much earlier work than theirs, provides evidence that is quite irrefutable. Why then has the myth been so long perpetuated? If the former and only recently changed Western attitude towards Tibetan Buddhism is accepted as a guide, it would seem that mistakes made very early on in contacts between the West and a hitherto barely known Eastern culture are repeated by writer after writer, giving the impression that later writers have had their minds made up for them in advance before they as much as enter upon their own first-hand studies.

The philosophy of Lao and Chuang is in any case worthy of our deepest reverence. Far from wishing to denigrate them, I esteem them above most other men. A handsome bronze statue of Lao-tzû occupies the place of honour on my desk and, just behind it, hangs a calligraphic scroll bearing my favourite passage from the *Tao Tê Ching*. During the year or so since I acquired them, I have found them an unfailing source of inspiration. There are plenty of works available on the teachings of those sages. Here I am concerned mainly with those aspects of the doctrine which are of prime concern in studying the development of the Taoist concept of immortality. Properly understood, the term 'immortal' connotes something similar to what Lao and Chuang meant by 'the True Man', 'the Perfect Man', 'the Sage', except that, in the writings of Huang Lao adepts, there is often an assumption that immortality cannot be readily attained without the assistance of yogic practices such as breathing yogas, the internal alchemy, etc. The title of this chapter is taken from the Chinese ideogram *p'u*, which occurs several times in the *Tao Tê Ching*. The dictionary defines it as meaning the 'substance of things' and as 'things in the rough' and I have used the second of these in translating Ko Hung's nickname, Pao P'u-tzû. In most other contexts, I prefer D. C. Lau's rendering in the Penguin version of the *Tao Tê Ching* – the 'uncarved block'. More than any other single word, *p'u* expresses Lao-tzû's conception of what a sage should aim to be (if 'aim' is not too suggestive of consciously directed effort to be fitting in a Taoist context). Here are some pertinent quotations:

Because he has no high opinion of himself, [the sage's] mind is luminous; not caring for status, he becomes illustrious; being without pride, he achieves success; unassertive, he is supreme. Because he does not strive, no one in the world can vie with his supremacy. There is an old saying: 'The imperfect becomes whole'. How true that is! To become whole and return [to the Source], one must be ever in accord with nature. . . . There is nothing in the world so weak as water, nor anything strong enough to overcome it. . . . The man of great wisdom is like water which, though benefiting all things, never strives. . . . That which is strong and hard gets put down; that which is pliant and supple is exalted. . . . As low ground forms a foundation for the high, so does humility form the foundation of regard. . . . He who stands on tiptoe totters; he who takes great strides cannot travel far. . . . The wise men of old who took goodness as their way possessed marvellously subtle powers of penetration; they were so deep that none could plumb their minds and, on this account, if forced to describe them we can only say that they moved cautiously like men fording a river; they were retiring as though shy of all around them; their conduct [to all] was respectful as though to honoured guests; they could adapt themselves like ice melting before a fire; they were as artless as blocks of uncarved wood.

Again and again Lao-tzû emphasises the unwisdom of seeking prominence, wealth or status; the wisdom of being simple and artless – hence that graphic image, the uncarved block. This image perfectly accords with what is meant by 'becoming an immortal' and underlies much of Japanese as well as Chinese art and culture. In the Far East, restraint and simplicity have long been regarded as the hallmark of true greatness, and this principle is inherent in the best of the poetry and visual arts of China and Japan, where the loveliest poems consist of a few bare syllables; the finest paintings are often executed with an astonishing economy of brush-strokes and with no colour but the various shades of watered black ink on a white surface; the most exquisite ceramics are notable for extreme simplicity; and the most elegant furniture owes almost the whole of its beauty to simplicity of line.

This love of the simple and unassuming derives directly from intuitive perception of the nature of the Tao. Formless and void, the

Tao is the source of all the myriad forms. Mother of the universe
and sustainer of all creatures, it is perfectly indifferent to – indeed
unconscious of – its bounty. Effortlessly it replenishes lack and
diminishes excess, accomplishing all that is required without fore-
thought, strain or hurry. It is at once both void and form, the one
aspect being essential to the other, just as voidness is essential to a
vessel, unimpeded space to a window or a door. For creatures to sing
the praises of such a Mother in the form of hymns or psalms is
simply to make a noise. The Tao is never obtrusive, demanding or
flamboyant. To sing of its glories would be a waste of breath; what
needs to be done is to observe the manner of its working and take
that for a model. To live by the Tao is to function like the Tao, to
conform with that marvellously effortless way of getting all things
done, and to produce what is of use to others as the Tao produces
beneficial rains and dews with never a thought of praise or thanks,
still less reward.

The secret of sagehood, which is also immortality, is acceptance;
hence Lao-tzû's injunction to become like a new-born babe accepting
things as they come without distinction. To tamper with their natural
progression is a sure way of courting sorrow and disaster; to go along
easily with things as they are is the way to tranquillity and wisdom.
Why resent this or that, why make distinctions? Without ugliness,
there could be no beauty; without evil, no good; without death, no
life. Alternations are necessary to existence; seeming calamities are
often benefits in disguise. Low has its usefulness no less than high,
last no less than first. Expansion implies contraction, straight implies
crooked, strong implies weak. Rising and falling, taking and giving –
each in its place serves a need. No storm lasts forever, no rain falls
unceasingly – so *why* worry? The sage is one who knows well that
acceptance of what is is always best; nature be may relied upon to
confer benefits in its own time and season; to tamper with its working
is to invite retribution.

Softness prevails over hardness as water prevails over all obstruc-
tions to its flow. Arrogance and contention violate the way of heaven,
bringing misery in their train. True sagehood, true superiority, is
never to be won by strife, but by letting things be. Resistant plants
get blown down or snapped; supple plants survive the gale. This is
what is meant by learning to accord with nature.

A corollary of letting things be as they are is leaving people free to do their own thing. Lao-tzû condemned the talk of benevolence, filial piety and loyalty that was so characteristic of Confucians, pointing out that insisting on the need for them is a sure sign of their being in decline. The way of the sage is to do just what is needed when things go wrong and then withdraw from the scene, wasting neither words nor thought upon what is now past. Laws, he felt, merely lead to an increase in the varieties of crime. This teaching contributed to the fondness of Taoist adepts for the solitude of the mountains where one can be free to act in accordance with the prompting of the heart, unfettered by laws or the usages of society.

However, tolerance and acceptance by themselves do not lead to sagehood, to immortality. There has of course to be a positive side to the adept's cultivation of the Way. Lao-tzû's main prescription for attainment is to be frugal, selfless and *still*. To paraphrase his teaching on this subject: colours blind, tones deafen, rich foods vitiate the palate, pleasures derange, greed for wealth perverts. Those who hold fast to the Way desire no satiety; where satiety is avoided, everything seems fresh and new. Nothing is worse than multitudinous desires: lust, distraction, greed disturb tranquillity. One must abide by the real, caring not at all for the merely ornamental. Artifice and eagerness for power or riches are nothing to a sage; it is by not attempting to hold on to things that he spares himself loss. To percieve the way to heaven, one need not go a step beyond his doorway. Discarding learning, discarding care, discarding desire, the adept cultivates stillness and, in that stillness, sublime perception of the Way will be attained. Then does the Real appear and he can reach to its utmost bounds; it is not to be seen, not to be heard, but to be apprehended in silence and stillness. The *Tao Tê Ching* is too tersely worded for the reader to be sure as to whether any kind of formal yogic practice is entailed in following this teaching. Do the words 'just sitting still' imply regular meditation practice or not? 'Stop up the orifices of lust, close their gates!' could be interpreted either way. Well, whatever Lao-tzû may have intended, the fact is that that injunction is difficult to carry out; for which reason all kinds of yogic regimens and devices were subsequently developed as aids to attainment, but such practical aids ought not to be considered a departure from or perversion of his teaching; rather, they constitute a much needed development, for not all men are equally gifted with a capacity for stillness. Furthermore, the absence in the *Tao Tê Ching* of specific instructions on contemplative and breathing techniques does not necessarily imply that Lao-tzû did not countenance them. In an exceptionally terse text dealing with basic principles, one would not expect to find detailed instructions of that kind. In the thirty-third section of that work there is, as a matter of fact, a passage that seems to be directly concerned with the yogic goal of immortality. It runs: 'To die and not to perish – [that is] immortality!' True, the Chinese term here rendered 'immortality' literally means no more than 'longevity', but among Taoists it is used with either or both those meanings and, in this context, 'longevity' would seem to make no sense. Not that the matter is of any real importance, for – except among the naive proponents of the doctrine of flesh-and-blood transmogrification to immortal state – 'becoming an immortal' and 'becoming a perfect sage' have always been regarded as virtually synonymous.

Chuang-tzû, who is thought to have lived about a century later than Lao-tzû, is so closely indentified with him that the term Lao-Chuang has long been used to denote them jointly; however, there are dissimilarities as well as many close similarities between them. Chuang-tzû's works, besides being much more voluminous, could almost be described as diffuse in comparison with the astonishing terseness of the *Tao Tê Ching*; what is more, they are full of chatty anecdotes and provide a feast of sly humour. The essential difference between the two sages is, however, of another kind. Whether or not Lao-tzû can rightly be described as a quietist without a well-defined mystical goal and a stranger to formal contemplative meditation is an open question, but there is a fair amount of evidence pointing to this as an apt description. With Chuang-tzû, it is different. I do not see how anyone who has studied his works can doubt that he was well acquainted with states of mystical rapture lying well beyond the frontier of quietist accord with nature. Yet many writers have suggested that both these sages sought only simple rewards for their practice of frugality, their love of stillness and their acceptance of nature's ups and downs without any wish that things be other than they are. According to this view, all they wished for was to be left alone by the authorities during a turbulent era when to attract attention was unhealthy, to live free from anxiety and revel in simple joys – a cool breeze, the sparkle of a mountain stream, the fruits of the field, the reflection of the moon in clear water, the warmth of sunshine, the purity of untrodden snow, the shadowy outlines of mountains lost in cloud, mist tinged with the rosiness of dawn rising from a lake, the music of wind in the pines, the rustle of bamboos. I, personally, doubt this even in the case of Lao-tzû, for many of his cryptic sayings point to a more transcendent kind of wisdom; but there is certainly no positive evidence that he was acquainted with the ecstatic joy that is attained in the stillness of contemplation when the inner light shines forth. Chuang-tzû's works, on the other hand, frequently communicate a sense of the ineffable bliss that arises when the yogin communes in silence and stillness with that which looms above earth and sky and is yet so close as to be found shining within the innermost recesses of his own mind. Ancient Chinese texts are so terse and leave so much room for varying interpretations that it is difficult to be sure about much less recondite matters than these; but, whereas a strong case could be built up for supposing that Lao-tzû was more of a quietist with mystical leanings than a fully fledged mystic, it seems clear to me that this qualification of mysticism does not apply to Chuang-tzû

Burton Watson, the wise and percipient translator of Chuang-tzû's complete works, does not agree with me. In his introduction he suggests, with becoming tentativeness, that Chuang-tzû sought no more than 'freedom from the world' to be attained by tossing away conventional values so as to escape both self-imposed and external bondage. In his view, if I have understood him rightly, the sage's philosophy can be summarised as follows:

Neither name, fame, status and high regard on the one hand, nor blame, disregard and failure to attain high rewards on the other, are worth a moment's care – this recognition confers immunity from troubles coming from without. Similarly, tossing away attachment, especially to wealth and unneeded possessions, enables one to break away from self-created bondage, since life's *real* essentials are – or were in his time – seldom hard to come by. Calm acceptance of natural ills, such as poverty, disease and death, as a necessary and not unwelcome part of nature's plan makes one invulnerable to sorrow. Man, as the author of most of his own sufferings, can banish sorrow by the simple expedient of refusing to allow his equanimity to be disturbed by whatever comes along. As to war, injustice, widespread poverty and other social evils, these would cease if men would refrain from falsely labelling things good and bad, desirable or otherwise. Purposeful, value-ridden activity should be eschewed in favour of *wu wei* – the spontaneous, mindless activity with which nature succeeds most admirably in accomplishing her ends. To indicate how satisfying this kind of activity can be, the sage adduces the work of skilled craftsmen: the expert wood-carver's knife flies instinctively to achieve the best results with a beautiful economy of effort; so it is with a skilled lumberman, a butcher, a swimmer – they do not need to ponder their actions to ensure perfection. To quote Chuang-tzû's own words:[1] 'He who practises the Way does less every day, does less and goes on doing less until he reaches the point where he does nothing, does nothing and yet *there is nothing that is not done!*' The wise man embraces simplicity, enjoying the sights and sounds that come his way; free from attachment, he welcomes their arrival, but lets them go without a care. Thus he wanders joyously through life; having no special aim, he knows nothing of disappointment or frustration. 'The mountains and forests, the hills and fields fill us with over-flowing delight and we are joyful. Our joy is not ended when grief comes rushing in.' Another passage runs: 'The Perfect Man uses his mind like a mirror – responding but not storing.' When something goes wrong, a hearty laugh will do more than save the situation. Chuang-tzû was fond of laughter and excelled in poking fun at pretentiousness and pomposity.

Seen thus, Chuang-tzû's teaching does look like mere quietism, mystical perhaps, but without any sense of a high mystical goal to be attained. However, there are passages in his works that are surely open to a mystical and even to a yogic interpretation. The descriptions of adepts who have become invulnerable to heat, cold, hunger and mishaps of every kind, and who are able to fly joyously above the stars, are clearly not meant to be taken literally, but what can they point to other than to the exhilarating mystical rapture and sensations of buoyant freedom that result from full success in yogic contemplation? Speaking apocryphally and in fun of Lieh-tzû, a fellow sage, Chuang-tzû derides him for doing no better than riding on the wind, saying that though this saved him the trouble of walking, he had still to depend on *something* to get him around, whereas the true sage, 'mounting on the truth of heaven and earth' and 'riding the

---

[1]   Dr Burton Watson's translation has been used throughout for quotations from Chuang-tzû.

changes of the six breaths', can wander throughout boundless infinity without having to depend on any sort of steed. Incidentally, this passage may also point to familiarity with yogic breathing techniques, of which one later on came to be called 'breathing through the heels' with reference to another passage in which Chuang-tzû mentions this practice as one of the accomplishments of the true sage. Elsewhere, however, he does castigate certain yogins who taught an over-complicated system of breathing and yogic postures, saying: 'To pant and to puff, to hale and to sip, to spit out the old breath and draw in the new, practising "bear hangings" and "bird stretchings", longevity their only concern – such is the life favoured by scholars who practise [the kind of yoga known as] Induction!'

Well, it is not in the least surprising that Chuang-tzû was opposed to over-pretentious yogic methods, but he himself gives some vivid descriptions of yogic contemplation and its results, one of which runs:

> The essence of the Perfect Way is deep and darkly shrouded; its extreme is mysterious and hushed in silence. Let there be no seeing, no hearing; enfold the spirit in quietude and the body will right itself. . . . When the eye does not see, the ear does not hear and the mind does not know, your spirit will protect your body and your body enjoy long life. Be cautious of what is within; block off what is without, for much knowledge is harmful. Then I will lead you above the Great Brilliance, to the source of the perfect *Yang*; I will guide you through the Dark and Mysterious Gate to the source of the perfect *Yin*. . . . You have only to take care and guard your own body; then other things will themselves grow sturdy.

In a humorously apocryphal account of a visit paid by Confucius to Lao-tzû, the Taoist sage is discovered thus: 'Utterly motionless, he did not seem even to be human.' Then Confucius exclaims in wonder: 'Did my eyes deceive me? A moment ago, Sir, you seemed to be as stiff as a long-dead tree, as though you had forgotten things, taken leave of men, and were fixed in solitude itself!' To which Lao-tzû is made to reply: 'I was letting my mind wander in the Beginning of things.'

In another passage, warm praise of meditation is put into the mouth of, of all unlikely people, Confucius himself:

You have heard of flying with wings, but you have never heard of the flying without wings. You have heard of the knowledge which knows, but you have never heard of the knowledge that does not know. Look into the closed room, the empty chamber where brightness is born! Fortune and blessing gather where there is stillness. But if you do not keep still – this is what is called sitting but racing around. Let your ears and eyes communicate with what is inside, and put mind and knowledge on the outside. Then even gods and spirits will come to dwell, not to speak of men!

Those Taoists who actually believed in physical transmogrification may have taken literally Chuang-tzû's description of a holy man on Ku-Shê Mountain 'with skin like ice or snow, and gentle and shy as a young girl', whose sustenance was dew, his steed a dragon; but though we cannot possibly suppose Chuang-tzû to have been naive enough to credit such stories, these words do conjure up the wondrous magical sensations that reward success in yogic meditation, and also the youthful appearance long retained by some yogins.

That he did not share the early Taoist dream of attaining immense longevity is apparent from several passages, such as: '[The True Sage] delights in early death, he delights in old age; he delights in the beginning; he delights in the end' and 'How do I know that loving life is not a delusion? How do I know that, in hating death, I am not a man who, having left home in his youth, has forgotten the way back?' On the other hand, he clearly did not suppose – as some people have alleged of both Lao and Chuang – that death is the end of everything, for he wrote: 'Life is the companion of death; death is the beginning of life' and 'Some day there will be a great awakening when we shall know that all this is a dream'. The latter saying is fully compatible with the mystical concept of 'returning to the Source', that is reabsorption into the undifferentiated Tao.

Whether one chooses to regard Lao and Chuang as quietists or as mystics, it is indisputable that their teaching inspired many others to take the path of mysticism. The interpretation generally given to inner stillness, goes far beyond the purely philosophical concept that man, as the master of his destiny for the duration of his lifespan, is the author of his own sufferings and can cure most of them by welcoming all that happens as part of nature's pattern. With inner stillness is associated the inner light best known to accomplished yogins.

Viewed in relationship to the problems of modern life, quietist teaching may seem inadequate, for it is obvious that man's needs are not fulfilled by nature's bounty if one happens to be living in the smoky brick and asphalt slums of Birmingham or Liverpool. It is long since more than a small minority of people have been free to wander effortlessly through life, and it would appear that this mode of living had its difficulties as far back as two millenia ago, for hermits wandering through the mountains on their own soon gave place to small communities of recluses with some means or other of support. And yet? Even allowing that most people have to earn their living by means that are more or less incongenial, there is still ample scope for ameliorating life's ills by applying the methods of Lao and Chuang. If being wealthy is taken to mean having the means to satisfy one's every want, all but the very poor can become rich as though at a single stroke of a magician's wand simply by ceasing to want more than is really necessary for sustaining life! By being content with little and not giving a rap for what the neighbours think, one can attain a very large measure of freedom, shedding care and worry in a trice. To these mitigations can, moreover, be added the tranquil joy that is won through meditation, and to this the ecstasy of mystical experience, followed by a world-transcending apotheosis.

The Ch'an (Zen) masters, who are as much the heirs of early Taoism as of Indian Buddhism, teach methods much closer to Taoist cultivation of the Way and therefore to the teaching of Lao and Chuang than is generally realised. Their terse aphorisms and characteristic humour are both highly reminiscent of those sages. What they mean by Mind and its indivisibility from individual minds is not different from what Taoists mean by the Tao as the Great Void and the Tao that is to be found within the individual when the mists of delusion have been swept away. The Ch'an doctrine that Enlightenment is to be attained in the Here and Now is precisely the Taoist doctrine of 'attaining immortality' properly understood. The Taoist word *shên* and the Ch'an Buddhist term *hsin*, the one meaning 'spirit', the other 'mind', are often interchangeable and, in later Taoist works, *hsin* often replaces *shên*. If there is any real difference in the two modes of cultivation, it is to be found only in the stress placed by Taoists on using physical as well as mental endowments as a means to attainment.

However, in comparatively recent times, it is among Taoists

rather than Ch'an Buddhists that the debt to Lao and Chuang has been explicitly acknowledged. I was often struck by the extent to which Taoist recluses reflected in their speech and conduct facets of the wisdom of those sages, sometimes by quoting their works – many could recite the *Tao Tê Ching* by heart – sometimes indirectly. Much of their sweetness, unobtrusiveness and gaiety gave one the feeling that they were deeply imbued with Chuang-tzû's spirit. Without the powerful strand of wisdom contributed by Lao and Chuang, Taoism might have lost its appeal for men of education and have suffered the fate of the Heavenly Teacher Sect in being almost entirely submerged in the ancient folk religion.

It is a pity that so little is known of the other Taoist sages who are thought to have flourished at about the same period as Chuang-tzû. Of their history one knows nothing and of their works only fragments survive. Outstanding among them was Lieh-tzû, of whose teaching the following aphorisms may give some idea:

To know the outcome, look to the root. Study the past to know the future.

When the road goes straight, I romp ahead; when it twists and turns, I make the best of it I can.

The ancients regarded death as a going back, life as having to leave home.

The sage keeps company with those who think of life and death just as one thinks of waking and sleeping, not with those who have forgotten the meaning of *return*.

It is no less a pity that one so seldom encounters the modern counterparts of those ancient sages. In the West today, Ch'an masters and Zen roshis turn up in the most unexpected places, but Taoist teachers are hard to find. It cannot be that all of them have suddenly vanished from the world of dust, though one likes to imagine that they escaped the red tide by winging their way to the realms of immortals. The true explanation is probably that they are shy and unassuming, that they live in obscurity, thus exemplifying Lao-tzû's words: 'The Tao has ever been nameless – an uncarved block.'

Taoist Humour
An appealing characteristic of Taoism is a fondness for clothing even sacred matters in the garb of humour. Chuang-tzû's works and others abound in amusing – but never cruel – aprocryphal anecdotes in which not only Confucius but even Lao-tzû himself is made to appear just a trifle ridiculous. The notion that piety should be sanctimonious is wholly absent. The following example, although of rather modern origin, is fairly typical:

Once Confucius happened to come upon Lao-tzû bathing in a stream. Disliking pretence and having not a shred of prudishness, the elderly sage emerged from the water to receive him stark naked. 'Sir,' cried the great moralist, hastily averting his eyes, 'I perceive you are lacking in a proper sense of human dignity. If humans were to go around unclad, in what way would they be distinguishable from birds and beasts ?' 'Sir', replied Lao-tzû, 'is it such a bad thing to put ourselves on the level of birds and beasts ? They are strangers to lust for fame, covetousness, stinginess, wallowing in luxury and countless other vices. You will excuse me if I go on with my bathe.'

Another day Lao-tzû, espying Confucius preaching to a handful of disciples on the subject of benevolence, came up to him flapping his arms and squawking like a crow, whereat the benevolent sage leapt up with a roar of anger, crimson as a man about to die of apoplexy. 'Sir,' remarked Lao-tzû, keeping nimbly out of reach, 'I was edified by what you had to say about benevolence. Now why this sudden change ? If humans were to go around tearing at the eyes of old gentlemen who like a bit of fun, in what way would they be distinguishable from famished tigers ?'

Upon a third occasion, Confucius chanced to see Lao-tzû tippling in a wineshop. 'Sir,' admonished the outraged sage, 'is *this* your sense of decorum ? Do you hope to teach the Way by imbibing in view of all and sundry ?' 'Sir,' replied Lao-tzû, 'do you not approve this demonstration of my being neither bird nor beast ? I have not heard that such creatures tipple.' 'But for a learned master to disgrace his grey hairs in public is *worse* than being bird or beast,' exclaimed Confucius. 'You must be joking, Sir,' replied Lao-tzû. 'Once you reprimanded me for behaving in the manner of birds and beasts; now you admonish me for *not* behaving like our befeathered and befangéd friends. Clearly you stand in need of some instruction. The Tao, you must know, is the progenitor of all and sundry, of you and me, of birds and beasts, of this wine-pot and this wine. Imbibing the Tao is a very fitting occupation for a Taoist, one would think. When you have learnt that everything beneath the wide canopy of heaven is imbued with holiness, *then* indeed you may call yourself a sage.'

'Wonderful!' cried Confucius, thunderstruck. 'Ah, what wisdom has this gentleman. His like will be hard to find this side of heaven! He is a very phoenix among crows!'

Chapter 4

Poems of Stillness
(Taoist Poetry)

The poems inspired by Taoist love of nature are a joy to read and most admirably convey the spirit of mountain-dwelling recluses, but it is difficult for the translator to capture more than a hint of their beauty. Their rhyme and even the original rhythms have to be discarded, for the verse forms most often chosen have just five or seven syllables to each line, and English with its *-ing*s and *-ed*s, its *a*s and *the*s, all of which are absent in the original, cannot be so compressed. Having wrestled with the problems night and day, I decided to use two (and occasionally even three) lines for each line of Chinese, so as to be able to keep the lines rather short than long and thus preserve something of the airy lightness which is one of the chief beauties of these poems. The rhythms of the originals, of which the first, second and fourth lines usually rhyme, may be represented thus: – – / – – – or – – / – – / – – –. Not all of the poets selected were consciously practising cultivation of the Way, but all were Taoist in the sense of possessing that special affinity with nature which, in China, is the hallmark both of Taoists and great artists.

In the reign of the Bright Emperor of the T'ang dynasty – that same Hsüan Tsung who posthumously confirmed Chang Tao-Ling's title of Heavenly Teacher and sent a Taoist off to the realms of immortals in search of the spirit of his beloved concubine, the Lady Yang – Taoism was greatly in favour at court. Moreover, the Emperor was such a lavish patron of the arts that poets, painters, actors and musicians flocked to the imperial capital, Ch'ang An, making it one of the most scintillating centres of beauty in the history of the world. Thither the great poet, Li T'ai-po, was summoned and there he enjoyed the splendours and comforts accorded to court favourites, but presently fell into disgrace and retired to a hermit's cottage in the mountains. According to a popular story, the circumstances which led Li to compose one of his loveliest Taoistic poems were as follows. During his exile, an official was sent to announce that he had been taken back into the Emperor's favour and so must hasten to return; but, to the elegantly attired and perfumed messenger, already dismayed by his journey into a place so wild and comfortless, the poet answered that he would not go.

'Eh?' exclaimed the flabbergasted courtier, lip curling as he surveyed the exile's hovel, 'What in the world is there to detain you in a place like this?' Li T'ai-po's answer is contained in a poem of just twenty syllables, very light and unassuming, but so charming (in the original at least) that Shigeyoshi Obata who translated almost all of Li's poems into English some fifty years ago, preferred it to any other. I do not remember his translation, so I have used my own:

> You ask me why I dwell
> Amidst these jade-green hills?
> I smile. No words can tell
> The stillness in my heart.
> The peach-bloom on the water,
> How enchantingly it drifts!
> I live in another realm here
> Beyond the world of men.

Knowing how greatly this poet was influenced by Taoistic thought, can we perhaps take the concluding words to suggest that his peaceful contemplation of nature had given him an inkling of what it is to attain more than human state? 'Stillness' is, in any case, the keyword of the poem; it often signifies the state of mind essential to intuitive perception of the Way. The fallen petals drifting on the water are, perhaps, just a random example of the manifold beauties of nature around him, beauties compared with which the glittering splendours of the court seem tawdry. Who knows whether the poet really had all this in mind when he dashed off the poem? Yet one may surmise this, for Li was so deeply imbued with the spirit of Taoism that many of his poems read like charming adornments to sermons on the Way.

Ch'üan Tê-yü who, like many other busy officials, enjoyed periods of seclusion in the mountains, describes a visit to the sacred mountain, Mao Shan. In Taoist poetry, curtains of mist or expanses of white cloud symbolise perception of the boundless void, the Tao in its undifferentiated form.

> Dismounting from my horse,
> Dusk falling on the wild,
> I hear amidst the silence
> The plash of a mountain rill.
> Birds sing and petals fall;
> Of men there is not a trace.
> The window of my hut
> Is curtained with white cloud.

Another poet, Shih Tê, celebrates the joys of seclusion in some charming lines entitled 'The Remedy'.

> How lovely this forest spring –
> Not a dwelling within miles,
> Just clouds of misty spray
> Above the plunging torrent.
> The path winds up to where
> Gibbons cry among the trees.
> A tiger's roar re-echoes
> Among the lonely hills,
> Hushing the pines' soft whisper
> And the cawing of the birds.
> Skirting the dripping rocks,
> I climb towards the peak
> Or rest on a pebbled bank
> To peer through tangled creepers
> At the distant moated walls
> Whence the city's din comes softly.

Ch'êng Hao, in a poem of just twenty syllables entitled 'Attainment' hints in veiled language at the supreme mystical experience.

> Serenity has fallen,
> All is tranquillity.
> I sleep on, though the eastern casement
> Reddens with the dawn.

Silently I contemplate
The myriad forms
Spontaneously brought forth
By nature's hand.
Sweetly the seasons reach their fullness
– And so with men.

'Among the Wu I Mountains' is the title of the following poem by Hsieh Fang-tê, known to history for his gallant resistance against the Mongol invasion in the thirteenth century. Perhaps he was driven into hiding among those lovely hills now famed for their fragrant tea-shrubs, but still very lonely and wild. The conclusion of the poem is so enigmatic that one cannot be sure of the thought that inspired it; but, whether he came upon a flowering plum-tree somewhere in those lonely hills or recalled one while thinking of the home he might never see again, it is certain that, for him, this plant was a symbol of a great achievement for which he had wearily sought in vain. Though a warrior by circumstance, he obviously shared that special feeling for nature in the wild that has characterised so many of his countrymen down the ages, whether Taoist hermits or scholars and officials.

It is ten long years since I
Even dreamed of going back home.
Now I stand alone amidst bluish peaks
On the bank of a turbid stream –
Earth and sky a vasty stillness
After the mountain rain.
Ah, how many lives of pruning
Ere the plum-tree is made to bloom?

In the next poem, a gentleman whose Taoist cognomen was Li Fêng Lao-jên describes a recluse of his acquaintance. According to the doctrine of *wu wei* (no calculated, profit-seeking activity), cultivators of the Way learn to achieve without striving. It is by stillness, never by strife. that attainment is won.

Cool as ice
His Taoist heart.
No vain strife
Towards the goal.

> The Tao arises
> Of itself,
> So still his mind –
> A shining moon-disc,
> Glistening, immaculate.

Another of Li F'êng's poems, entitled 'The Willow Immortal', speaks of the tranquillity that follows upon meditation during which the mind soars above the world.

> Over range upon range he wanders,
> Insubstantial as a summer cloud.
> Returned to his body, he lies gazing
> At the mistily veiled moon.
> A breeze, pine-scented, whispering softly,
> Pervades him with its blissful chill.

This poem is full of Taoist symbolism. The spirit wandering away from the body during meditation may be taken either metaphorically or literally, for many Taoists believe that it is possible to create a spirit-body that can leave its mortal frame at will. The mistily veiled moon symbolises the Tao which, perceived in all its shining clarity during meditation, is once more veiled now that the meditation is over, but the memory of it still lingers. The breeze is *ch'i* (cosmic vitality).

Again Li F'êng seeks to convey the bliss of meditation:

> Faintly upon the breeze
> Come the scents of cassia and pine.
> The moon's cold radiance
> Bathes the temple hall.
> Lapped in stillness,
> The hermit sits
> And flies beyond the world.
> To him, all sounds are silence
> And there is nothing else at all –
> Just all-pervading coolness.

The followers of most religions clothe their concepts of the ineffable with such epithets as brilliant, glorious, blazing, splendorous, magnificent; whereas Taoists prefer such terms as cool, shadowy, mysterious, hidden, vast, silent, tranquil, still. It is this which gives Taoist writings their characteristic flavour. Even at moments of triumph and exhileration, Li P'êng's language is restrained. In the following poem he describes the very moment of attaining the 'sacred elixir', here used as a synonym for the supreme mystical experience that sets the adept free for ever from bondage to egotism, passion and desire.

> The sacred elixir
> Is his for ever!
> His tranquil mind
> Gleams like a hidden mirror
> Dispersing the phantom shapes
> Of the world of dust.
> His body, freed from bondage,
> Idles like a floating cloud.

Chinese poets, as students of Ch'an (Zen) well know, are fond of comparing the mind of a sage to a mirror that reflects the passing show without receiving the least stain, no matter what evils or horrors have been enacted. Unlike the longings of unenlightened men for what is seen and loved, these reflections do not linger. Taoists are fond, too, of comparing men of high spiritual attainment to floating clouds, beautiful phenomena which *are* but make no effort to *be*. The filmy lightness of an idling summer cloud is suggestive of the sensation of weightlessness that characterises immortals, a sensation born of absolute freedom from care and anxiety.

Of the poems rendered so far, except for the longer 'Remedy', all consist in the original of just twenty or twenty-eight syllables. This verse form is ideal for capturing with a few masterly strokes a momentary sensation or appearance, a single throb of feeling. For conveying the essence of the doctrine, longer poems are required. One of these is Lü Yen's 'Nature's Laws'. In Chinese it has a powerfully alchemic flavour, much of which is necessarily lost in translation. For example, the original of 'Life happens just because our parents choose to mate' would, if rendered literally, yield: 'Life's brink is just in a *yin-yang* tripod'; my phrase, 'the natural course of things' is a paraphrase of 'sun-moon revolutions'; 'our human form' stands for 'eight-trigram vitality' (a reference to the trigrams in the *Book of Change*); and 'man's elements' paraphrases 'radiance of the five activities'. I should dearly have liked to retain this alchemical language because it is so typically Taoist, but the result must surely have been quite incomprehensible. As it stands, I am rather proud of having rendered the original one hundred and twelve syllables in only slightly more than double that number without, I hope, losing much of the meaning.

> Though pent for years
> Within this world of dust,
> I neither work nor worry,
> Leaving all to nature's plan.
> Life happens just because
> Our parents choose to mate
> And the rest of it then follows
> The natural course of things.
>
> Still, our human frame conceals
> A precious gem within;
> Man's elements, though coarse,
> Embody pure spirit.
> When the mulberry field's[1] transmuted
> To self-existent Being,
> A worldling then becomes
> A world-transcending sage.
>
> It's a joke when people ask
> Whereabouts my home may be.
> With my magic cloud-tipped staff
> I draw dawn-clouds from the sky.[2]
> All that talk of an 'inner light'
> That the meditator sees
> Shining out between the eyes[3]
> Is by no means idle gossip;
> But it would not do to boast
> That my 'golden flower' has bloomed.[4]
>
> A three-foot wooden staff
> Is all my worldly gear.

[1]   An alchemic term for the spirit-womb.
[2]   I have no home, but use the sky as a tent wherever I happen to be.
[3]   A yogic reference to the 'mysterious portal', an area situated just behind the mid-point between the eyes, from which inner radiance issues during meditation.
[4]   That I have attained the Way.

> A pot of mellow wine
> Is the acme of my wants.
> On dragon back I fly
> To the Islands of the Blessed.
> Within that faery realm
> When the night begins to wane,
> One may see immortals sport
> With the rings around the moon!

Another longish poem which I think well worth including, despite immense difficulties for the translator, is Lü Yen's 'Stanzas', which sets forth in verse the essentials of cultivating the Way. The single word *p'in* provides a good example of those difficulties. Commonly meaning 'poor' but also 'Taoist priest', I have felt it necessary to translate it here by 'the Taoist priests who seek that kind of goal' – ten syllables to translate one! In a few other places I have had to paraphrase almost as lavishly in order to bring out the whole meaning. Moreover, there is one four-lined passage which I have omitted in despair. Literally it runs: 'In the morning he [or 'one' or 'I' ?] tours the North Sea, in the evening visits the blue *wu*-tree. The gall of the green snake carried in his [or 'my' ?] sleeve produces only a coarse kind of *ch'i*. The triply intoxicating peak *yang*-essence is virtually unknown. Its effects excel the exhileration of flying over the Tung-t'ing Lake.' Clearly the general idea is that the accomplished meditator, having attained the Way, can fly at will in or above the world. The green snake's gall is probably one of the ingredients used by inferior sages in compounding the golden elixir. Even so, the meaning of the passage as a whole eludes me. As for the rest of the poem, though less charming than the others, it is full of wisdom.

> With nature's course and man's
> I'm really not concerned.
> I do not scorn belief
> In immortality,
> Nor yet the Taoist priests
> Who seek that kind of goal;
> But were I asked how best
> To cultivate the Way,
> I'd say: 'Just till the mind
> And tend the body well.'

When one wanders on high peaks
Letting his gaze roam wide,
The universe seems vast,
Its people numberless.
Yet, alas, there are but few
Who win to true attainment.

To those who know the secret,
'There's not a single thing'.[1]
They learn to give things up
And simply practise stillness.
Closing their gates at dawn,
They read till evening falls,
Then sweep the floor and light
A stick of fragrant incense.
All day they battle with
Six robbers called the senses
Until they recognise that shapes
And forms are wholly void,
Then awaken to the truth
That 'there's not a single thing',
That the 'magic mirror stand'[2]
Exists only in the mind.
When sense reaction's cut,
Self-transformation follows.
Then stillness dawns, and form
Is recognised as void.[3]
'The Buddha is your mind;
Your mind is just the Buddha',
Green mountains are white clouds
In a passing transformation.

Discard your jade and gold;
You'd best forget such dross.

[1] A reference to a Buddhist classic, the Diamond-Cutter Sūtra, which stresses the essential voidness of phenomena.

[2] In the Buddhist classic, Sūtra of the Sixth Patriarch, a monk compares the mind to a mirror-stand that must be kept free from the world's dust. The future Sixth Patriarch replies that there is no mirror-stand on which dust could possibly collect, the point being that 'mirror' and 'dust' imply a duality between pure and impure, mind (mirror) and objects (dust); whereas in truth all is mind and no duality exists.

[3] A reference to a passage in the Buddhist Heart Sūtra: 'Form is void and void is form.'

Spring blossom, autumn frost
Are worthier of attention.
Disciples like to boast
Of immense longevity,
Yet ten thousand years of life
Pass like a lightning flash!

On the days when flutes shrill forth
Before the Tower of the Yellow Crane[1]
And a riot of summer blooms
Decks the margin of the lake,
Can one really cast off sadness
And obliterate desire?
Who but the summer breeze
Or the radiant moon can tell?

This poem reveals the writer's knowledge of both Taoism and Buddhism. While recognising the value of the yogic methods employed by many Taoists, he prefers a wholly spiritual approach, relying on mind rather than on the transmutation of essence, vitality and spirit. He perceives that the higher forms of Taoist cultivation are, if the yogic alchemy is discarded, identical with the Ch'an (Zen) methods which resulted from what has often been called a marriage between Taoism and Buddhism. Both systems stress the essential voidness of objective things, meaning that none of them is permanent nor can exist independently of other objective things, all of them being analogous to waves which, appearing on the surface of the ocean, have but a transient identity that is soon merged in the ocean that gave them birth. Just as there is no real and lasting difference between two sea waves, so is there no real difference between objects, since all arise from and revert to the universal 'non-substance' variously known as mind or spirit.

For all that this poem is full of interest, it strikes a didactic note and thus loses some of the peculiar charm one has come to expect of Taoist poems. To redress the balance, here is a poem about Wu I Mountain which carries no message at all, nothing but exuberant joy in nature's beauty. It was written by a Taoist hermit who chose to be known as Pai Yü Ch'an, meaning 'White Moon Toad', an animal who lives in the moon and is ceaselessly at work on compounding the golden elixir.

[1] I do not know the significance of this reference.

Swiftly runs the stream, greenly tinged
By fragrant grasses.
The ancient pines are dyed
With the bluish tint
Of distant mountains.
Standing where the water gushes,
I raise my flute.
Child immortals gather in the cave
To hear its music.
Below the cliffs, mist clusters thickly.
Still no one comes!
Softly white clouds descend,
Oh softly,
Veiling the greenish moss.
The pines have thickly carpeted the earth,
Hushed now the birds;
A light breeze fans my wanderer's pillow
Bringing dreams.

The following lines, penned by Ch'ang Chao during his pilgrimage to the Garden of the Sacred Cliff, touch upon the contrast between Taoist recluses and the inhabitants of the world of dust.

Tinkling, twinkling mountain rills
Bring to mind a courtier's lute;
Whirling, twirling autumn leaves
Scatter gold upon the ground.
The dwellers in these wooded hills
Seldom care for rank or wealth.
How sad that people by and large
Know nothing of this wisdom!

Writing of Wu Hsiang Szû (the Temple of Formlessness) to which he had paid a visit, the Confucian scholar Wang Yang-ming, who could not help feeling a lifelong affection for Taoism though he believed it was his duty to oppose it as a rival to Confucianism, expressed himself in a thoroughly Taoistic manner. In just twenty syllables, he hints at the equanimity of mountain-dwelling recluses in the face of both the beauty and savagery of nature.

Under the cliff lives an ancient recluse;
Pine and bamboo encompass his dwelling.

Birds sing at dawn and at evening is heard
The companionable roar of a cliff-dwelling tiger.

Another of Wang Yang-ming's poems, called 'Magic City Monastery', celebrates a night passed in a Buddhist monastery standing so high that it was bathed in moonlight though rain was falling below. The reference to a dragon is not quite clear to me. Certainly for many Taoists dragon and tiger form a pair scarcely eclipsed in importance by *yin* and *yang*, but here the dragon may have been a falling meteor or perhaps a cloud formation. Speed and strength are well conveyed by wind sweeping through the branches of the trees as the cliff-dwelling tiger rushes by. I regret having failed to capture the meaning of the last two lines more felicitously; Wang Yang-ming's idea is that the lamplight *befriends* a monk who might otherwise be lonely while reciting his solitary prayers.

Set high and deep among the hills,
Stands Magic City
Leaning upon the void; its towers
Invade the realm of gods.
Beyond, a bright moon voyages
Through a cloudless autumn sky;
But the world below is darkened by
Fine rain like spring-time mist.
A dragon from the sky swoops down;
Clouds rise to form its throne.
As the tiger to its cliff returns,
Wind rushes through the trees.
I love this mountain-dwelling monk,
So faithful to his tasks;
At the ev'ning rite, the lamps lend warmth
To his solitary chant.

Yet another poem by this Confucian scholar who showed such unusual fondness for Taoists is called 'Passing the Night in a Hermit's Cell on Fragrant Mountain'. Though my rendering falls woefully short of the beauty of the original, I have included it as an example of a favourite Chinese technique; the poet seeks to convey the sum total of his feeling by sketching a series of unconnected details, each of which adds its quota. From the third line onwards, each pair of lines conveys one of the ingredients of the tranquil atmosphere surrounding a Taoist hermit's dwelling.

I came to this solitary vale
Seeking otherworldly feelings.
From afar the stone-hewn gateway
Points to where some white clouds gather.
Through the forest now and then
A woodsman's axe resounds.
This monk at the mouth of the valley
Is a friend whose name eludes me.
In the pool a young moon sails
Across an inverted sky.
Aloft a cloud-formed stairway
Rises to heaven's smoothness.
Who but a Taoist would dwell
So high above the wild grasses?
From the moonlit peak there sounds
A stone bell's sweet-toned chime.

The remaining four poems are representative of the full flowering of Taoist mysticism. Two of them combine mysticism with evocation of nature's beauties. The first and third do not attempt this, but are of such importance in their different ways that it would be a pity to omit them. Wang Ching-yang's poem, 'Shedding Light Upon the Way', has the flavour of Ch'an (Zen) poetry; at a certain point the paths of Taoists and Buddhists naturally converge, the distinction between them vanishing progressively. Verse 2 warns us that to confound the Void with mere nothingness is wrong. Nothingness is the opposite of existence and both have their place in the scheme of things, whereas the Void stands beyond both of them, or rather it *is* both of them seen in the light of a higher level of truth whereat both 'is' and 'is not' cease to be meaningful concepts. Verses 4 and 5 reveal that distinctions spring from our own minds; when false distinctions are not made, everything is as it is, neither good nor bad, neither this nor that.

The line in verse 1 which I have rendered 'very easily get lost' is much stronger in the original Chinese, which conjures up the agonising experience of suddenly losing hold of one's own identity. The 'magic pearl' in verse 2 is Truth. The last line of verse 3 refers to the perfect freedom and sense of self-existent being enjoyed by the realised sage. The first two lines of verse 4, perhaps taken from a famous Buddhist classic, mean that the real neither comes into being nor ceases; only the transient appearances mistaken for reality spring into being and vanish. The 'radiant moon', occurring towards the end of that verse, points to a mystical experience that accompanies attainment of the Way. The second, third and fourth lines of the final verse mean that, in order to attain to full realisation, one does not have to *do* or to *become* anything whatsoever; what is needed is just to *be* what in fact one really has been from the first.

1   Do not prattle of the Void
Not knowing what it means;
For those who seize upon it
Very easily get lost.
Should you really wish to know
The truth about the Void,
It's a vast and undivided
Expanse of shining mist.

2   The nature of the myriad forms
Is void, not nothingness.
Whereas nothingness contains
The workings of creation,
Within the Void no grain
Of dust finds place to lodge.
There's nought but golden light
Where the magic pearl is seen.

3   A student of the Way
Seeks the truth of life and death;
For, else, he longs in vain
To win immortal state.
But he who knows life's source
Discerns death's meaning, too,
And thenceforth is set free
To live spontaneously.

4   From first to last there is
No dying or being born;
From a flash of thought a myriad
False distinctions spring to mind.
But when you know just where
Those thoughts arise and vanish,
A radiant moon shines forth
In the temple of the mind.

5   Then before you lies the truth
    That's there's nothing to be sought.
    Of *themselves* the hills are green;
    Of *themselves* the waters flow.
    Let the mind by night and day
    Embrace this single thought –
    By thought wherein there's no thought
    Must one cultivate the Way.

Li Fêng, some of whose verses occur earlier in this chapter, is the author of the remaining mystical poems. In the first, he pays homage to a recluse called Great Master of Wonderful Clarity. The 'coral clouds' symbolise the beauty of a mind about to pass beyond the realm of form; the 'veil of white mist' is the very last curtain to be parted when the adept attains full intuitive perception of the Tao.

> Wreathed by coral clouds,
> The mountains stand out vaguely.
> Still clad in mortal frame,
> He lingers on the blue-green slopes
> Of his solitary valley,
> Veiled in white mist
> Where none disturb him.
> Soon he will win
> To a spiritual body
> And be seen no more.

The next poem recalls Lao-tzû's famous words 'Banish the wise, away with the learned!'

> Seeking out masters,
> Visiting sages
> And painfully conning the *Ts'an*[1] –
> Why this infliction,
> This senseless restriction
> On mind's freedom to roam where it lists ?
> Unlimited chatter
> And mystical natter
> Had best be swept out of the way.
> Then the radiant orb
> Of wisdom's moon
> Will emerge from behind the hill.

[1]   The *Ts'an T'ung Ch'i*, an abstruse yogic manual.

In the final poem, Li P'êng pays homage to a sage from Kansu province in the far north-west of China, through which Lao-tzû must have passed when he rode his ox towards the Central Asian wilderness. The poet speaks to us again of nature's beauties and of the joy of mystical attainment. The cinnabar-coloured mists swirling at the gates of heaven hint at the alchemic yoga in which cinnabar, understood literally or symbolically, plays an important part.

> He gazes from afar
> Towards Tung-nan.[1]
> Standing midst whirling leaves,
> The whole sky autumn-tinged,
> He is driven by the autumnal chill
> To don a warmer robe.
>
> This aged immortal,
> Having won to full attainment,
> Has seen the mists
> Of cinnabar that swirl
> At heaven's gates.
> Idly he joins the pines[2]
> In drinking in
> The mountain hues.

[1] South-eastwards across the length and breadth of China.

[2] Now that he has attained, there is nothing left for him to do but enjoy his kinship with nature.

Bronze statue of Lao-tzu with his special emblem, a fly-whisk; he also carries a gourd, the Taoist symbol of wishes magically fulfilled. The smaller statue in the foreground represents Chung Li Ch'üan, one of the Eight Immortals; it is made of scarlet lacquer.

Representations in bone of the Eight Immortals.

A delightful earthenware figure of the poet,
Li T'ai-po.

Ho T'u

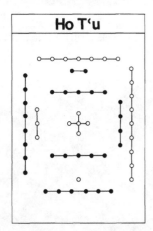

Lo Shu

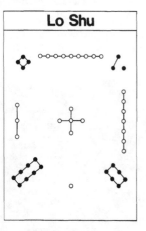

The Ho T'u (Plan of the Yellow River) and Lo Shu (Lo
River Writing), the most ancient of Taoist magical
diagrams.

A Vietnamese wood-block print in which the man and the woman represent 'Green Dragon White Tiger'; besides being a delightful example of Vietnamese folk-art, it probably refers to the practice of Dual Cultivation.

OVER PAGE

Top: Copy of a masterpiece from the imperial collection representing a Taoist magician in the act of changing his staff into a dragon.

Centre: A Taoistically inspired painting in which one can perhaps trace the course of dragon veins.

Bottom: A glimpse of an immortal realm.

Chapter 5

 The Mysterious
Portal
(Legends of Immortals)

*Entering the Hsüan Men, the Shadowy Portal, they pass
beyond the world of dust into a realm of immortals*

(old saying)

This is a chapter of curious stories, different in character, but all
concerning immortals, of whom there are several kinds. I was once
presented with a peach-stone on which had been incised the ideogram for immortality. Laughingly the recluse who placed it in my
hand exclaimed: 'There! Now the whole of Taoism lies within your
grasp!' At the time, his words seemed obscure, but indeed they were
very apt. Simple people who seek eternal life in the courts of heaven
or as transmogrified flesh-and-blood immortals, philosophers who
acquire the wisdom of acceptance in the manner of Lao-tzû, adepts
of the yogic alchemy and mystics who pursue the exalted goal known
as return to the Source, one and all describe attainment with the
words *ch'êng hsien* – becoming an immortal.

True immortality is described thus by Professor Chou Shao-hsien:

His spirit wise, his essence holy, he illumines the mysterious and
subtle, comprehending the workings of the Real. While still at a
distance, he perceives himself and the entire universe as one, as
partaking of the same eternal nature. Nothing in earth or heaven

hinders his goings and comings. Swimming through the blue vault of the sky, he gazes down upon the yellow springs [portal of death]. Though he wander through the universe from end to end, neither his spirit nor his essence will undergo further change. For him there is no birth and death, nor joy or sorrow worth mentioning. Such is the true condition of an immortal, to which even the most gifted cannot easily attain, for it is not to be found through knowledge, whether human or divine. Neither virtue nor vice, nor yet perfect understanding of nature's workings leads to its attainment. The one way to reach it is to master the subtle laws set forth in the *Tao Tê Ching*, the *Nan Hua Scripture* [Chuang-tzû] and that called *Merging with the Void* [Lieh-tzû]; even then the guidance of a teacher, wise and virtuous like the ancients, must be sought.

In the classic entitled *Attainment of the Hidden Mystery* is a similar passage, but couched in such terms as have often led the unwary astray, causing them to believe in miracles of a more spectacular kind:

The man of great attainment is serene, free from idle thoughts and cares. His roof the sky, the earth his chariot, he drives the seasons as his steeds and makes *yin* and *yang* his coachmen. Ascending through the clouds, he soars beyond the Milky Way, a compeer of the Creative [Tao]. Pressing forward, mind unclouded by inordinate desires, he passes to the heavenly regions, walks without using his feet, swiftly yet unhurrying, using the rain to smooth his path, the wind to blow away the dust. With lightning for a whip and thunder for chariot-wheels, he wings aloft to bathe in the river of the Milky Way, descending thence through the Gateway of Infinity.

Ko Hung, after describing immortals in similarly poetic terms, deemed it necessary to add – rather amusingly, I think – the following caution:

As for recluses famed for such meagre attainments as being immune from pillage by wandering soldiery, subduing demons, being invulnerable to poison and disease, being able to travel safely through the mountains unbeset by savage beasts or to wade streams unharmed by crocodiles and dragons, being immune from epidemics, becoming invisible when danger threatens – all these are trivial matters, though one needs to be aware of them.

Yet it is not surprising to discover that such warnings were not always heeded. The lofty concept of immortals as beings who have undergone spiritual rebirth, thus passing beyond their fellow beings to a spiritually deathless state in union with the Tao, is not as easy for simple people to envisage as the possession of magical powers. They were much more attracted by such passages as one finds in a work entitled *Histories of the Immortals*. For example:

Tsêng Ying, having attained the Way in his eighties, regained the glossy black hair of his younger days and such litheness of body that his arrows would hit a mark set up at a distance of a hundred paces. In a single day, he could walk several hundred *li* at a pace that made it difficult even for youngsters to keep up with him, and once he fasted for fifty days without being assailed by hunger.

We feel more sympathy with unsophisticated men avid for such wonders when we recall that, even supposing such descriptions to be exaggerated, there is a basis of truth to them. Many people have attested that Ch'an Master Hsü Yin, who died not long ago when well into his hundred-and-twenties, could outwalk young people until only a few years before his death; and this I can vouch for, having been one of the young men he outwalked in his late nineties! Then again, there is the story I have told elsewhere of the first Tibetan lama to become my teacher: once, having bought some loaves of fresh Chinese bread, he entered into meditation, from which he emerged ready for lunch, only to find that so many days had passed that the bread had become mouldy!

It is the popular concept of immortality, rather than the mystical one, which has inspired Chinese poets and painters through the ages. Everyone familiar with Chinese art has been enchanted by those groups of colourfully attired figures of benign appearance who disport themselves against a background of shadowy mountains amidst fantastic rock formations, picturesquely convoluted trees and exotic flowers, sometimes with fairy-like pavilions crowned by gracefully upturned roofs rising in the distance. They form a charmingly varied medley – one or two bearded sages, with bellies bared to the winds of heaven, a handsome old scholar wearing elegant silken robes, little ladies who might chance to be less demure than they appear, a beggar-man perhaps, and youths with marvellously satiny skins and pink and white complexions, an old fellow carrying a peach who has an extraordinary dome-like head, and so forth. Always they are seen in the postures of idlers joyously at ease with themselves and the world around them. A couple may be playing *wei ch'i* (an antique kind of chess); some may be drinking thimblefuls of wine (or is it dew or liquid moonbeams?); one may be crouched over an earthenware tea-stove, lazily fanning the glowing charcoal, or playing a flute while a fellow immortal accompanies him on a moon-guitar. More rarely one sees them teasing a pet dragon or riding astride an enormous crane or a chubby Chinese unicorn; often they are laughing or just sitting still in shining-eyed contentment. How can one fail to wish oneself a part of such a joyous band?

A rather different concept is that of immortals as grave old gentlemen who would certainly not wish to be seen drinking (even moonbeams) in public, still less with rounded tummies and fleshy nipples bared to the winds; for the term 'immortal' is also used of the Taoist equivalent of the Confucian Princely Man, a sage of exalted virtue and transcendent wisdom so attuned to the Way as to be beyond the ordinary joys and vicissitudes of life. Here the emphasis is on virtue (though not quite in the Confucian sense) and on wisdom, but there is usually an implication that beings with such vast spiritual accomplishments must certainly enjoy supernormal powers, though reticent and disinclined to use them except for some exalted purpose. Nevertheless, Taoists mostly possess a keen sense of humour and it would be unthinkable to depict a Taoist sage as a pompous looking person.

One of the excitements for travellers in places at once remote and beautiful was the possibility of encountering *real* immortals – not, of course, beings flying about on dragons, sages returned from a trip to the Milky Way or playful jugglers with the rings around the moon, but men living in retirement who really had succeeded in attaining immortal state in the sense of being able to commune with the Tao, having conquered death and finding nothing left to do but patiently await the day of liberation from their perishable bodies. I truly believe that a few of the recluses I encountered could be so described – several of them aged men, one of them astonishingly young.

It stands to reason that few immortals would care to continue living in the world of dust, that they were most likely to be encountered among the solitary hermits or small bands of recluses who lived deep in the mountains far from the abodes of ordinary men. The insistance of Lao and Chuang on spiritual withdrawal from the world doubtless contributed to the notion of actual physical withdrawal. The Taoist True Man, unlike his Confucian counterpart, had no desire to involve himself in the task of reforming society; and it was obvious that the conquest of desire could be carried out more easily in the solitude of the mountains than in densely populated towns and villages. Taoists bent on cultivating the Way usually did inhabit solitary places. Indeed, the Chinese ideogram for 'immortal' also bears the connotation 'mountain man', being written thus 仙, of which the part to the left (人) means 'man' and the part to the right (山) means 'mountain'. From an early date, the Taoist ideal was of a sage who, besides being inspired with intuitive understanding of the Way, loved to wander alone among majestic peaks, with the sun and moon for lamps, the sky for his roof and the softly waving grasses for a bed. The idea of virtue in a *worldly* sense was absent. Certainly the immortals were held to be virtuous in the sense of having conquered passion and desire, those main bastions of the ego; but no virtue was seen in meddling with the affairs of human society or government. Immortals observed the principle of *wu wei*, of leaving well alone so as to let everything take its natural course. This, thanks to Lao and Chuang, was firmly embedded in the Taoist mind.

Confusion as to the real meaning of immortality was worse confounded by the absence – at least in the minds of ordinary people – of a boundary line between immortals who had risen from mortal state by reason of their great attainments and mythical immortals who, according to professors of the popular folk religion, were a separate order of being not very different from what we in Europe mean when we speak of fairies, except that they were not thought of as a tiny folk, but rather as resembling superlatively handsome humans. Some of these lovely beings were rumoured to be the genii of pools and streams and ancient trees; others were believed to dwell in remote mountain regions, upon islands in distant seas, in the clouds, on the moon and so forth. As some branches of Taoism became more and more closely merged with the popular folk religion, so did the difference between 'immortals by attainment' and 'immortals by race' tend to be lost sight of. What was possibly a loss for Taoism was most certainly a gain for art, such themes as the Islands of the Blessed (P'êng Lai Shan) and their shining, super-naturally beautiful inhabitants providing wonderful material for poets and painters.

Simpletons who supposed that human beings could actually transcend nature's laws and subsist thenceforth on wind and dew were seldom ridiculed by adepts who understood the true significance of immortality. Such folly, besides being amiable and harmless, had its uses. In the first place, the popular beliefs provided a protective colouring for enlightened followers of the Way who felt it necessary to guard spiritual and yogic knowledge from profanation and abuse; this should on no account be transmitted to those unworthy to receive it. There is no doubt that mystical and yogic practices really do lead to the acquisition of hightened powers which, wrongly applied, are dangerous both to the wielders and their victims. The rumour that Mao Tsê-tung and Chou Ên-lai owed much of their stupendous success to secret mastery of the science of *yin* and *yang* strikes me as being sinister rather than ridiculous. Another advantage of the popular supposition that cultivators of the Way were expert in magical practices and the performance of miracles was that this belief stimulated a wide interest in cultivation; the ingenuous people who turned their backs on the world of dust in the expectation of winning magical powers culminating in flesh-and-blood immortality would, if they had spiritual possibilities that made them worthy of instruction, presently come to distinguish false from real. Their aspirations could be diverted towards the goal of true immortality. They could gradually be taught how to co-ordinate and develop the full potentialities of body and mind in order to achieve the sudden spiritual transformation known to Buddhists as Enlightenment – whereat the real self, identical in nature with pure undifferentiated being, emerges and shatters the illusion of individual selfhood. This transformation, expressed in traditional Taoist terms, is wrought by refining and transmuting essence, vitality and spirit into purified *yang*-spirit which, uniting with the cosmic *yang*-spirit, results in immortality in the true sense of the term. Meanwhile, erroneous thinking gives place to intuitive wisdom, the bonds of passion and desire are sundered and true virtue arises, that is to say both eagerness and power to benefit all living beings with pure impartiality.

In China, legends and anecdotes concerning immortals are innumerable and pertain to the varied concepts of immortality ranging from the somewhat grotesque and highly fanciful to the inspiring and sublime. Writers and story-tellers, unlike painters and the carvers of wood, lacquer, ivory and jade, are not limited to portraying immortals as a kind of fairy-like folk, for they can describe spiritual qualities and experiences not easy to express by means of the visual arts. However, as there are other chapters detailing the paths to true immortality, the stories given here have been chosen for their picturesque qualities rather than on account of any spiritual content. Like myths, legends and fairy-stories, they can be read for fun.

The Lesson of the White Mist

In the reign of the Emperor Shên Tsung (1573–1620), a scholar surnamed Fan, who was a native of I Ping, so distinguished himself in the public examinations that he received a succession of high appointments in various parts of the Empire. No matter where he went, his duties brought him into contact with the evils of society – greed, avarice, lust, vanity, cruelty and oppression. Having taken leave of absence in order to spend the period of mourning for his deceased father in his native town, he decided not to return to official life but to retire to the solitude of the mountains and cultivate the Way. In the vicinity of Mount Omei he acquired a small hut where, during inclement weather, he shut himself up with his books and devoted hours a day to meditation. A nearby stream trickling amidst moss-encrusted rocks and clumps of fern provided him with clear, sweet water; for food he had brought a few sacks of rice and one or two jars of oil, to which slender resources he added the bounty of the forest – silver tree-fungus, bamboo shoots and all sorts of delicious, nourishing plants. In fine weather, he rose early to enjoy the panorama of floating clouds richly tinged with coral, pink or crimson and edged with gold, then wandered amidst peaks and valleys searching for medicinal herbs and titbits for his table, often sleeping out beneath the stars. Within three years, his heart had become attuned to the more ordinary mysteries of nature; yet the Tao eluded him. 'I see it is there. I behold its transformations, its giving and its taking; but, shadowy and elusive, how is it to be grasped?' Though known to his few neighbours as a skilful healer and accomplished immortal, to himself he was a wanderer who had left the world of dust in vain.

One day he had a visitor who, though dressed coarsely like a peasant, had the sage yet youthful aspect of a true immortal. Broaching a jar of good wine he had left untouched since the day of his arrival, Fan listened to his guest with veneration. Said the visitor: 'I have the honour to be your nearest neighbour, being the genie of the stream running behind your distinguished dwelling. May I venture to inquire how it happens that a scholar of such high attainment as your good self has failed to find the starting-point of the Way, especially as it lies right in front of your nose?' Then, pitying Fan's confusion and wishing to put him at his ease, the genie added: 'It is a sign, sir, of your lofty intelligence. There are recluses in plenty who persuade themselves they have found the Way, but who would be hard put to it to substantiate that claim. Look for it not in the radiant clouds of dawn and sunset, nor in the brilliance pouring down from cloudless skies during early autumn. Seek it in the mists that shroud the valleys at which, hitherto, you have scarcely condescended to glance.' With these words, the genie made him a handsome bow and departed.

Thenceforward our scholar spent his mornings seated upon a knoll gazing down at the white mist swirling in the lower valleys. No spiritual illumination followed, but he persevered. Another three years went by. The woodsmen round about, seeing him sit for hours as still as the rock beneath him, blessed heaven's benignity in sending an immortal to dwell among them. Timely weather was attributed to his virtue; untimely weather was presumed to have been at least mitigated thereby; Fan himself knew otherwise. Then came a day when he hastened joyfully to where the stream bubbled out from an underground cavern and called upon the genie, who straightway appeared clad in a summer robe of brocaded gauze worn over garments of fine silk.

'No need to tell me!' boomed the genie in a voice like muted thunder. 'You have found the Way! May I venture to inquire how you did so?'

'Ha-ha-ha!' laughed Fan. 'Why did you not tell me sooner? I did not *find* but suddenly realised that I had never lost the Way. Those crimson dawn clouds, that shining noonday light, the procession of the seasons, the waxing and waning of the moon – these are not majestic functions or auspicious symbols of what lies behind. They *are* the Tao. To be born, to breathe, to eat, to drink, to walk, to sit, to wake, to sleep, to live, to die – to do this *is* to tread the Way. When you know how to take what comes along, not bothering with thoughts of joy and sorrow, wearing a quilted or unlined robe not because it is the fashion but because nature prompts the change, gathering pine seeds or mushrooms not for the taste but because hunger must be stayed, never stirring hand or foot to do more than passing need requires, letting yourself be borne along without a thought of wishing something to be other than it is – *then* you are one with the valley mists, the floating clouds. You have attained the Way, taking birth as an immortal. Wasting years on seeking what was never lost really is a joke.'

The cavern before which they were standing now echoed and re-echoed with their laughter. Then the genie composed his features. The skirts of his brocaded robe and the ribbons of his silk gauze hat streaming in the breeze, he bowed his head to the earth nine times, as to an emperor, crying joyfully: 'At last, at last, I have met my master!'

The Isles of the Blessed

Hsü was one of those who had turned his back upon the world for a merely trivial reason – disappointment in love. With a beginning so inauspicious, it was not to be expected that he would easily become immortal. Anyone could have told him that a charming girl is as likely to turn into a shrew as any other, that moth eyebrows and willowy grace seldom come up to expectation, that beauty's flower begins to shed its petals on the wedding night, and that he would have had better reason to cry if he had lost a good cooking-pot or tea-kettle. Still, he was happy to leave the scene of what he imagined to be a tragic loss. Taking up his abode on Mount T'ai, famed for the panorama of clouds that come sweeping in from the Eastern Sea at dawn, he visited the dwellings of recluse after recluse, importuning them for instruction in the Way. The only sage who proved willing to receive a disciple of such poor calibre kept him hard at work from dawn till dusk gathering fuel upon the sparsely wooded slopes or performing similarly arduous labours in return for very little teaching. As for the true immortals who dwell upon that mountain, easily recognisable by their shining eyes, carefree expressions, unwrinkled faces and a swift, easy gait that gave them the appearance of deer skimming over the rock-strewn alpine slopes, though they did not flee at his approach, their courteous manner cooled when they learnt how trivial was his reason for desiring to cultivate the Way.

Sadly Hsü departed thence to seek out the profounder solitude of the rocky hills girdling the coast where in ancient times the Emperor Wu had gone searching for the secret of the golden elixir. Here he encountered a sage who welcomed him as an assistant. Behind his dwelling was a lofty cave furnished with cauldrons, tripods, receptacles and stores of liquids, powders, chopped up roots, leaves, bark, gums, minerals and so forth. During the second year of Hsü's apprenticeship, this sage climbed a neighbouring hill and vanished, leaving behind a pair of shoes as a sign that a search for his bodily remains would be fruitless and a paper making over all the contents of the cave to his disciple. In the cave was found a book of instructions for compounding a golden pill and another detailing the method of transmuting base metals into gold. Either one of those would have proved a welcome legacy were it not that the names and quantities of certain vital ingredients had been omitted lest the instructions fall into unworthy hands. Such pills as poor Hsü managed to produce caused giddiness and sometimes fever accompanied by sensations of icy chill.

Having nearly destroyed himself by consuming what he took to be a perfected golden pill, Hsü greeted the dawn one day by kneeling with his face towards the pearly cloud-screen that veils the Isles of Bliss from mortal eyes and crying into the wind that came up from the mist-curtained ocean: 'Dog-flesh immortals selfishly immersed in the rapture of carefree spontaneous existence, I declare you to be detestable deceivers. If your hearts are not made of bronze, I demand as a gift one of the peaches of immeasurable longevity. Having laboured long and faithfully for other dwellers in seclusion, I deserve more than a trifle of consideration. Remain silent and I shall know that you and your peaches and your golden pills are but idle dreams fit for laughter. For the sake of your own reputation, you had better accede to my reasonable request.'

As he spoke, the sky darkened. The clear blue was blotted out by dense banks of cloud. Thunder rolled and raindrops the size of crab-apples came drifting down as an earnest of a threatening storm. Aghast at his own temerity, he made to rise, but a heavy hand descended on his shoulder and, looming over him, stood a burly recluse of menacing mien and piercing gaze.

'Blockhead! Turtle's egg! Who gave you permission to create a disturbance? Had the wind carried your words *over there*, do you suppose you would be alive now or have an instant more to live? Get up and follow me!'

The stranger led off in such haste that Hsü stubbed his toes and twice fell headlong in his efforts to keep up. Presently a sudden turn in the path revealed an altogether unexpected sight. Upon a small upland plateau enclosed by walls of rock stood a group of palatial buildings with elegantly convoluted roofs glistening with porcelain tiles of emerald green. Set in the magenta-coloured walls was a pair of handsomely lacquered gates, and the whole place had an air of splendour more suited to the capital than to this wild and lonely place. From within came the sound of ritual music – the high-pitched song of flutes, the throbbing of a drum and the pure chimes of jade tablets hanging from silken strings.

Half swooning with fear, Hsü was taken past the gateway and led to an inner chamber, where he fell to his knees before a very old man with cheeks as ruddy as peaches, a snowy beard falling to his waist and eyes like pools of light.

Having listened to the burly fellow's report of Hsü's conduct, this venerable sage remarked: 'It seems to me, young man, that you were in something of a passion. What did you hope to gain by such unseemly conduct? As a follower of the Way, you should know better.'

While Hsü related his sad story, the sage stroked his beard reflectively. At the end, he said: 'The peaches of immortality are not given for the asking. Who ever heard of such a thing? They are so carefully guarded that, if I myself wanted one, I should either have to steal it or pay a heavy bribe to one of the celestial gardeners. Even then, its absence would be noticed and there would be a fine old uproar in the courts of heaven. You must have read the 'Record of a Journey to the West' and remember how it was when Monkey set about stealing some. As to your laboratory, had you not the sense to realise that the ingredients of the golden pill of immortality are all inside you? Don't try getting at them with a knife, you rash creature, or there will be little left of you to benefit from the experiment. The only effective furnace is the one you carry behind your navel and the only safe receptacle for the completed pill lies within your skull a few hair's breadths from the crown.'

Then did the sage instruct him in the secret alchemy, teaching him how best to use his own endowments of essence, vitality and spirit. Thanking him humbly, Hsü begged to know whom he had the honour of addressing.

'Well,' replied the sage, 'I seldom reveal my name to people. If I did, most likely I should be taken for a liar. I don't mind telling you, though, that I was on a visit to the Islands of the Blessed, attending the birthday festival of the Dragon King of the Eastern Ocean, when you so ill-advisedly shouted defiance of the beings there. If I had not come back in time to give you a warning, things might have gone ill with you sooner or later.'

After walking out from the lovely precincts, Hsü turned back to have a last look. Not altogether with astonishment, he perceived that they had vanished. Wind stirred the grasses of the highland plateau. The only beings in sight were sea-birds.

Returning to his cave for a store of food and other necessities, he moved to a smaller cave overlooking the sea. Every day, he interrupted his yogic practice only for long enough to gaze towards P'êng Lai Shan and give thanks for the kindly response to his passionate yearning. Within a year, he had perfected the golden elixir without resource to external aids. Waking from a deep sleep during the night following upon his attainment, he went to scoop some cold rice from the pot to make congee for his breakfast. On raising the lid he saw, resting upon the congealed mass of rice left over from the day before, a luscious peach ripened to the point of perfection. It seemed, as it were, to be begging to be eaten!

A Gift from the Moon Goddess
This third story is at the level of popular Taoism intermingled with the folk religion. For all that it contains no moral teaching or mystical implications, it possesses a certain charm which, especially as it is typical of a thousand such legends, makes it worth recording.

In the early years of the Ch'ing dynasty (1644–1912) a commotion once occurred in the city of Kuang Chou on the morning of the festival in honour of the birthday of the Moon Goddess. A pedlar came walking down the street pushing a barrow loaded with fine pears. He was followed closely by two hefty louts from the magistrate's *yamên* (official residence) who presently helped themselves to a good share of the luscious fruit, meaning to walk off without payment. Much to their surprise, they had no sooner turned away grinning over their loot than their heads were knocked sharply together like a giant pair of wooden clappers! Cheeks red with shame at receiving such a punishment from an elderly man and one of low degree, they promptly arrested him and took him off to the lock-up. Now it happened that one Shên Ch'ing-yao, a youthful scholar with the degree of *hsiu-ts'ai*, witnessed the whole affair and, approaching the magistrate as one scholar to another, was able to procure the pedlar's immediate release. That night, as he sat reading by candle-light in his study, the erstwhile pedlar, now dressed in a seemly Taoist robe, paid him a visit and, greeting him with a courteous bow, remarked:

'Young sir, I owe you a debt, but before we speak further of that, pray answer me this riddle. What place in all the universe would you choose to visit if a convenient opportunity occurred ?'

Taking this for a joke, Shên replied: 'The shining banks of the Milky Way – no, no – the ice palace in the moon to offer birthday greetings to the Moon Goddess, who is reported to be a divinity of exceptional beauty.'

'Very well,' replied the Taoist as though the other had suggested a jaunt to some nearby beauty-spot such as White Cloud Mountain, 'May I trouble you to brush a circle on a piece of paper to represent the moon ?'

Sure now that his visitor was a joker, Shên willingly complied and, following a further instruction, fastened the drawing to the wall. Instantly the Taoist blew out the candle whereat the room, instead of being plunged into darkness, grew bright; for the 'moon' pasted to a wall-beam now glowed like the real sky orb with a milky white radiance and began growing bigger and bigger.

'Be so good as to walk this way,' remarked the Taoist and, a trifle bemused by the turn things had taken, the young scholar followed his new friend into a gleaming white landscape where the ground was so soft and springy that he felt as though his shoes were winged. Passing through a 'rockery' of ice pinnacles skilfully arranged to resemble a chain of mountains, they came to a moated palace with battlemented walls, turrets and multi-tiered roofs all constructed of glittering ice. Great gates of beaten silver swung open at their approach and obsequious footmen arrayed in ceremonial gowns conducted them through a labyrinth of courtyards to a spacious chamber wherein a venerable toad of prodigious size, its body seemingly composed of lustrous white jade, sat working with the kind of pestle and mortar used by druggists.

To the Taoist's greeting this animal replied: 'Brother, you know I cannot stop now' and, taking no further notice of his visitors, it continued pounding some gleaming crystals from which arose what looked like the rainbow mist one sometimes sees above a waterfall on a sunny day. Presently the Taoist signed to Shên and they left the industrious toad to its labours, the rhythmic sound of the pestle following them *p'ang p'ang p'ang* down the corridor leading to a handsome inner courtyard. Open to the sky, this courtyard was partly roofed by the contorted branches of huge old cedars with silvery-white trunks that reflected the radiance of a triple-roofed hall constructed of glittering ice like the rest of the palace. The great doors stood open and a throng of splendidly dressed courtiers of both sexes pressed forward to kneel before its principle occupant and offer their birthday greetings. Shên and the Taoist were carried along by the tide of visitors and soon they, too, were kneeling before a throne of intricately wrought silver whereon was ensconced that proudly austere and chaste divinity, Chang Ô, Goddess of the Moon.

This most lovely of divine beings wore her hair, which was blacker and glossier than the coat of one of the imperial 'midnight steeds', elegantly piled in the phoenix-tail mode. Dripping with pearls and further ornamented with turquoise pins, it formed an exquisite contrast with her skin, which resembled white marble tinged with rose and coral. Her elongated, delicately tilted eyes shone like moonlight reflected in dark mountain pools. So brilliant was her gaze that Shên tremblingly lowered his eyes, hardly daring to contemplate as much as the tiny satin slippers peeping from beneath a graceful robe of white and silver brocade edged with pearls.

'Your Immortality,' she murmured, graciously addressing the Taoist in accents purer than the music rung upon tablets of fine jade, 'We are pleased to reward this young scholar for his timely aid – though why you should travel about the weary world of mortals masquerading as a fruitmonger is beyond Our understanding. Your companion, We perceive, is dismayed by these unfamiliar surroundings and will feel more at ease when he finds himself safely back at home. Therefore, not forgetting to present him with the trifling token of Our regard which We have set aside for him, find means to send him back without delay.'

Nor was that all, for she condescended to honour Shên with a few happily chosen words of courtesy, bending her radiant gaze upon his face the while, so that he felt as if his veins were pulsing with liquid moon-fire. Before dismissing him, she enjoined him not to reveal to his fellow mortals aught of what had transpired since he had stepped into the moon, keeping silent until his lifespan drew close to its end and his disciples – of whom there would be many – came to take their leave of him.

Leading him from the throne hall, the Taoist uttered some curious syllables, whereat the scene changed magically and the young scholar, as though waking from a dream, found himself back in his study. Yet it had not been a dream; for, lying upon the table among his books and writing materials, was an alabaster box of curious design which the Taoist had handed him at the moment of parting. Bemusedly he set his tea-kettle upon its tripod above the charcoal brazier and, having infused a fine quality tea to do honour to the occasion, ceremoniously drew from the box its contents – two crystals of a shimmering white substance that emitted rainbow-coloured rays. These he placed upon his tongue and imbibed them with a sip of tea. Once again it seemed that liquid moon-fire ran racing through his veins.

Thereafter the young scholar abandoned his sterile study of the Confucian classics, betook himself to the solitude of the mountains and became wholly immersed in contemplation of the Way. It is recorded that, even in extreme old age, his brow was smooth and the ruddiness of youth still tinged his cheeks, so that the grandchildren of his first disciples beheld him as a man still in the full vigour of his early years. In his 163rd year, he bade his pupils farewell, ascended the peak that sheltered his rustic dwelling, and departed thence for celestial regions, discarding his robe upon the summit as a sign of his final attainment.

Breaking Down the Walls

This final story of immortals is very different from the others, being no legend but a factual account of the attainment of immortality in the true Taoist sense of that word. I heard it years ago from a Taoist of Mount Hêng and, though I cannot recall the actual examples he gave me of the 'double talk' with which Taoists clothe their secrets, I can vouch for the closeness of my version to the original in spirit if not in detail. The recluse who related the story, told me that he was a 'third generation spiritual descendent' of the White Heron Immortal.

In the reign of the Hsien Fêng Emperor (1851–62), there lived on the slopes of Mount Hêng a recluse known as the Narrow-Waisted-Gourd Immortal, more commonly called Hulu Wêng, the Gourd Ancient One, or it may have been Hu Lao-wêng which has the same meaning. Besides a few middle-aged disciples, he was attended by two children who were supposed to be boys, though some said they were his granddaughters, the offspring of a son conceived before he retired from the world of dust. Strangers coming to pay their respects were invariably received by one of these children, who had some skill in distinguishing false from real. Those whom the children reported to be unlike followers of the Way were generally told that the Immortal, being deep in meditation, might not be able to receive them for several days to come. If, however, these guests persisted and asked that lodging be provided until such a time as the Immortal found it convenient to bestow some of his precious time on them, then coolness vanished and they were made welcome. Perhaps their desire would be fulfilled that very evening, the Immortal suddenly emerging from his inner chamber, crying: 'Well, well. How may an old and ignorant fellow serve Your Honours?'

One day there arrived from the capital a scholar surnamed Pai who, at the age of 30, was already a little stooped and short-sighted from too much study of the Confucian classics. He seemed at once distraught and impatient, so it was just as well that the little girls reported favourably on the state of his heart and mind. Upon coming into the Immortal's presence, he was with difficulty restrained from kneeling and knocking his head on the floor as before a Confucian dignitary. 'I come to Your Immortality', he cried, 'as a very last resort. Either you must show me the face of truth or I shall dispatch myself here and now to the yellow springs with the help of my silken girdle. All my life I have been searching for truth, pouring over the classics, listening to so-called sages in vain and cultivating the company of eminent Confucian scholars. A brilliant official career lay before me until, all of a sudden, I realised that all that talk of benevolence, filial piety and propriety is so much claptrap! What can *li* [propriety] conceivably have to do with the Great Way? Does cultivating the Tao require that we walk or bow in this way or that? Of course not! Your Immortality must help me to make up quickly for wasting my whole life upon such nonsense!'

Impressed by his sincerity, the Gourd Immortal invited this official to stay for a while and receive 'such poor teaching as an ignorant old fellow has to give'. Pai was delighted, but the next day a horrible disappointment awaited him, for the Immortal spoke to him in terms that seemed utterly at variance with his own conception of sagehood and wisdom. This was the substance of Hulu Wêng's first lesson to the bewildered scholar:

'I cannot describe to you the indescribable, but I can teach you several by no means inconsiderable arts – invisibility, flying without wings, invulnerability to sword or serpent's fang – you know the kind of thing. Here, then, is your syllabus of study. Seeking the Mysterious Portal, you must first provide yourself with the wherewithal to bribe the guards and render yourself invisible that you may slip through unnoticed. That sort of thing is not to be mastered in a day. Next you will have to learn how to fly thence to the courts of heaven, make your way to the central chamber, surprise Lord Lao [Lao-tzû] at breakfast, snatch up his flask of golden elixir, slay those who will come running in to rescue it, break down the walls of the sky-castle and return to earth an immortal! A man of your determination has but to follow my course of instruction to be certain of success.'

Hoping with all his heart that the Immortal was just having a little joke at his expense, Pai gazed at him earnestly, trying to read his expression. Alas, his face was calm and solemn, and his eyes shone with an unearthly lustre that made Pai wonder if he were not dealing with a dangerous fanatic. Had he travelled post-haste from the capital, scarcely dismounting for weeks on end, forgetful of food and sleep, merely to be told the kind of nonsense that any child can find for himself in the sort of books he borrows from servants without letting his parents know? The thought was intolerable. The next day, long before dawn, he rose and packed his few belongings, meaning to slip away without having to make embarrassing excuses. He was just tying up his bundle when one of the little girls came in with a pot of tea. Seeing how things were, she smiled and said: 'Please, Uncle, do not leave us so soon. If you do, I shall get the blame for not looking after you properly. You would not like that to happen, would you, Uncle? I know why you are angry. The Immortal said something you did not like, isn't it so? Have you never heard of mountain divinities pretending to be horrible red-tongued demons just to test the pilgrims' courage? *You* wouldn't be taken in, would you, Uncle?'

Rather than cause trouble for the friendly child, Pai decided to delay his departure for a few days, since it would be quite impossible to admit the true cause of his wanting to leave. Meanwhile the lessons continued, arousing such interest that the few days became many and, in the end, Pai never left the hermitage again, staying there in all for some seventy or eighty years!

Since a prerequisite for flying without wings is weightlessness, the first lessons were directed at 'throwing things away'. Unlike many others, Pai had discarded greed and ambition before coming to the mountain, but he still had cumbersome baggage to be disposed of – excessive ardour, for example, over-eagerness to succeed and over-anxiety lest he fail. He was taught to lose all sense of hurry, to subdue his tendency to strain. He had to learn to let himself be borne along like a floating cloud on the *ch'i* of heaven. Simultaneously, he set himself to acquire the art of invisibility. For this, stillness was required and the capacity to be as unobtrusive as a lizard on a branch, mingling with the pilgrims who came on festival days – there, yet unnoticed. The bribe to be offered to the guardians of the Mysterious Portal turned out to be a vow that, if the golden elixir were won, Pai would not depart into final bliss before founding and nursing a line of disciples capable of passing on the recipe for immortality to future generations. As to the Portal itself, he learnt that it stands in a region known as the Precious Square Inch lying just behind the mid-point between the eyes. There came a day when he could at any time behold the rays of heavenly light that are forever streaming through this gate but remain invisible until the adept has learnt how to develop his inner seeing. Learning to fly proved the longest and most arduous task, requiring that his physical endowments – semen and subtle essence, breath and blended personal and cosmic vitality, spirit both personal and cosmic – be transmuted into a spirit-body able to soar, during meditation, beyond the stars. Entering the courts of heaven meant achieving at will a state of ecstatic trance. Passing into the central chamber was the fruit of a yoga for drawing up the final product of blended essence, vitality and spirit from the region below the heart to the *ni wan* cavity just below the top of the skull; snatching the golden elixir from Lord Lao meant causing the perfected elixir to descend (and reascend) the central psychic channel running between the pelvis and the *ni wan*. Slaying the guardians was a term for countering the illusory ego's final struggles to retain the recognition hitherto given to it as an individual entity. Breaking down the walls was the supreme act, destruction of the last barriers between the adept's being and the Source of Being, so as to attain immortality in the true and only meaningful sense of those words. It signified, in fact, 'return to the Source', the be all and end all of Taoist endeavour, of cultivation of the Way!

The former Confucian scholar, having by devoted labour and with the unstinted help of his teacher attained to immortal state within a mere decade of his distraught arrival, was destined to make the Gourd Immortal's hermitage his permanent home. Its former owner, before 'soaring among the stars on the back of a dragon', confirmed Pai as his spiritual successor. Pupils of Pai's pupils were still to be found there in the 1930s and it was probably *their* pupils who were turned away when the red tide reached Mount Hêng around 1950!

Chapter 6

The Jade Emperor's Court
(Taoism as a Popular Religion)

Everything to do with Taoism is paradoxical. It may be said to have a pantheon so vast that no one has ever known the names of all its deities; or it may be said to have no deities at all, recognising no supremacy but that of the sublime, impersonal Tao. At its higher levels Taoism is a religion in the sense of embodying exalted mystical aspirations, not in the sense of acknowledging a God or gods; it is also a philosophy and way of life, a way of self-cultivation. Even Lawrence Sterne – author of *Tristam Shandy* in which the hero is not so much as born until we are half way through its several hundred pages – would scarcely have attempted a book on Christianity in which neither God nor Jesus, neither saints nor angels appear *at all*, yet Chou Shao-hsien's *Taoists and Immortals* which contains the very essence of the voluminous Taoist scriptures (*Tao Tsang*) has not a single paragraph on deities! What is more, that omission is perfectly in order. The fact is that deities entered the body of Taoism more or less accidentally and may be regarded or disregarded at will.

The Chinese have seldom subscribed to the view that adhering to one religion precludes adherence to another – or several others! Traditionally, most Chinese have been simultaneously Confucian, Taoist, Buddhist and followers of the ancient folk religion that never achieved a name of its own. Until the last century, there was indeed no word for 'religion' in the language, the three just mentioned by name being collectively known as the Three Teachings, a convenient term often extended to cover – rather vaguely – the folk religion as well. Foreigners in China are inclined to classify all temples which are not obviously Buddhist or (much more rarely) Confucian as Taoist and the Chinese seldom contradict them because they find it difficult to grasp the point of such distinctions and see no need for them. In early times, those Taoists who were intellectually advanced or gifted with spiritual perception paid no attention to gods. Lao-tzû just mentions them in passing and was clearly unconcerned about them; probably all Taoists at that time *believed* in gods, just as we believe today that there are polar bears near the north pole, an order of beings that exists but has no personal importance for ourselves. On the other hand, less intellectually or spiritually gifted Taoists naturally did feel some concern about the gods they, like other Chinese, had inherited from the folk religion to which they adhered without making any particular distinction between it and Taoism proper. At a later stage came a development which helped to bring about a marriage between popular level Taoism and the folk religion on an institutional basis.

The early followers of the Way lived as hermits or wanderers, perhaps with small bands of disciples; but this must presently have become economically difficult, for hermits gave place to small communities of recluses, each community with a fixed dwelling in some remote and unusually beautiful spot. However frugal their mode of living, a modest income was necessary if the communities were to flourish, and the traditional mode of self-support – selling herbal medicines and practising the physician's art – must often have brought in very little in places far away from large villages and towns. An additional sourse of income was needed and there proved to be one comparatively easy remedy. The peasants needed the services not only of healers able to deal with diseases caused by physiological disturbances or malevolent devils, but also of intermediaries likely to be on good terms with gods and spirits, men who could assist in such matters as funerals, obsequies for the dead, obtaining divine aid for worldly projects and either placating or subduing hostile demons. To these peasants, a holy man was a holy man whatever faith he might belong to, so it was natural for Buddhist monks and Taoist recluses (both popularly assumed to enjoy divine favour by reason of their austerities) to be called upon for such services. Buddhist monks, however, tended to lead people gradually away from the worship of indigenous deities, admonishing them to offer their devotion to the Buddhas and Bodhisattvas; and thus it fell to Taoists to function as the priests of the traditional divinities; this, Taoist communities with incomes adequate to their small needs were not always prepared to do, as priestly functions would take up some of the time they preferred to devote to the all-important task of self-cultivation. Most communities, however, had no regular source of income and so priestly functions came increasingly to occupy a proportion of their time. Moreover, as Buddhist institutions grew in numbers and in splendour, Taoists found it necessary to beautify their shrines and make their rites more spectacular in order to compete with the Buddhists for the often slender amount of financial support available.

To complicate matters, at an early date the Heavenly Teacher Sect drew closer to the folk religion than to the heart of Taoism; moreover a large number of city temples and other easily accessible institutions of the folk religion usurped, as it were, the name of Taoist, dressed their priests in Taoist robes, called them by Taoist names and even claimed that some of them were genuine immortals! No fraud was intended, its professors (mainly peasants) being almost certainly unaware that what they professed was not in accord with the real teachings of Taoism; in their simplicity, they assumed all religious doctrines to be more or less the same! All of this has led to a good deal of confusion. Self-cultivation is a private matter about which adepts maintain a modest reserve, whereas priestly functions are public, so it is often difficult to judge at first sight whether one has come upon a Taoist institution in which priestcraft plays a subordinate role, or a shrine given over to dealings with gods and demons among whose servitors self-cultivation is largely absent. As a result of this confusion, some people have come to suppose that living Taoism is altogether degenerate, that the only 'Taoists' worthy of respect are the Tao Chia, that is to say admirers of the philosophy of Lao and Chuang who are for the most part uninterested in supernatural aspects of Taoism. In my opinion, the dividing line – if there have to be such tiresome divisions – should come not between the Tao Chia philosophers and the Huang Lao Taoists as a whole, but between the Tao Chia plus the genuine seekers after immortality (in its higher senses) on the one hand and the priests who merely make use of the name 'Taoist' on the other. However, such a line would be very hard to draw. It is only when one gets to know individual communities or individual recluses that it is possible to decide whether or not they are genuine Taoists in the sense of pursuing self-cultivation. In general, one can say that most city temples and many places of pilgrimage on the more accessible of the sacred mountains were, during the earlier part of this century, Taoist only in name; but that, in the smaller and more remote hermitages, devoted cultivators of the Way were by no means rare – this point has been overlooked by so many writers that I almost despair of being believed, except by the few people who, having visited such places, know the truth for themselves.

In any case, there was so much overlapping of the various levels that it would be wrong to write a book such as this without devoting a chapter to popular Taoism, all the more so as some believers, originally drawn to the priesthood by the opportunities for making an easy living and therefore paying only lip service to Taoist ideals, later developed into genuinely devoted Taoists fully intent on cultivating the Way.

A description of Taoism at the popular level should perhaps start with the pantheon.

Divinities

The Chinese have been called a materialistic people on the grounds that the popular conception of the heavenly regions is of an astonishingly close replica of the structure of the Chinese Empire in the world below. However, this judgement ought to be reversed, the traditional Chinese view being that the entire universe is composed of spirit and that the Chinese Empire was a replica of heaven – not the other way round. To Chinese literati of the old school, heaven was a more or less abstract moral principle governing the world of beings, and thus virtually synonymous with the Tao. To the ordinary people, however, the heavens and hells were actual realms ruled by an intricate hierarchy of spirit officials; these regions, being enormous, were presided over by several emperors, all of them under the supreme jurisdiction of Yü Huang Shang Ti, the Jade Emperor. Though it seemed appropriate to dedicate this chapter to His Celestial Majesty, there is really nothing to be said about such superlatively august figures, since they are altogether too exalted for one to know anything of them as characters. For this reason, the divinities most often sought after by the faithful belong to subordinate categories. Among them, the Pole

Star Deity and the rulers of the adjacent stars have been popular from very ancient times and were probably worshipped before anyone came to hear of the Jade Emperor and other divinities of imperial rank. A lady deity known as Queen of Heaven and Holy Mother (not to be confused with the Jade Empress) is also a favourite, but the deities closest to the hearts of the people are mostly historical figures posthumously deified, not by heavenly command, but by one or other of *the real-life Chinese emperors*, acting each in his capacity as Son or Viceroy of Heaven! Of these, the most widely popular is Kuan Kung (or Kuan Ti), a Chinese general remarkable for absolute fidelity to his country, friends and sworn brothers who, after being executed by his enemies, was posthumously promoted to the rank of god by one of the T'ang emperors. Since his elevation he has been a celestial patron of both literature and commerce. Cheeks red as the sun, he is nine foot tall, has a magnificent beard and eyebrows like 'sleeping silk-worms'. A deity more feared than loved is Yen Lo Wang who presides with impartiality over the judgement of sinners, some of whom are sentenced to very fearsome hells of fire and ice, but the sentences are exactly in proportion to their sins; heinous though these may be, none of them undergoes *eternal damnation* and this barbarous sentence is not included in the statutes, nor is there any record of its having ever been passed.

Besides the governors of the celestial regions – the Emperors of the East, South, West, North and Central Realms – and their vast retinues of subordinates, there are also stellar deities as well as deities who live in or partly in the world of men – the gods of thunder and lightening; the gods of mountains, rocks, seas, rivers, streams, trees and flowers; the gods of earthly cities (whose effigies were occasionally taken out into the fierce sunshine and beaten by order of the local magistrate if, in time of drought, they failed to bring rain); the domestic divinities of kitchen, stove, storehouse and garden well; the divine patrons of professions such as literature, tailoring, gambling and prostitution; and such uncountable billions of nature spirits that not a rock, pool, stream or tree on earth is without its guardian genie. Some exalted beings have sprung from surprisingly humble origin; thus the present Queen of Heaven was formerly the daughter of a humble seaman, a native of the China coast.

Evil spirits are scarcely less numerous, but on the whole less powerful, than benign deities. Some are the ghosts of people subjected to

violent death or of childless couples with no progeny to conduct rites
on their behalf; others have been fiends since the first and would
dearly love to attain human state, for which reason they occasionally
murder humans so as to be able to inhabit their bodies; yet even the
most hideously malevolent fiends generally possess redeeming qualities and have been known to requite kindness with devotion and
faithful service. All are responsive to affection.

Few of these beings, whether divine or demonic, have much to do
with cultivation of the Way. In ancient times, Taoist hermitages
often had no special shrine room and the hermits' only connection
with spiritual powers was that, as healers, they had to set about subjugating the demons of disease. However, with the growth of huge
and ornate Buddhist monasteries, the Taoists were forced to compete
for the revenue derived from pilgrims. Thus big Taoist temple halls
were erected in some places. To match the three large Buddha images
in the main shrine halls of Buddhist temples, there came into being a
trinity known as the Three Pure Ones; but the fact that the identity
of the members of this trinity is by no means identical in all temples
is clear evidence of their relative unimportance among recluses dedicated to *self*-cultivation! One can hardly imagine Christians arguing
as to whether the members of their trinity should include the Holy
Ghost or the Virgin Mary, there not being room for both! Commonly the Taoist trinity consists of:

Ling Pao	Yü Huang	Lao Chün
Heaven's Marvellously Responsive Jewel, embodiment of *yin* and *yang* interaction and of past time	The Jade Emperor, embodiment of the Primal Cause and of present time	Lao-tzû, embodiment of Taoist doctrine and of future time

These statues have esoteric significance at different levels of understanding, not all of which are disclosed to chance visitors. Among
other things they represent the 'real Taoist trinity', namely *ching*,
ch'i, *shên*, essence, vitality and spirit.

The most delightful of the genuinely Taoist divinities, as opposed
to those inherited from the folk religion, are not really divinities at all
but charming embodiments of the popular conception of immortals.
Wherever Chinese artefacts are assembled will be found effigies of
the Eight Immortals, two or three of them beautiful, others majestic,

and at least one of them amusingly grotesque. Painted on wall-scrolls, fans, silks, vases, teapots and utensils of porcelain or lacquer; modelled as figurines in earthenware, porcelain, wood, bronze, ivory or jade, they are ubiquitous. Among them, only Lü Tung-pin is actually invoked in connection with divination and some yogic practices, but a Taoist hermitage with no representation of the Eight Immortals for decorative purposes is hardly imaginable. They are listed below with the distinctive emblems they *sometimes* carry given in brackets after their names:

Chung Li Ch'üan (a fan), also known as Han Chung Li, usually has his large tummy bared to the winds of heaven. A Han dynasty general sent to subdue Tibetan rebels, he was severely trounced and ran off into the wilderness where a wandering Taoist imparted to him the secret of longevity. Overjoyed, he cried: 'War is human devilry. I agree with Lao-tzû that the lucky fellow who escapes the battlefield with life and limb intact is the real victor. To kill a thousand men is a victory not worth mentioning beside the conquest of desire.'

Chang Kuo Lao (a section of bamboo containing two stick-like objects), very elderly and long-bearded, wears any headgear from a handsome hat to a cabbage leaf. He possesses a white mule that can be made small and folded up like a handkerchief, ready to be revived at any time by being sprayed with a mouthful of cold water. Commenting on this animal, a sage once remarked: 'Chang's mule is a poor mount after all, for it needs four legs; whereas I, riding on the *ch'i* [vitality] of the universe during meditation, can reach the Pole Star before Chang has ridden a single *li*.' To this, Chang replied: 'So can I, but I don't care to boast about mere trifles.'

Lü Tung-pin (a sword) is a handsome bearded figure in the prime of life. Though a sword is strapped to his back, he is no warrior; for, as he said himself of that weapon, 'Besides being useful now and then in rendering me invisible, it lops off passions and desires in no time.' While yet a mortal, though a great scholar, he failed in the very first round of official examinations, being unable to overcome his disgust at the pretentious style of the eight-legged essays required by the Confucian examiners.

Ts'ao Ku Chiu (a pair of musical clappers made of wood) is a bearded and rather prosperous looking figure, often dressed in official garb with a winged hat. Brother-in-law to one of China's Mongol emperors, he owned a token that ensured handsome treatment at no charge wherever he chose to wander. Chided by a Taoist mendicant for making use of this golden disc to get free drink, meals and transport, he carelessly tossed it into the river. Questioned about the whereabouts of the Tao, he pointed to heaven. 'But where is heaven *really* ?' continued the immortals who had propounded the first question in the hope of catching him out. This time, he pointed to his heart and the immortals burst out laughing as they exclaimed: 'Ha, this is a fellow who knows the Way!'

Li Hsüan (a bottle-gourd and iron staff) is more commonly known as T'ieh-Kuai Li or Iron-Staff Li. Born a very handsome fellow, he suffered a misfortune which explains why, far from having the appearance of an immortal enjoying perpetual youth, he has one leg shorter than the other and cannot walk without his staff. While as yet an ordinary mortal, he learnt to send his spirit forth on journeys, from one of which it returned to find that his trusted servant, summoned to the bedside of a dying mother, had left Li's body to be devoured by wild beasts. Needing a substitute instantly, the spirit had to take up its abode in the crippled body of a newly deceased beggar. In spite of this, he is a jolly fellow with a fine disregard for keeping up appearances.

Han Hsiang-tzû (a flute, sometimes carried in a soft embroidered cover) is a youthful looking immortal, occasionally depicted as a child. A scholar disgusted by Confucian pedantry, he was from the first fond of music and poetry. In a poem composed prior to his attainment of immortal state, he describes the joys of living in a cave veiled by a misty torrent, sipping midnight dew, breakfasting off rosy dawn-clouds and melting pearls by the power of music.

Lan Ts'ai Ho (a flower-basket) is a pink-and-white complexioned youth who wears his hair in side-buns and is often mistaken for a girl by the unlearned in these matters. His youthful appearance is a reminder that, as a mortal, he learned the secret of youth perpetually renewed. In those days, he was fond of roaming the streets with one foot shod, the other bare, his clothes thick in summer, thin in winter, to show his contempt for convention. In short, he was the original flower-child or hippy. Once, while drinking in a tavern, he heard unearthly music coming from nearby; whereat, throwing off his rags, he leapt upon a crane and soared into the empyrean.

Ho Hsien-ku (a long-stemmed lotus-leaf or magic fungus) is the only lady in the group. Having attained immortality while still a child by imbibing 'cloud-mother' [mica?], she vowed herself to chastity. Forced to the point of marriage by a wicked stepmother, she vanished, but left her slippers behind as a sign that she had departed for celestial regions. Asked whether she felt a need for female company, she replied: 'My fellow immortals, having found the Way, possess all the accomplishments of both sexes.' 'Still, Iron-Staff Li can hardly be called a beauty,' remarked a wit. 'He would seem so to you if you had beauty in your inmost self,' was the strange reply.

Another group of immortals known to all lovers of Chinese art consists of figures representing the three principle desires of ordinary people – Fu (wealth), Lu (rank) and Shou (longevity). Lu is dressed in the winged hat and belted robe of a high official and carries a jade sceptre indicating ministerial rank. Fu, standing on the right, bears a kind of cornucopia, but wears a simpler gown as befits a merchant. Shou, on the left, is identifiable by several symbols of longevity – an extraordinarily high, bald cranium, a staff of peachwood, a peach, a crane, and a spotted deer nuzzling up beside him. Millions of people long for the blessings they personify, but two of these blessings illustrate how far away in spirit is the folk religion from genuine Taoism, wealth and rank being two curses of humanity that followers of the Way seek to avoid! Nevertheless, paintings of the venerable Shou, Fairy of Long Life, are often very charming and he, at least, represents a thoroughly Taoist ideal, the more so if one takes 'long life' to be a synonym for immortality, as it often is.

Rites
Over the years Taoists have evolved elaborate rites somewhat resembling those practised in Buddhist temples. The blaze of votive lamps and candles, the swirling clouds of perfumed smoke and the richly coloured ritual garb of the officiants sometimes produce a

powerful effect, especially if the voices are good and the sweet music of flutes replaces the rather harsh music of clarinet, drum, cymbals and 'wooden-fish drum', although this, too, may be impressive. In large temples devoted to priestcraft, the rites are apt to be garish, whereas in the smaller hermitages, where recluses are sometimes scholars with notable artistic skills, they can be at once beautiful and spiritually moving. Music and slow ritual dances are vehicles for expressing the ecstatic sensations and longings of mystics, whose intimate acquaintance with nature, moreover, has made them adept at reproducing nature's sounds. Birdsong is best reproduced by flutes, whereas the exciting noise made by a flock of birds rising suddenly in alarm is a favourite theme for the classical lute; this has seven silken strings on which many recluses could play exquisite melodies. Some of the songs and chants have an eerie beauty, especially those used during the evocation of demons; they are so charged with melancholy that it would be no surprise to see among the shadows in the corners of the shrine hall the sad white faces of wandering ghosts! Except at festivals when rites are performed in honour of various deities, by far the most frequent ceremonies are those connected with sickness or with funerals and the obsequies which precede or follow interment. Individual suppliants may come to seek divine aid at any time, lighting incense and bowing to the floor; very seldom are the benefits thus sought of a spiritual nature, being chiefly connected with such mundane matters as business troubles, illness, barrenness, buying lottery tickets, and so forth. Here again, the link with Taoism is very tenuous.

Evocation of Gods and Spirits

This important aspect of priestcraft relates wholly to the ancient folk religion which was originally of the kind known as shamanistic. Mediums, who may be of either sex, deliberately induce a trance state during which they tremble, shudder, speak in strange voices and are certainly unconscious of what they do and say. Taking the god or spirit invoked to be actually present in the medium's body, suppliants bow to the earth to ask questions that are answered usually by the god speaking through the medium's mouth; but sometimes by means of trance writing, which is really puzzling for one can see it performed by mediums known to be illiterate! No doubt, both in this and other matters, fraud is sometimes practised;

but, apart from the fact that the mediums and their assistants are often sincere believers by whom counterfeiting the voice or actions of the god would be regarded as an act for which they would have to answer with their lives, there is the evidence of one's own eyes and ears, as when one asks a question of an entranced medium – or rather of the god inhabiting his body – and receives an answer revealing insight into matters known to oneself that could not by the wildest stretch of imagination be supposed to be known to the medium! Besides, very few mediums are accomplished charlatans; they can be seen at any time of the day in ordinary states of consciousness and often prove to be people of low rather than abnormally high intelligence.

From time to time, mediums and other devotees give demonstrations of invulnerability to injury (at least in some degree) by walking over burning coals without as much as blistering their skin, or piercing their flesh with skewers, hooks, axes or knives. However deep the wounds, very little blood – if any – is shed and they heal with astonishing rapidity, leaving no scars! When I reflect that my fourth right finger and lower lip are scarred by relatively minor wounds inflicted by glass some fifty years ago, I cannot agree with Leon Comber who, in a book on such phenomena among the Chinese community in Singapore, tries to explain away the mystery by saying that the wounds inflicted are 'nothing more than lacerations'; for that is a good description of my wounds which are still visible after fifty years, whereas the scars left by a skewer pierced through both cheeks disappear altogether within a few days! So it is with the unscarred feet of the fire-walkers; on my arm I bear the scars of twelve very tiny lighted incense sticks affixed to the skin during an initiation undergone over forty years ago; those scars remain, whereas the fire-walkers, exposed to great heat over the entire surface of their soles, show no marks at all! Then again, those mediums sometimes sit, while in a state of trance, on chairs of which the seats consist of rows of knife blades, or they roll about on similarly constructed beds. Mere athletic skill cannot explain the absence of damage to their flesh, for novices would suffer horrid lacerations while acquiring that skill; moreover, the slight lacerations that do sometimes occur, though certainly not very deep, are renewed so frequently that one would expect the mediums to be permanently scarred – which they are not! The explanation given by the mediums themselves is that nothing can harm them seriously during the times when they are possessed by gods or spirits.

Closely connected with this kind of self-induced possession is another kind – unsought possession by malignant spirits! Demonic possession strikes the modern mind as too bizarre for one to have much faith in the possibility of its occurring. Yet there are cases which have all the appearance of that phenomenon, and it seems that Western medicine has been more successful in finding names for such conditions than in providing cures, whereas in Taoist monasteries one could find recluses able to perform cures in an astonishingly short space of time. Patients would be brought up the mountain in a condition attended by many of the horrors portrayed in such films as 'The Exorcist', detained for a day or two and then sent home again apparently quite normal. Whether the cures were permanent I had no means of knowing, nor was I permitted to observe the treatment used; all I can say is that the change in the patient's condition was sometimes striking enough to appear miraculous. In the minds of the Taoist healers themselves, there was not the least doubt as to the cause of this type of illness; the blame rested squarely on the shoulders of invisible demons. As to the methods employed for healing diseases of non-demonic origin, these lie within the domain of Taoism proper, being in some cases by-products of the external alchemy discussed in the next chapter.

Magic Charms

Ever since the epoch of the Five Emperor-Sages, charms have been esteemed for medicinal and other purposes, the art of preparing them having been inherited by both Taoists and adherents of the ancient folk religion from the same source. Although this is a matter with no bearing on cultivation of the Way, even scholarly Taoists in the old days set store by these remedies for ills, as well as by auspicious luck-bearing charms. The most ancient charms of all are two magical diagrams, the Ho T'u (Plan of the Yellow River) and Lo Shu (Lo River Writing). Each consists of a different arrangement of tiny black and white circles joined in series by straight lines, the black representing *yang*, the white, *yin*. The Ho T'u is believed to symbolise the state of things prior to the birth of the universe and also the creative activities of nature during the first half of the year; whereas the Lo Shu symbolises the state of things subsequent to the universe's birth and also the dying or *yin* aspect assumed by the 'five activities' during the second half of the year. Unlike so many Taoist charms, these two can lay no claim to beauty; their interest lies in their immense antiquity (*at least* 3,000 years) and in the curious fact that the central arrangement in the Ho T'u, namely ⚛, is of wellnigh universal religious significance. Besides forming the heart of the principal Tibetan mandalas, it is essentially a cross – a symbol common to the Ancient Egyptian and Christian religions among others – and is, of course, related to the swastika of Hinduism and Buddhism. From this one may surmise that it is of profound archetypical significance. Like the eight trigrams in the *Book of Change*, it represents one of those hidden verities inherent in the workings of spirit and of matter (if making a distinction between these two has any real validity, which Taoist philosophers deny).

As to charms in general, it is believed that the sages of high antiquity were able to imbue those they transmitted with some of their own spiritual power. In speaking of them, Ko Hung said: 'Charms received from Lao Chün are written in the "script of heaven", for he was one who attained to the spiritual radiance whence these charms are derived. Indeed, Lao Chün *is* the radiance of heaven!' Another source recommends: 'To obtain charms, provided you have won to the Way, rise at dawn, burn incense in your courtyard, offer prayers and rites, then visualise a lovely youthful lady immortal richly dressed and girdled with a belt of jade. In her hand she grasps the "Genuine Jade-Clarity Purple Cloud Charm of the Sun Emperor". Beholding it, your mind will become one-pointed, free from idle thoughts. Then will the truly efficacious charm you seek appear in your mind.' Chou Shao-hsien tells us that 'These charms are called "Spontaneous Inscriptions of Jade-Clarity". One sees them in the mind written on red and coral clouds. Ordinary people never behold them; yet, to a holy adept who has made the necessary preparation, it will appear that they must be visible to all' (i.e. they will seem to him to exist objectively before the eyes). Here we are not dealing with the trumpery magic of charlatans, but with the mind of an enlightened adept as the source of efficacious charms. It is not surprising that a realised adept, a man of profound spiritual insight, should find within his mind symbols of great yogic or psychological significance. It is a pity that this passage from Ko Hung's writings was not commented upon by C. G. Jung.

The reference in the preceding paragraph to the 'script of heaven' may be intended to point to the origin of the secret scripts widely used by Taoist charm writers, such as the *shên shu* (divine script) and *yün shu* (cloud scripts), which can be understood only by initiates. Some of these scripts are beautiful; all are curious and excitingly enigmatic, recalling patterns seen in nature such as wave patterns or the footprints of birds. In Taoism, nothing of that kind is arbitrary, but the result of close observation of nature's workings. There are all sorts of legends about the origin of the various scripts. Some, it is said, were incised on gold with a stylus of white jade and 'hidden in the Dark Terrace of the Seven Treasures' where only those who had attained to the Way could come upon them. This is a saying which may, like so many others, have a special significance for initiates.

Faith and Self-Cultivation

Taoism resembles Buddhism in being entirely free from dogma. Nevertheless, both these religions demand faith – not in particular principles, for then dogma would be present, but in the existence of a higher good, a higher state of being to which it is possible to attain. What distinguishes true understanding from what passes at the popular level for understanding is recognition that faith, though essential, is never enough; Immortality or, in the case of Buddhism, Enlightenment has to be won by great and sustained effort; neither divinities nor sages have the power to bestow it; attainment or failure rests squarely with each individual. This is a vital truth largely ignored at the popular level. Followers of Heavenly Teacher Chang, for example, set great store by magical or divine aid; whereas, among serious cultivators of the Way, self-mastery and self-attainment are recognised as the sole way to success. A little anecdote culled from the *Tao Tsang* conveys the popular notion of the power of faith. We are told that a country fellow with a deep longing for the Way but no idea how to set about attaining it could think of nothing better than to kneel all day, month after month, year after year, before a withered tree, begging it to bestow the boon of immortality. All day long he cried to the tree 'Give me immortality! Give me immortality!' Not surprisingly, this went on for many years without having the least noticeable effect. However, such was his tenacity that at last the withered tree was constrained to put forth lovely blossom and exude a liquid sweet as honey. On the advice of his friends, the simple fellow ate and drank of these and was straightway transmuted to immortal state!

On the face of it, this anecdote is so nonsensical that one might think it surprising to find it included in the sacred *Tao Tsang*. In fact, however, it possesses a certain poetic truth, as do many of the Western fairy stories it so much resembles; for single-minded repetition of a formula is an effective method of so concentrating the mind that the senses are sealed against contaminating inflows, with the result that profound mystical insight is attained. This is recognised not only in China, but by mystics everywhere; there are Buddhist, Hindu, Christian and even Moslem versions of this practice. Thus the way of faith may become the way of self-attainment.

I shall now relate three longer stories that provide insight into Taoism at a level at which it is heavily intermixed with the folk religion. The first is an amusing illustration of the extent to which the celestial and nether regions are popularly held to resemble the world of men. The second, with its combination of magical and moralistic elements, represents the kind of Taoism that emanated from Dragon-Tiger Mountain, headquarters of the Heavenly Teacher Sect whose members were seldom greatly concerned with self-cultivation. The third gives us a glimpse of a secret world of immortals.

Spirit Money

Li Hua, a wealthy and respected merchant, owed the foundation of his fortune to his having when a youth defrauded a widow of her whole property, driving her to hang herself to escape utter penury. Not a living soul was in the secret, but 'no crime goes unnoticed by the eye of heaven', as the proverb truly says. When Li Hua was at the point of death, two shadows darkened the door of his chamber and he was horrified to recognise the awful beings who now entered as lictors dispatched, no doubt, by one of the assistant judges of the dead! 'You *must* not take me yet', he blustered. 'There is a crime on my conscience I have always been meaning to pay for in some suitable way, but somehow the matter slipped my memory until now. I shall need at least a year to amass a store of merit by way of redressing the balance.' 'Be sure we know all about that,' snarled a hawk-headed lictor, snapping his iron beak ominously. 'The lady you defrauded has laid a plaint before His Excellency, who detests oppression of the weak and helpless. Still, you need not fear that his detestation will make him unduly severe. His Excellency – ha-ha-ha – always sees to it that the punishment *exactly* fits the crime. You will probably be sentenced to merely impalement upon a red-hot sword-tree for precisely the number of years cut from the virtuous widow's life on account of your cruelty. To compensate for the interest on the principal which has been accumulating during all those years, I dare say I shall be instructed to exercise my iron beak on your flesh several hundred times a day; or my friend here with the bull-head may be ordered to give you a daily lesson in virtue. Who knows ?'

Alas, reflected the shuddering merchant, if these two were human lictors, I could buy them off without the least trouble, but what use have these creatures for bars of gold ? Stay! At funerals a lot of paper imitations of golden ingots are burned to provide the departed with sufficient means to purchase a fitting establishment in the celestial regions. It stands to reason that the terrible judge Yen Lo Wang or one of the assistant judges would be glad to accept a sufficiently handsome sum paid in genuine spirit-money. And of course these two unspeakable wretches must have their share. Ah well, ten thousand 'gold ingots' made of paper will cost my sons two or three silver pieces at the most. Hurriedly he laid this plan before the lictors, to be answered with brazen laughter and a sharp command to finish dying, so as to be ready for his last journey.

'Ah, gentlemen, stop, stop! I pray you! Give me just a moment to think clearly. My mind is all at sixes and sevens. There, I have it! You have no right to stand between that poor widow's spirit and an opportunity to improve her circumstances in the celestial regions very considerably. If you haul me off without giving me time to arrange things, the judge will have something to say to *you*! I undertake to make full restitution in spirit currency of the sum I – er – acquired from her, together with *full interest* for all the years which have elapsed since that unfortunate event. I must be allowed a few minutes to make the arrangement with my sons.'

Putting their hideous heads together, the demon lictors conversed in harsh metallic undertones. Recognising that the poor widow's spirit had nothing to gain from this vile spirit's sufferings, however entertaining, they agreed that a handsome sum of spirit currency remitted through the Celestial Bank would decidedly improve her standing among her heavenly neighbours and enable her to buy a pleasant property with a garden full of celestial fruit trees.

Accordingly, with some trepidation, they permitted Li Hua a further hour of life, although the extension had not been sanctioned by His Excellency. The lictors vanished. Li forthwith sent for his sons and, without disclosing the disreputable reason, commanded them to have such and such a sum of paper spirit-money burnt during the course of his obsequies. This done, he peacefully submitted to death and accompanied the lictors on their downward journey to the awe-inspiring nether regions, where the only music to be heard was the shrieks of convicted criminals and where the very breeze was tainted with the stink of charred flesh.

No sooner had their father passed away than the eldest son said to his brothers: 'It seems our honoured parent was wandering in his mind when he issued his august commands. It is true that paper ingots cost no more than a copper for ten, but would not the neighbours think it vulgar to make such a great show of burning paper money? They might even suppose that our esteemed parent had it in mind to bribe his way out of any trifling difficulties that may await the spirit of a man so upright. That would not look well for us.'

'True, Elder Brother,' replied the second son. 'As you say, our dear father's mind was wandering towards the end. It would not be undutiful to disregard instructions given under such circumstances. Let us agree to say no more about it.'

During the splendid obsequies that followed, only the customary amount of spirit money was burnt – no more than a tenth of the sum proposed by the late Li Hua. Who knows what price he had to pay for his children's unfilial conduct? In this world of dust, even a dying man cannot rely upon the filial piety of his children!

The Younger Brother of the Pole Star Deity

During the Liang dynasty, a strange young man appeared in one of the provincial towns of Lu, where he revealed himself as a devotee of worldly pleasures – gambling, wenching, wining and dining night after night. Everybody took him for a wastrel and the citizens were careful to keep their daughters out of sight, for he was a youth of notable charm whose smiling pleas even a well brought up girl might find it difficult to resist. Once when dining late in a tavern, he fell foul of three ruffians. Judging from the quality of the jade ornaments about his person that he could have sufficient gold in his sleeve to make it worth their while to take the risk of dispatching him to the world of ghosts, they engineered a quarrel. Upon some trumped up pretext, they closed in with weapons drawn and, beating down his spirited defence, made an end of him there and then, before fleeing into the night. The pursuit was half-hearted, for the authorities deemed that the rogues had done a considerable service to the fathers of pretty girls in the neighbourhood. Meanwhile, the robbers, having divided up the jade and gold, went their several ways; but no sooner did the new owner of the finely carved jade belt-buckle lie down to sleep than the buckle remarked pleasantly: 'I think you will agree that you came by me dishonestly. You had better put things right before punishment befalls.'

'Put things right?' stammered the unlucky rogue. 'Short of restoring your previous owner to life, there's really not much we can do about it, is there?'

'Well,' replied the buckle, 'that's for you to decide. It is you who will have to suffer the consequences of omission. My advice is go off into the mountains, leaving all worldly possessions behind, and cultivate the Way. I rather think you have about three days in which to make up your mind.'

The next morning, the unfortunate rogue, meeting his two fellows in the market place to plan some further enterprises, discovered that each had had much the same dream. One had received admonishment from the dead youth's jade bangle, the other from the jewel that had ornamented his hat. Thoroughly alarmed, they hurried off into the mountains where, after wandering miserably and hungrily for some days, they came upon a hermit residing alone in a dilapidated hut. 'Just what I was hoping for!' exclaimed the bearded sage. 'Three strong fellows like you should be able to help me build the fine stone hermitage I need for housing some disciples who are due here on the seventh day of the seventh moon.' With that, he gave them a good meal, then set them working grievously in return for nothing but enough rice and vegetables to keep them from starvation. Rocks had to be prised from a cliff, carried to the site and hoisted into position. One day of such labour was more than enough for them; but, whenever they desisted, the hermit ran among them with his stout staff raised on high to rain blows on heads and shoulders until they wept for mercy. Nor could they hope to run away from a master whose supernatural powers included thousand-league vision and thousand-league hearing.

Miserably they worked from dawn to dusk, longing for the sun to set; yet even then they could not rest, for the hermit would spend the hours from nightfall to midnight discoursing of the Way. But at last the building was completed and the hermit, smiling amiably, said: 'Return whence you came and fetch any little trinkets you may have in the form of jade, golden coins, silken garments and suchlike that we may make ready to welcome my disciples lavishly.'

Disconsolately the robbers hastened home, knowing it would be folly to disobey, and returned some days later with all the valuables looted from the body of their unfortunate victim together with the loot of some previous crimes. 'Quite satisfactory,' remarked the hermit and, turning his back on the others, arrayed himself in the dead youth's finery. When he turned towards them again, they were appalled. The bushy beard had vanished revealing a face they remembered all too well – that of the wastrel they had slain!

'Well now,' said the hermit, smiling pleasantly, 'we are quits. You gentlemen did me a disservice followed by a service. The debt is paid. You may go home.'

With one accord the robbers bowed to the earth, crying to him to allow them to remain as his disciples.

'So that's how it is, my friends – just as I expected. Today, as you gentlemen may recall, is the seventh day of the seventh moon. You, by the way, are the disciples for whom this handsome hermitage was built.'

He now revealed himself as the renowned immortal known far and wide as Younger Brother of the Pole Star Deity. Having perceived with his all-seeing eye that three teachable young gentlemen had fallen into bad ways, he had taken care not only to save them from retribution by exacting payment for their crimes, but also to instruct them in the Way. All attained immortality thanks to his instruction and went to dwell with their master in the Pole Star Deity's palatial dwelling.

Would that all rogues could meet with such an amiable judge!

A Hidden Realm

Governor Wu of Kiangsi, a distinguished member of the Han Lin Academy, had four sons all scholars like himself, but the youngest, Wu Lien, unaccountably conceived an aversion for the holy sage, Confucius, and spent his time immersed in the histories of immortals.

Shocked by such impiety, the Governor first remonstrated several times and finally struck his son; whereat the boy, having bowed at his father's feet, walked out of the house never to return. Some days later, the garments he had been wearing were found on the shore of the P'o-Yang Lake. It appeared to be one of those cases all too common in Confucian society – suicide by a son unable to bear the remorse occasioned by being reprimanded for unfilial conduct.

Several years later a rumour spread that in the Wu-I Mountains was sometimes seen a young immortal who marvellously resembled the missing Wu Lien. Concealing his joy, Governor Wu ordered his most trusted subordinate to gallop off and investigate. This Lo Chu arrived in the vicinity of Wu-I with a military escort, but was told by some villagers: 'He is shy and elusive, Sir, and detests soldiers. Go in company with armed men and you will not get a glimpse of him.'

In those days, the Wu-I range was well wooded. Lo Chu wandered for days without coming upon the youth he sought. One day, however, while stooping to drink from a mountain stream, he observed a rainbow mist rising from among the tumbled black rocks whence the stream welled forth. Filled with awe, he climbed to investigate and came suddenly upon – his master's son! But was he so ? Though the likeness was striking, this youth wore an expression so full of self-assurance and his eyes shone so brilliantly with the light of transcendent wisdom that it was impossible to sustain his gaze; added to this was the extraordinary effect produced by the rays which, streaming from his person, formed a nimbus like those rainbow mists that hang above a plunging torrent when sunbeams play upon the spray. He was at once lovely to behold and yet so awe-inspiring that Lo Chu had to turn away his eyes and was tempted to turn and flee.

The Immortal, though poised for instant flight, had allowed him to approach and now suddenly broke into a radiant smile. 'Uncle Lo, how good of you to come! I did not expect you so soon. As my parents and brothers are well and youngest sister's malady is not serious, my father might have spared you such a fatiguing journey.' Here was a new wonder! The youth, instead of inquiring anxiously about his family, spoke as though he were the one to have just arrived from Nan-Ch'ang. It was now that he seemed to become conscious of his nimbus, for he blushingly withdrew the rays. Together they walked through the trees to his dwelling, a grotto with a smooth stone floor whereon were arranged a pile of blankets, a tea-stove, several books and a very few household necessities, of which only the books had the air of having been recently in use, Through the wide sunlit entrance, brightly plumaged birds and gorgeous butterflies flew in and out, but were too respectful to deface the floor with the usual droppings. It was spotless. Sitting still to encourage these creatures to perch on him, the Immortal briefly related his story.

On leaving home, he had left behind seeming evidence of suicide, knowing that his father would rather believe him dead than think of him as a 'Taoist beggar-man'. The fame of the Crystal Spring Immortal had brought him hastening to the Wu-I mountains and he had enrolled among the great man's disciples. 'Last year, on the night of the summer equinox, my Master ascended to the clouds, leaving us to disperse, but not before favouring me with such precious knowledge that I have attained in a few months what took him a lifetime of effort. Forgive my seeming to boast, for it is better that you know the whole.'

To all Lo Chu's entreaties that he return to Nan-Ch'ang the youth returned a smiling refusal. Rather, he persuaded the secretary to remain for a while to enjoy the '*real* sights of the mountain'; and, whereas hitherto Lo had seen naught but wild scenery and a woodman's cottage or a hermitage or two, he now beheld wonder upon wonder. In many a hidden grotto or cavern dwelt shining creatures in whose very existence he had never quite believed. In one they found a pair of glorious phoenixes with plumage so dazzling that the long tail-feathers looked like streamers of coloured flame. In another they disturbed a brood of new-born dragons, as yet no more than two feet long from whisker to tail, their skin an unlovely pink where the scarlet scales had still to form. More often these hidden nooks were inhabited by *ch'i-lin* (Chinese unicorns) or *shih-tzû* (long-haired lion-like creatures) with gleaming, varicoloured coats – sky-blue, jade-green, crimson, pink or yellow. 'Why did I glimpse none of these creatures when I was wandering about on my own?' inquired Lo. 'They are shy, Uncle, and hide themselves from the eyes of mortals. You would not wish to see those baby dragons chained in a rich man's garden or placed in a gourmet's cooking-pot?'

Some of their visits were to immortals – sages clad in shimmering robes, some of whom displayed an innocent vanity in the splendour of their long silky beards. They were usually ready for a game of *wei ch'i* or of elephant chess or prepared to exhibit their virtuosity with flute or *shêng* (a mouth organ composed of varying lengths of bamboo reed bound tightly together). However, not all of them passed their days in idleness, but could be seen standing round a steaming crucible in which lay some glowing substance that exuded a mysteriously perfumed golden mist. Now and then they would throw in small quantities of coloured powders and watch eagerly for a result that never seemed to materialise; then they would laugh softly and poke gentle fun at one another's ineptitude. None of these immortals was seen to eat, much less answer a call of nature. 'No, Uncle, you are wrong. They do require nourishment, but a drop of honey or as much dew as you would find upon the petals of a single flower is enough to last them for a month or so. There is one who still has a craving for rice and shocks his friends by consuming as much as four or five grains at a single meal, an unfortunate appetite that tends to dim the lustre of his nimbus, but – ha-ha – he does not care. Vanity about the brilliance of a nimbus, he says, is the sign of being a newcomer to immortality. As a senior contemporary of Lord Lao, he feels he has been immortal long enough to be allowed a certain indulgence. Would you care to feast with some demons, Uncle? *They* have excellent appetites and will drink with you cup for cup until your legs give way.'

'D-demons?'

'Why yes. You need not be afraid. Though treacherous beyond imagining, they know better than to make trouble for *my* friends.'

Lo Chu could hardly contain his impatience, reflecting on the sensation he would cause in Nan-Ch'ang by relating the details of a banquet attended by demons. The following dawn found them at the top of a high peak, where the Immortal spent some time collecting cosmic *ch'i* in a small leather bag he had brought for the purpose. Back at the grotto, he recited some words over it and made several magic gestures; then, unfastening it and holding it upside down, he scattered its mind-created contents on the ground outside. There tumbled forth from the narrow neck at least a dozen carcasses of beef done to a turn and a vast number of richly stuffed chickens and wild-fowl, to say nothing of that demon delicacy – enormous white rats cooked in honey.

As the sun went down, the guests began arriving. Most were hideous beings with horrendous fangs and claws, lolling scarlet tongues and grotesquely distended bellies, but at least they bore a vague resemblance to humans; whereas some others were just dark shapes with no distinguishable features apart from a cavernous red mouth in what, on other beings, would have been called the region of the belly. A few were animal-headed or had several eyes; one looked like an uncommonly pretty girl as far as her face was concerned, but otherwise there was nothing of her but hanging entrails. All behaved with reasonable decorum in the Immortal's presence, if one made allowances for their manner of eating, which was to tear the flesh apart, stuff great gobbets into their mouths, and pick up the bones and crunch them to powder. By way of recompense for so fine a feast, they gave an exhibition of demon dancing to the music of clashing bones and such a moaning, wailing and shrieking as may be heard when the wind howls among mountain caverns. What the dance lacked in elegance was made up for by the dancers' prodigious agility.

On their last night together, the Immortal took Lo Chu to a moon-viewing terrace and, fixing his eyes upon a brilliant star, caused it to draw nearer and nearer to the world. Presently the radiant orb was so close that they could wave and bow to a band of immortals who were dancing in front of a lovely pavilion built of pearl and coral cloud. One of them, a white-bearded sage, gazed at them as he danced, lips wreathed in smiles. The youth bowed his head to the ground in his direction, ordering Lo Chu to do the same and whispering that this was his old teacher, the Crystal Spring Immortal.

In the morning, Lo begged with tears in his eyes to be allowed to remain as the youth's disciple. 'No, no, Uncle. That would not do. My father has lost a worthless son, but must not be troubled by the loss of a valuable secretary. Here is a box containing a powder that will instantly cure youngest sister's malady. And here is a book for you, Uncle. Study it well and, when you reach retirement age, come back again. You will have plenty of time in which to cultivate the Way.'

Chapter 7

白 青 Green Dragon
White Tiger
虎 龍 (Taoist Alchemy)

'Green dragon white tiger!' With this poetic phrase are associated
many curious meanings. Like '*yin* and *yang*' it denotes various pairs
of opposites – especially male and female, it being the task of the
Taoist magician, alchemist, yogin or mystic to fuse them into an
indivisible unity. Often these four words hint at some secret rarely
disclosed to non-initiates. Their merely magical meanings do not
concern us here, although Taoist magic is a fascinating subject, both
because of the tantalising secrecy that shrouds it and because it so
often seems to *work*! Is its working wholly psychological, or is it
really possible for magicians to manipulate hidden forces and bring
them to bear as Mao Tsê-tung and Chou Ên-lai are alleged to have
done in secret? I do not know. Ah, but how much less dull the
modern world would seem if we could believe that it was not dreary
dialectics but green dragon white tiger that brought those gentlemen
their phenomenal success; for, were that really so, there would be
some prospect of a return to colourfulness, romance and mystery to
relieve the drab uniformity they have created.

The Ts'an T'ung Ch'i
How strange it would be to come upon a single volume whose
meaning could be so variously interpreted that it could be taken to
pertain simultaneously to the anthropomorphic doctrine concerning
the gods of Mount Olympus, to the Christian religion with its
emphasis on eternal life in heaven or hell, and to Buddhism with its

concept of casting away ego-born delusion and plunging into the ocean of Nirvana like raindrops returning to their source! Taoists, though, would not be even mildly surprised to hear of the existence of such a book, for they have one on which even more diverse interpretations can be placed! The *Ts'an T'ung Ch'i,* a work which on the face of it seems to set forth an alchemic process for transmuting base metals into gold, has been taken by some to be exactly what it seems; by others to contain instructions for compounding a golden pill able to confer perennial youth, immense longevity and perhaps flesh-and-blood immortality; by yet others to teach a method of creating, by sexual or non-sexual means, a spirit-body capable of enjoying eternal life; and by mystics to be the key to that shining apotheosis whereby one becomes pure spirit, free to plunge into the luminous undifferentiated ocean of the Tao; not to mention a fifth interpretation which makes of it a manual of the arts of government and war! What a catalogue of aims from un-Taoistically avaricious to incomparably sublime! That any one volume could possibly be taken to inculcate all of them results from two peculiarly Taoist concepts of the nature of existence: (1) the indivisibility and indeed identity of spirit and matter; (2) the identical working of nature's laws at every possible level and in every possible mode of being.

As to the history of this extraordinary work, it is recorded that it was composed soon after the beginning of our era by a recluse known as the Immortal Hsü; yet it may in fact be very much older, for the title he gave his version was *The Ancient Dragon and Tiger Classic.* Why *ancient* if he himself was the author? A century later, the great Wei Po-yang revised it and added an important commentary; since then it has been known as the *Ts'an T'ung Ch'i* – a virtually untranslatable title sometimes rendered the *Union of Three.* In its revised form it has survived without further alteration other than the addition of further commentaries. The extent to which it is revered may be judged from its being classified as a 'prior-to-heaven' work, meaning that it pertains to the state of things before the universe was born, or even that it springs from the divine wisdom inherent in the Tao.

The doctrine propounded in the *Ts'an* is based on the premise that within the human body, as within the macrocosm termed 'heaven and earth', exist three treasures – *ching* (essence), *ch'i* (vitality) and *shên* (spirit). By the transmutation of these three from coarse to subtle form and by their subsequent interaction, a mysterious elemental 'something' is created. If this alchemic process is carried out within the body, that 'something' is an embryo spirit-body or, according to some interpretations, pure spirit. If the same process is applied to physical substances, a highly purified form of matter (e.g. gold) is obtained. Exactly how the *Ts'an* is understood depends upon how it is interpreted by the accomplished master who supplies the essential orally transmitted key to its meaning. As we have seen, there can be no *conflicting* interpretations (unless by ill-instructed persons), only interpretations appropriate to different levels or different modes of being. It contains many references to the blending of *yin* and *yang*, which are sometimes given a sexual connotation pointing to the blending of the male and female essences within the yogin's body; but they are more often interpreted to pertain to an internal yoga for which no sexual partner is required. Always there is the idea of getting back to something called the 'original'. One passage runs:

> The holy sages of old clung to the 'original' and embraced it in unsullied form, nourishing their bodies on the nine-times refined elixir, a pure substance formed from a seething liquid. Conserving their essence and nourishing their bodies, they attained to the marvellous virtue that characterises heaven, earth and man in their pristine state; and, by following the principle of secreting their essence so that it ran out through the pores, they caused flesh and bone to be transmuted into a holy substance. Abandoning erroneous methods, they rectified their vitality and thereby made it everlasting, thus passing from mortal to immortal state.

In his remarkable book, Chou Shao-hsien makes the point that the *Ts'an* and similar yogic manuals seem to advocate 'simultaneous production of the inner and outer pills', meaning that self-cultivation is to be carried on as an internal process (yogic and mystical) and external process (alchemic in the literal sense) together. Thus, for example, the Taoist yogin may ingest alchemically compounded drugs as a subsidiary means of purifying and transmuting his being, but recognise such aids to be of small account in comparison with spiritual cultivation. There are passages in the manuals into which it is difficult to read any spiritual significance; in the case of the

Ts'an, one may wonder why great sages such as the Immortal Hsü and Master Wei Po-yang should have included them. One possibility is that they involve analogies not recognisable as such by the uninitiated; but it is more probable that they result from the Taoist conviction that identical natural laws are at work in everything from the tiniest particle up to the great macrocosm itself, from which it follows that the same techniques are suited to every conceivable level of activity. Should one desire to attain the highest possible spiritual goal, well and good; should one have merely worldly aims or believe that the transmutation of metals is relevant to spiritual transmutation, why not? A Taoist would not be a Taoist if he presumed to lay down hard and fast rules for other people's conduct; everyone must be free to 'do his own thing'; if he prefers to use his secret knowledge of nature's workings for trivial ends, that is his own affair. Meanwhile it is the duty of a sage to manifest nature's marvellous powers as a whole. How can an enlightened sage permit himself to make distinctions and yet preach, as he is bound to do, that full attainment involves the reconciliation of opposites? Gold, however much abused by the avaricious, is no less imbued with Tê, the virtue of the Tao, than anything else one may care to mention. According to a well-known Taoist poem, there are three thousand six hundred gates for entering upon the Way. How foolish to claim that this or that is not the Mysterious Portal of the Ultimate!

The general principle of the alchemic process, whether applied to spiritual development or to the transmutation of base metals into gold, can be expressed thus:

Essence, vitality and spirit continually interact. The sequence of their interaction in nature leads from void to form, from the universal to the particular, from the subtle to the gross. A sage is one who knows how to reverse this sequence, proceed backwards from gross to subtle, and thus regain original perfection for the substance or non-substance worked upon. There is an exact parallel between the transmutation of the gross powers of body and mind into pure spirit and that of base metals into the pure element, gold.

The complexity of the terminology used in the manuals and the difficulties facing the translator may be gauged from the following sample sentence, which happens to be taken from the *Book of the Elixir*: 'With heaven as your cauldron, earth as your furnace, take the black hare medicine and heat it.' One needs to know that 'heaven' signifies the heart, 'earth' the body, 'black' the *yang* principle and 'hare' the *yin* principle; and, knowing that, to understand exactly how that knowledge is to be applied – hence the vital importance of the oral key supplied only to initiates.

Before describing the internal alchemy, a true means of achieving spiritual perfection, I shall touch upon two versions of the external alchemy, the first of which – sexual yoga – is closely related to the internal form.

Dual Cultivation or Sexual Yoga

'From the union of the green dragon and white tiger energies in the cauldron of the body arises the lucent vapour of pure spirit in rainbow-coloured clouds.'

The ingredients are cinnabar (female essence) and mercury (male essence). The body of either partner may be used as the cauldron. The fusion of cinnabar and mercury reflects the union of heaven and earth, the birth of the myriad objects in the womb of the formless Tao. Therefore must lust be wholly eschewed, lest the adept be ensnared and deflected from cultivation of the Way. He or she should select a partner robust in health but not so alluring as to cause the stirring of passion – an eventuality which makes this yoga dangerous to spiritual health. In Chou Shao-hsien's view, this practice, though of some benefit to married couples, cannot compare with restraint or abstinence, since cultivation within the adept's own body (the inner alchemy) is a greatly superior way of transmuting *ching*, *ch'i* and *shên* into pure spirit. Master Ko Hung declares that dual cultivation practised without full understanding of the Tao's profundity leads erring couples to 'exhaust their energy (*ching*) and tire their spirit (*shên*) without attaining success after a whole lifetime of endeavour'. In another passage, this great master of yoga states that, since strict continence is for most young couples extremely difficult, rigid chastity may cause illness and will certainly result in tumults of spirit more likely to shorten than to lengthen life; hence dual cultivation is sometimes employed as a remedy for sickness or in order to lengthen one's lifespan; however, most adepts are sincere in desiring to blend and raise the essence (to the *ni-wan* or 'upper cinnabar field') so as to vitalise the brain (or seat of *shên*, spirit). This indicates that the Master favoured dual cultivation when practised with sincerity; yet he seems to have had doubts about it, for he wrote elsewhere that adepts of the yoga are sometimes people labouring under a dreadful misapprehension, or libertines using it as an excuse for sensuality, or even pretended yogins eager to lure women into adultery on the pretext of accomplishing a high spiritual purpose. In his later writings, he revealed a still more sceptical attitude, declaring that dual cultivation may have some therapeutic value and be a good way of avoiding wasteful expenditure of semen (since the adept must always stop short of ejaculation), but that it is not to be relied upon as a sound method of spiritual cultivation. I myself found this opinion general among Taoists; yet it had its devotees right up to the coming of the red flood, for there are recorded cases of its suppression by the communists who, whatever they may say about the 'iniquities' of Confucius, share fully in his puritanism.

This yoga, since it is dangerous for adepts who have difficulty in freeing themselves from bondage to the senses, must be undertaken if at all, in conjunction with contemplation of the real nature of the alchemic process. It is taught that this body, like the universe, had its origin in non-being; that the original cosmic essence was responsible for its coming into being and that, by a reverse process, blended male and female essence can be used to create a spirit-embryo that will endow its owner with the power to return to the original state of non-being by merging with the Source. Thus there is a correlation between a biological process (viewed with misgiving by strict Confucians, though not with the disgust exhibited by the fathers of the Christian Church) and the process of achieving man's highest spiritual goal. To Taoists with their perception of the identity of spirit and matter, there is nothing surprising in such correlations. The notion that sexuality is gross does not occur to them, their only fear being that spiritual endeavour may be overwhelmed if free rein is given to the passions. Such doubts as some of them have had on the subject of dual cultivation have been on this score only. It was the prudery of the Confucian authorities rather than a change of heart among Taoists that led some centuries ago to a diminuition in the practice of a yoga popular since the days of the Yellow Emperor.

Having never at any time received instruction in this yoga, I cannot pretend to speak of it with authority. To the best of my understanding, it proceeds along the following lines:

Pure *yang*-spirit pertains to heaven and is not present in this *yin*-world in unadulterated form. To create it within one's body, it is first necessary to refine one's natural endowment of coarse essence, vitality and spirit. The vehicle of coarse essence is sexual fluid (or, as some Taoists would say, coarse essence *is* sexual fluid). This must be most carefully conserved and transmuted into subtle *ching* by causing it to interact with *ch'i* (vitality) and *shên* (spirit). Their transmutation can be facilitated by the following means. The flow of coarse *ching*, having been aroused during the act of coition, is restrained at a crucial moment, that is to say the moment at which the sexual partner achieves orgasm. By a secret yogic method, the partner's *ching*, together with that of the adept, is drawn up into the lower cinnabar field (below the navel) where the two are blended and, being blown upon by the wind of *ch'i* (vitality, breath), transmuted into subtle form from which, by further operations of *ching*, *ch'i* and *shên*, what is variously described as a spirit-embryo or golden pill is formed and thereafter drawn up the median psychic channel to be lodged in the *ni-wan* cavity close to the top of the skull.

In practice, this process is far from simple and needs great yogic skill. At the outset numbers of subsidiary requirements have to be mastered – certain postures, certain rhythms of performance, certain times of the day, month and year, a particular regimen of diet and bathing, all of them conducive to restraining the adept's outflow of *ching*, ensuring full expenditure of the partner's essence, facilitating the first stage of their blending and making sure that the blend is drawn into the 'crucible', namely the 'lower cinnabar field' two inches below the navel, where upon further stages are entered upon with the assistance of yogic breathing and of the art of visualisation. The textbooks giving instruction in these matters are compositions of various dates, the authorship of some of them being credited to the divine beings who taught the Yellow Emperor how to master the esoteric bedroom art. These teachers, most prominent among them the Plain Girl (Su Nü), are said to have provided him with some ninety secret recipes. Unfortunately most of the books bearing such titles as 'Classic of the Plain Girl's Secret Way' have been virtually lost to China for several centuries owing to the prudery of the Confucian authorities; they can, however, be found in a few public and private libraries in Japan.

This art, sometimes called 'the secret Tao of *yin* and *yang* interaction', has been described as 'assisting men in winning immortality; assisting women in overcoming a hundred maladies', a quotation which suggests that the benefits for men are greatly superior to those for women; in fact, however, that is not the case. Numerous texts claim for the art the pow   to prolong youth and promote longevity for adepts of either sex, though it stands to reason that only the 'receiving' partner can benefit, the other being a 'giver' who must remain unrewarded except by the consciousness of having conferred an inestimable benefit; for, since success depends on absolute continence achieved by stopping short of orgasm over a period of several months or years, the 'giver' cannot expect to benefit at all. There is an unpleasant story about the goddess known as the Western Royal Mother to the effect that she was a mortal who achieved immortality by exhausting the energies of a thousand young men driven to perish by their ardour to sacrifice their strength on her behalf; but I rather think that the story is a sly joke aimed at people who make dual cultivation an excuse for licentious conduct.

Compounding the External Elixir
From remote antiquity, the search for drugs conducive to perpetuating youthful charm and vigour has been popular with certain kinds of Taoists. The ingredients of the elixirs compounded in the days when flesh-and-blood immortality still seemed a credible goal included poisons; yet, despite such mistakes, Taoists contributed a great deal to the development of traditional Chinese medicine, a system with remarkable achievements to its credit, as can be gathered from the fact that the Chinese communist government has retained it, for communists are too pragmatic to have made that decision unless satisfied by results. This system still contains traces of the Taoist 'five activities' doctrine, illness being diagnosed largely in terms of preponderance or deficiency of one or more of those 'activities' (or 'elements'), and drugs are classified as being, among many other things, rich in *yin* or *yang* elements. The idea is that, if the balance of *yin* and *yang* or the smooth interaction of the five activities is disturbed, illness results. Whatever one may think of this method of diagnosis, the fact remains that a high percentage of cures is obtained and that, for some disorders (including high blood pressure, severe haemorrhoids and certain stomach diseases), it is demonstrably more effective than Western medicine. Then again, though

the pursuit of immense longevity or flesh-and-blood immortality may seem absurd, until we remember our own ignorance during those long gone-by centuries when belief in them flourished, there is no doubt that Taoist alchemists made scientific advances remarkable for their day and age, as Dr Joseph Needham has abundantly revealed in recent years.

Though what is generally held to be the highest form of Taoist alchemy is an internal yoga requiring no external aids at all, faith in the helpfulness of certain mineral and vegetable substances was at one time widespread, and there were alchemists who spent their lives trying to compound an elixir able to rejuvinate the old, prolong youth and promote immense longevity. The earliest hermits conceived the notion that, if certain drugs keep illness at bay, then it should be possible to discover even more powerful compounds that would stave off death for centuries! Was it not written that the Yellow Emperor, having partaken of a nine times refined elixir, had attained immortal state? Ancient Taoist recipes make much mention of a 'red pearl' or 'pill pearl', the ideogram *tan* meaning either 'red' or 'pill', which was probably a derivative of cinnabar. The *Pen Ts'ao*, oldest of Chinese medical works, declares: 'People have long been taking cinnabar to brighten their faculties, maintain their youth and make their bodies light.' Ko Hung, learned scholar that he was, spoke highly of this substance, saying: 'The longer you refine cinnabar, the more wonderful its transformations; as for gold, it can be refined five hundred times and not change its composition. These two can assist in attaining immortal state.' The lists of ingredients proposed for the magical elixir generally include cinnabar, gold, silver, varieties of a kind of plant called *chih* (which is also the name for sesame), jade and pearls.

The elixir to be effective had to undergo nine transmutations, hence the frequent use of the phrase 'nine times refined'. The trouble was to know exactly what ingredients were required, for the lists varied from master to master, sect to sect, and the names of the drugs were often deliberately changed or given in code so that only initiates would understand. According to Ko Hung: 'This Tao (Way) is of immense importance, but is transmitted only to men of holiness and wisdom; unless one is a fit person, he may pile up a great mountain of jades and still not be rich enough to buy the secret.' Herbal medicines alone would not suffice: 'With guidance on the use of herbs, you may achieve longevity, but still you will have to die; only imbibe the holy elixir and your present body will become immortal, lasting as long as heaven and earth; you will climb among the clouds, ride upon a dragon up and down through the azure canopy.' The Yellow Emperor is said to have declared: 'He that desires to compound the sacred pill must seek the solitude of deep mountains or extensive marshes, places where people do not venture. Should you be constrained to compound it in an inhabited place, see to it that your walls are high and sturdy. Let neither those who dwell within your house nor those who dwell without see what you are doing; only then will your efforts prevail.'

There are other important conditions to be observed:

Helpers must not number more than two or three. You must fast for seven days and bathe in scented water around noon when the sunlight is beneficent. The fifth day of the fifth moon is the most favourable, the seventh day of the seventh moon comes next. First compound the substance called 'mysterious yellow'; for this, place ten catties (about twenty pounds) of mercury and twenty catties (forty pounds) of lead in an iron cauldron set upon a fiercely burning fire, so that a purple or yellowish gold vapour is emitted; collect this with an iron spoon, place it in a bamboo container and steam it a hundred times with sulphide of arsenic and liquid cinnabar. Steam them together.'

Further instructions as to ingredients and processes follow; then: 'Mix these in an iron receptacle, heat them for nine days and nights on end', etc. 'The most sacred kind of pill is called "red flower" – that is the real thing. . . . Altogether there are nine kinds of pill, none without cinnabar and the five precious minerals.' These instructions are partly of a practical nature, partly magical. One must suppose that the alchemists were often filled with holy awe, feeling themselves to be on the brink of witnessing one of the secret workings of nature hitherto known only to the gods. One detects in such writings a fondness for flames and vapours of many colours, these being phenomena likely to be seen in the secret places where nature is at work mysteriously creating form from void! Always there was this sense of holiness and mystery. Those were days when there was still poetry in science!

Proponents of these material means to immortality were apt to be laughed at by their wiser contemporaries. As one writer said: 'Using pills instead of one's own body requires five metals, eight minerals, cinnabar and mercury for their compounding! The true way is *formless union with the void*. The so-called "nine-times refined pill" means in reality union with the void. The basis of the pill is the nature of real void, mother of all great medicines!' (Clearly this means that health and longevity come to those who sit still communing with the limitless Tao, not from eating pills.) It was also said: 'Students of the Way longing for immortality, you may eat the "nine times refined pill" if you wish – and suffer the consequences!' (Many alchemists and their clients actually died of lead or arsenic poisoning!)

Ko Hung was forever pointing out that the attainment of immortality is impossible without a good teacher. He wrote that those who really had become immortals lived so far from the habitations of men that it was hard to obtain the true teaching, which was the reason why genuine recipes for 'compounding the elixir' had long ago been lost.

The various names for herbs and minerals to be found in all textbooks of the external alchemy are not very helpful because of wide differences of interpretation. In some lists the *chih* plants already mentioned are given as fungi. According to one school of thought, the five most valuable minerals are 'red sand' (cinnabar), 'cock-yellow' (sulphide of arsenic), 'mother of the clouds' (mica), 'mineral flower' (quartz) and 'love milk' (various kinds of stalactite). In the most ancient writings there is much mention of powders compounded of the five minerals, but there has never been agreement as to what those minerals were. A certain Ho Yen says: 'Powders compounded of the five minerals, besides regulating the body, brighten the mental faculties.' It was believed that, after ingesting them, one must keep walking about, hence the name 'walking powders'. The exertion would arouse warmth, but a feeling of chill would follow, whereupon it was the custom to disrobe and sprinkle oneself with cold water, eat cold foods and drink mulled wine, hence another name for the invigorating substance – 'cold food powders'. After ingesting them, one had to be cautious about bathing, wear light loose garments and patterns instead of shoes and socks, 'lest skin and flesh change to leather'!

That such drugs were dangerous was well known, but this did little to deter people who had set their hearts upon longevity. Several emperors were among the victims. A 'miraculous drug' caused one emperor to sink into such a melancholic mood that he was barely restrained from suicide, and several other Sons of Heaven actually died from overdoses of the poisonous ingredients. Aside from fatalities, two other drawbacks to ingestion were recognised. The medicines were held to be too drastic for people with delicate constitutions and they were so enormously costly that only very rich men could afford them in sufficient quantity. In the T'ang dynasty when Taoism was in high favour at court, there were a number of imperial fatalities. Hsüan Tsang, the Bright Emperor who had sent a Taoist in pursuit of the shade of the Lady Yang, was among the victims. On one of his successors, Wu Tsung (841–47), the elixir had the effect of arousing his passions to such an extent that he died in a violent fit of rage. Tu Fu, the great T'ang poet, wrote an amusing poem dealing with the deaths of a number of people who had taken magic drugs *to prolong their lives*, which ends with the words: 'And I alone, who do not seek long life, am like to reach the ripeness of old age!'

That belief in the efficacy of such drugs lingered until the present century may be gathered from an item in China's leading newspaper, the *Ta Kung Pao*. In 1939 the following news item appeared:

A gentleman of Wan Hsien, Szechuan province, born in the last year of Ch'ien Lung's reign [1796], worked during the final years of the following reign as secretary to the military authorities in charge of the Yangtse River Region. After retirement, he went off to Tibet in search of medicinal plants, disappearing for so long that he was given up for lost. However, in the autumn of 1931, at the age of 135, he returned to his native district where many aged residents recognised him as someone they had known when still very young. Despite his grizzled hair, he looked no more than 50 and had scarcely changed at all.

This curious item brought journalists flocking to the scene and the same newspaper came out with a photograph of the Wan Hsien magistrate in company with the sturdy looking ancient. A few months later, he left on a second journey to Tibet and was not seen again. This story may seem hard to believe, yet I myself have encountered at least two Taoist adepts whose colleagues put their ages at around 150 years. There seemed no reason to dispute their claim, the more so as I remembered meeting a Turkish gentleman who had visited Cambridge at the age of almost 140, but I do not recall now whether those aged Taoists attributed their longevity to the use of medicinal drugs.

Historical records can be quoted in favour of and against ingestion. For example, whereas Wang Hsing, an illiterate fellow from Yang-chou, dosed himself regularly with a particular nostrum and lived so long as to be known to several generations of his fellow townsmen in turn, his contemporary, the Emperor Wu of the Han dynasty, was reduced to a permanent state of melancholia within two years of beginning to take that very same drug regularly and died prematurely of its effects. I found that the general feeling among the Taoists I questioned was that ingestion is not safe as reliable prescriptions have not survived. Moreover, Chinese physicians have always laid more emphasis than their confrères in the West on the fact that, since no two people are alike, there is no prescription exactly suited to two victims of the same disease; the same principle applies to ingestion; what may benefit one may harm another and have no effect upon a third. The same is true of systems of yoga and meditation – and, indeed, of such modern remedies as penicillin.

Both the methods set forth in this chapter lie beyond the scope of my personal knowledge. Lacking both instruction and first-hand experience in the matter of dual cultivation, I cannot pronounce upon its usefulness to the modern yogin, but agree that it should not be attempted without a competent teacher and that, in general, strict sexual continence is best suited to those engaged in high spiritual endeavour. As to ingestion, most of the tales told of it relate to the remote past and are inclined to be magical in content rather than spiritually illuminating, but they are not without charm and some of them are thought-provoking, as is sometimes the case with our own legends and stories. The following example is fairly typical.

The Pine Kernel Youth

The Pine Kernel Youth was known to inhabit a grove of pines that crowned a rock too steep for anyone to be able to climb up and pay him reverence; but often and often he was seen standing negligently on the very brink of that perpendicular slope smiling down at the pilgrims toiling past its foot. Some held him to be a faery, the genie of a hidden cave or spring; others declared they knew him to be servant to an Immortal who sat rapt in meditation, never appearing in public lest visitors intrude upon his solitude. But as the years passed by and former pilgrims to the temple lying further into the mountains came again bringing marriageable sons and daughters who had grown up in the meanwhile, it began to be whispered that the Pine Kernel Youth was himself an immortal of great age, for his appearance had never changed. Seen from a distance, he still looked about 14; he had glossy black hair only partly concealed by a carelessly tied headcloth, a smooth white skin, cheeks touched with the colour of ripe persimmons and a lithe figure clad in coarse blue cotton. Whenever he appeared, people shouted friendly greetings, whereat he would smile delightedly and nod his head, but he was never heard to speak.

The district magistrate, becoming curious about this youth, more than once sent runners to question him, but none could find a means of access to the pine-crowned spur; so, on the nineteenth day of the ninth moon, he had himself arrayed in formal attire and carried in a chair to the temple, as though to pay a birthday visit to the Goddess. Ordering the chairmen to stop below the spur as though to rest, he stepped down from his palanquin and stood gazing respectfully towards the top of the cliff. There being no response, he lighted nine sticks of incense, placed them in a rock crevice, made three respectful bows and went forward towards the temple to complete his pilgrimage. The courtyard was thronged with worshippers, who hastily made way for their magistrate to perform his devotions in comfort. When he had done, the abbot hurried forward and begged His Honour to accept 'a poor collation of cold spring-water and coarse vegetables' in the privacy of a small pavilion reserved for distinguished guests. The 'poor collation' turned out to be a veritable feast of mountain delicacies, as the worthy magistrate had happily anticipated when accepting the invitation.

Taking a few cups of heated wine 'against the autumn chill', he inquired whether there was any means of coming face to face with the Pine Kernel Youth.

'It is strange that Your Honour should ask,' replied the abbot, 'for he has sent to say that he is expecting you to honour his humble abode and receive his thanks for burning incense to him while attired in full official regalia. He was deeply touched by Your Honour's condescension. Besides, it would hardly be fair not to give him a chance to reciprocate such a notable courtesy. On your way back, dismount at the turn where the rivulet is carried through a pipe under the pilgrim path. Send your bearers forward round the bend and, choosing a moment when you are unobserved, enter the passage between the dripping rocks and follow the track that winds round and upwards from there. As it starts by taking you in the opposite direction, no one has ever thought of seeking the Pine Kernel Youth by that route, especially as the gap between the rocks is, ahem, not always there!'

Taking his leave a full hour before the general descent of pilgrims began, the magistrate followed these directions and was amazed to discover that the hidden track led through a magnificent cave beyond which lay a most extraordinary landscape. In the foreground were the expected gold and crimson tints of autumn; to the south lay a hilly region where, for an inexplicable reason, the brilliant greens of summer lingered; to the east, the willow trees were actually clad in the green haze that betokens spring leaves just on the point of burgeoning; and, strangest of all, to the north lay a range of hills covered with winter snow! As he stood lost in wonder and half afraid he had drunk too many cups of heated wine, the Pine Kernel Youth suddenly appeared. To do honour to the occasion, he was now attired in a ritual hat and robe of elaborately patterned brocade, with a green dragon spewing forth a stream of silvery white on one side and a white tiger emitting a stream of molten cinnabar on the other; these shimmering streams poured into a golden tripod depicted on the skirts of the robe, from whence arose a cloud of rainbow-tinted mist. Even an emperor might have been proud of a garment so exquisite and rare.

As the magistrate made to prostrate himself, the youth threw out his arms to restrain him and together they entered a lacquered pavilion with octagonal windows latticed with strips of painted wood inset with squares of translucent mother-of-pearl.

'Well,' remarked the youth in enchanting accents, 'I hardly expected the pleasure of entertaining Your Honour in my humble abode, but then who could have imagined that a Confucian scholar clad in his official regalia would condescend to offer incense to a humble mountain man? Had it not been for the pilgrims, I should have leapt down to return your gracious bows. Since you have taken the trouble to visit my insignificant dwelling, the least I can do is to ask what is your pleasure and see if my poor arts will enable me to fulfil whatever wish lies nearest your heart. We mountain men have no great talent in performing unusual feats, but if you would care for some trifle as a memento of our meeting, such as a sweet little concubine, an early promotion, a tablet of flawless jade for your official cap, or an inexhaustible gourd of the best Persian wine, I am sure I could manage that much.'

'Your Immortality is exceedingly generous,' replied the magistrate, blushing at the unerring accuracy with which the youth, judging from the order in which he had mentioned these prospective gifts, had read his mind. 'But if you will excuse my presumption, there is a gift I should cherish even more than any of the delectable choices you have offered, namely – '

'No, no!' cried the youth in accents of distress. 'The secret of perpetual youth is not within my power to bestow. That is to say, it cannot be decorously imparted to Your Honour, unless you are prepared to resign your office and enrol among the pupils of – er – my Master.'

To this the magistrate could not with propriety agree as, coming from a family steeped for generations in the perfume of books, he was in duty bound to remain in the imperial service. The spirits of his ancestors would never brook his becoming a wandering Taoist. Yet such was his eloquence that he prevailed upon the kind-hearted youth to impart the secret he desired, though with such reluctance that it was pitiful to witness his discomfort. The formula proved to be so simple that the winning of immortality unexpectedly appeared to be almost a trifling affair. All that was needed was to imbibe on certain days of the lunar calender a decoction of herbs into which had been stirred a spoonful of powdered cinnabar and a powder to be made from pulverised lumps of the stalactite and stalagmite that abounded in the cave through which he must return. Seven times seven doses taken over a period of seven months would rejuvenate the elderly, ensure perpetual youth and guarantee immense longevity, provided that the adept's heart were set single-mindedly upon the Way.

'That I can promise,' cried His Honour, excited to the point of rashness. Before returning to where the chairmen, now deeply concerned over his long absence, were on the point of asking some pilgrims to hurry to the city and report His Honour's disappearance, so that someone would come to instruct them what next to do, the magistrate broke off two lumps of the precious material he came upon in the cave and concealed them in his sleeve. The processes of pulverisation and infusion were entrusted to his Third Lady, a pretty child recently acquired from poverty-stricken parents of reasonably good family who had been eager to secure for her a comfortable future. Supposing that he was suffering from constipation or some other complaint too embarrassing to relate, she did not press him to reveal the reason for his meticulous instructions, but set about following them to the letter.

For several months, all went well, with His Honour feeling younger and stronger with every passing day. Who knows what thoughts passed through his mind of the brilliant career lying before a capable official to whom centuries would be less than years to other men ? Or did he perhaps dally with the thought of adding considerably to his modest household of three ladies ? All that can be known for certain is that something presently diverted his heart from the Way; for the first dose taken in the fifth of the seven months produced sweating followed by nausea. The next dose caused his sudden collapse and, within a day, his twin souls had parted from his body!

The Third Lady being suspected by the senior wives of having poisoned her husband, a thorough investigation was ordered, from which it emerged that the departed had started taking doses of a curious medicine since very soon after a brief but mysterious disappearance while on his way back from the temple on the birthday of the Goddess. Though the chairmen attested that one of them, fearing to let His Honour stay alone by the wayside, had turned back to keep watch over him and seen him vanish into a cleft between two dripping rocks, a search revealed that there was no way of passing through the cleft nor any other means of leaving the path in the vicinity of the mountain stream. For lack of evidence, the case against the Third Lady was dropped, though not without such damage to her reputation as to cause her to take to a Buddhist nunnery and seek to expiate by her austerities whatever unknown crimes had brought her dear husband to an untimely end.

The story breaks off with the terse comment: 'Easy to say; hard to do.'

Chapter 8

黄白 The Yellow and the White
(The Secret Yogic Alchemy)

To the uninitiated, 'the yellow and the white' is no more than a poetic synonym for alchemy. Even to initiates it may signify either the transmutation of metals into gold, or else internal alchemy of the kind described in Lu K'uan-yü's enlightening work, *Taoist Yoga*. Here, however, it is used in a special sense to denote a form of yogic alchemy which only superficially resembles the one described by Lu; for in his work the analogy between alchemy and yoga is taken rather literally and there is much talk of the furnaces and cauldrons to be found within the yogin's body, whereas here the analogy does not go beyond retaining the words 'refinement' and 'transmutation', the rest of the vocabulary of alchemy being discarded as irrelevant. What now follows is, I believe, the first attempt to give an account in English of a practice which many Taoist yogins regard as the very core of their cultivation of the Way.

Born of the Tao and permeating the cosmos are three marvellous energies – *ching, ch'i* and *shên*. These are the life-giving powers wherewith the Tao sustains the universe, causing within the limitless void the coming into being, the rise and fall of the myriad entities that constitute the realm of appearances. In their subtle 'cosmic' or 'original' form, these energies are pure and holy, the very source of light and life, creative powers that bring about stupendous transformations. Only a sage of the highest attainment can gauge their unsullied perfection.

Man, like all else, is imbued with a stock of these three treasures; but, owing to the effects of passion and inordinate desire, his endowments are of a coarser nature and need refinement to restore them to their original purity. Hence the importance of this secret yogic alchemy. Though the goal is identical with what Buddhists call the attainment of Enlightenment, this method of attainment is uniquely Taoist. For Western students of the Way to employ it to the full, an accomplished teacher would be essential; yet this written account, hugely incomplete as such accounts are bound to be, may be judged to contain valuable guidance with which to supplement their current practice. Since it is based on the work of Chou Shao-hsien, who supports his presentation of the yoga with a wealth of quotations from the *Tao Tsang*, its authenticity is – as far as it goes – unquestionable. Its defects relate to the glossing over of certain matters which have traditionally been transmitted from teacher to disciple in secret.

An attempt to describe the extraordinary metamorphosis resulting from successful practice will be found in the next chapter; here the main concern is the separate stages of the yoga. First we must be clear about the meanings of those somewhat ambiguous and variously used terms *ching, ch'i* and *shên*.

The Three Treasures

	Coarse Form	Subtle Form	Cosmic or Yang Form
Ching (Essence)	Not precisely identical but closely associated with, and conveyed by, the male and female sexual fluids.	That within the body which gives matter tangible form and substance.	That within the cosmos which gives tangible form to what was originally undifferentiated void.
Ch'i (Vitality)	Not precisely identical but closely associated with, and conveyed in, the air breathed in through lungs, kidneys and pores.	Vitality indistinguishable (except by temporary location) from its cosmic counterpart.	Cosmic vitality seen as *Tê*, the virtue of the Tao with which each object is imbued.
Shên	Spirit not yet	Unsullied spirit	Cosmic spirit,

The Three Treasures

	Coarse Form	Subtle Form	Cosmic or Yang Form
(Spirit)	cleansed of the impurities of the senses and of erroneous thought.	released from the contamination of passion and sensuous longing.	void, pure, undifferentiated being.

(Each of these three terms is employed in yogic texts sometimes in all its senses simultaneously, sometimes in but one of them, and sometimes even in some other sense; e.g. *ching* may mean actual semen, *ch'i* may mean actual air or breath, and *shên* may in some texts mean mind. Therefore, where necessary, I have selected or placed in brackets the English term most fitted to the context; but it should be remarked that the distinctions are not always as precise as this usage would imply.)

The Theoretical Basis of the 'Alchemy'

The version of the internal alchemy given here rarely makes reference to the equation of parts of the body with furnaces, cauldrons and so forth that is such a feature of many other versions, for here the approach is more nearly what we should call spiritual rather than material, were it permissible in a Taoist context to make such a distinction. It would be wrong, however, to suppose this version superior to the others, for the question of superiority does not arise, since different yogic methods suit different individuals. What can be said is that the present version is easier for Western students of the Way to follow, especially if they lack previous experience with yogic alchemy. That a close analogy between parts of the body and the apparatus of external alchemy is needless is revealed by the following passage from an ancient work:

'Let *T'ai Hsü* [the Great Void] be your cauldron; let *T'ai Chi* [nature's own Dynamic Principle] be your furnace. For your basic ingredient, take stillness. For your reagent take *wu wei*, no activity [that is not spontaneous and free of involvement]. For mercury, take your natural endowments [of *ching*, *ch'i* and *shên*]. For lead, take your life-force. For water, take restraint. For fire, take meditation.' It is written that the real elixir thus compounded will, even if of inferior quality, bestow longevity and the retention of youthful vigour; that, if of superior quality, it will enable the adept to 'transcend the world of mortals and attain to holy state.'

Another authority, the Green City Hermit, states:

What is known as partaking of the golden pill does not signify bedroom arts [dual cultivation], but drawing upon cosmic essence, vitality and spirit to add to one's own store. It is by cosmic transformation that bodily transformation is wrought; it is cosmic life that prolongs one's own. Cosmic vitality acts unceasingly; so will it be with our own. Cosmic transformation continues without end; so will it be with ours. Cosmic life is free from defilement; so will it be with ours. Heaven and earth are unceasingly renewed; so will it be with us. Cosmic life endures to eternity; so will it be with ours.

This passage provides a key to the true nature of the internal alchemy, which is to become immortal not solely by our own efforts, but by achieving harmony – unity, even – with the eternal Way.

Nevertheless, what mystics of other faiths deem to be a wholly spiritual process requires, according to the Taoist masters, realisation of the full potentiality of *all* our endowments, physical as well as mental and spiritual. In the *Book of the Golden Elixir* it is written:

With the transmutation of *ching* [essence] into *ch'i* [vitality], the first barrier is passed and perfect stillness of body supervenes. With the transmutation of *ch'i* into *shên* [spirit], the middle barrier is passed and perfect stillness of heart supervenes. With the transmutation of *shên* into void, the final barrier is passed and mind and Mind are unified. Thus is the elixir perfected and immortality attained. This is the true significance of [all that has ever been written or spoken about] the sacred practice of cultivating and nourishing [*ching, ch'i* and *shên*]; it has nothing to do with compounding an actual pill.

Of the many warnings against over-literal interpretation of the yogic manuals, the following is a typical example:

Long ago there lived two sworn brothers, who each contributed a catty [about two pounds] of mercury and fired it in a hall near

Yang Chou for three years on end. One day this mercury fell into the fire and emitted rainbow-coloured light. Convinced that they had stumbled upon the true elixir of immortality at last, each of the blood brothers then and there consumed two ounces of the precious substance, whereupon their legs gave way beneath them and they died within a hundred days. How is that for an elixir reputed to confer immeasurable *longevity*?

Not all learned Taoist masters utterly rejected the use of fortifying medicines in connection with the cultivation of true immortality, for they held such drugs to be useful in achieving two of the by-products of the yoga, namely longevity and prolonged youthful vigour. Such a combination of what we should call spiritual and material means is in line with the cardinal Taoist principle that identical natural laws operate at all levels of existence. Often, however, the term 'culling ingredients for the elixir' has an esoteric meaning as can be seen from another of the texts which supply a key to the real meanings of various alchemical terms. The writer begins by recommending stillness as the most essential ingredient of the alchemy, adding that stillness should not be taken to mean suppression of the feelings so that one comes to resemble such mindless objects as earth, rocks, grass and trees; that *wu nien* (literally 'no thought') means 'real thought' or thought that is like light turned back upon itself causing *shên* to rouse *ch'i* and transform it into a spirit-substance that congeals; that 'lead' and 'mercury' really refer to *shên* and *ch'i* and that it is only in inferior forms of the yoga that one actually uses material ingredients. He goes on to say that where texts speak of 'culling herbs for the elixir' the meaning really is 'bringing mind and body under control'; since only when the mind is still will *shên* and *ch'i* be complete and 'ready for compounding the elixir in the cauldron of the body'.

The Yogic Regimen – a Preliminary and an Accompaniment to the Eight-Stage Yoga
No matter what his background, an adept cannot hope to practise the yoga successfully unless he is prepared to impose on himself a reasonably strict regime. After all, simple athletes are prepared to undergo the rigours of training for a much more ephemeral goal. Without adequate control of mind and body, no amount of ardour will produce the desired results.

Nourishing the Body. Making the body a fit vehicle for the yoga requires attention to such matters as diet, clothing, sleep, bathing and exercise. In the words of Ko Hung, 'there must be moderation in everything'. Food should be sufficient to satisfy hunger, but not abundant and there should be no fussiness about its flavour. Wine may be taken, but not in such quantity as to cause undue excitement or lead to the misapprehension that 'people cannot wait to hear one sing'! Clothing should be suitable for the weather, neither too thick in summer nor too scanty in winter. As to sleep, too little of it is as harmful to yogic progress as too much. One should not go to bed or get up at irregular times, nor sleep in the open if there is likely to be heavy dew. As to bathing, different schools of yoga have different rules, the main point being to strike a balance between bathing too infrequently and allowing it to become unnecessarily luxurious. Excercise, though good, should not be overdone and strain must at all costs be avoided. Ko Hung spoke of the folly of trying to become abnormally strong, declaring that over-exertion is as harmful as sleeping too much, or straining eyes or ears. He laid down that one should not foolishly brave bad weather by exposing himself to storms or to extremes of heat or cold. To be simple is one thing, to be spartan another. (Chuang-tzû's description of immortals as 'not partaking of the five grains, but supping wind and sipping dew' led to the avoidance of all grains by certain yogins in the past. According to one old text, here quoted merely as a curiosity: 'Vegetables, though healthful, cause dullness; meat, though strengthening, causes people to be overbearing; grain, though conducive to wisdom [food for the brain?] hinders longevity; whereas he who lives on *ch'i* emits light from his body and never dies.' This last may be true, but how far must the adept progress before he can do without food other than *ch'i*?)

According to another authority, nourishing the body involves making five sacrifices:

Attachment to wealth and fame brings worry – give it up! Excess of joy or fits of anger disturb serenity – give them up! Strong attachment to the pleasures of the senses produces disequilibrium – give it up! Worrying about success in cultivating the Way brings failure – give it up! Wasting one's precious stock of *ching* [semen] debilitates mind and body – give it up! These five forms of abstinence will help you to live longer – be sure of that, but not so foolish as to imagine they guarantee longevity!

Yogic Breathing. With most forms of yoga, Chinese, Indian or Tibetan, great emphasis is placed on special types of breathing. Its importance is due not merely to the physical advantages to be gained from the regular practice of deep breathing, especially in the early hours of the day when the air is thought to be at its purest, but also to recognition that *ch'i* (the exact equivalent of the Sanskrit *prana*) is conveyed into the body of the yogin by the air he breathes. Details of the types of breathing taught in connection with Taoist yoga will be found under the heading 'Nourishing the *Ch'i*', prefacing the fourth stage of the Yoga of Eight Stages (p. 145). Before that yoga is embarked upon, the adept should have made himself proficient in the simpler types of breathing, but even these can be dangerous if performed without supervision from a competent teacher. For example, preliminary exercises include inhaling and exhaling through the nose, each time holding the indrawn breath for a count that gradually rises to 120! The yogin learns to breathe so softly that the passage of breath through the nostrils is inaudible even to himself and so smooth that the fine hairs within the nostrils remain motionless. There are records of adepts having retained their breath for a count of one thousand – a highly dangerous proceeding for the yogically untrained.

When breathing yoga is practised regularly, diet should be light and consist mainly of good fresh vegetables, for it is written that such a diet 'strengthens the *ch'i* and inhibits passions inimicable to the gathering of cosmic *ch'i*'. The hours from midnight to noon are deemed favourable to breathing yoga, those between noon and midnight unfavourable, that being the part of the day when '*ch'i* expires'.

Yogic Exercises. Different teachers propound different forms of exercise. Among the most graceful are those comprised in the art of *t'ai chi ch'üan*, a kind of dance-like shadow-boxing well suited to people of all ages. Some of the others require considerable athletic prowess; for example, one stands on a low stool with a bucket of water on the floor at one's feet, bends down to seize the handle between the teeth and regains an upright position without either bending the knees or spilling a drop of water! I have met Taoist recluses who, though well into middle age, were capable of performing extraordinary feats such as jumping from a great height and landing on the feet as nimbly as if the height had been negligible. Kung fu was originally a Taoist art and judo, kendo and so on can all be regarded as offshoots of Taoist methods of armed and unarmed self-defence. The judo principle of utilising an opponent's weight and strength to overthrow him is typically Taoist. However, some of the exercises taught in connection with yoga are very odd and seem to have a solely ritual significance perhaps derived from the marriage between Taoism at the popular level and the folk religion; these involve numbered blinkings of the eye, grinding of teeth (upper upon lower, never from side to side) and swallowings of saliva. I should be inclined to regard them as mumbo-jumbo but for the fact that the Taoist yogins I met were seldom men of mean intelligence who could easily be persuaded to do what is manifestly useless, so I feel bound to keep an open mind. According to some teachers, all yogic practice should be preceded by grinding of the teeth followed by a single inhalation and swallowing of the saliva – why, I do not understand.

An example of what appears to me to be a mainly ritual or magical practice not quite in keeping with the rest of the yogic instructions is as follows:

> With clasped hands resting on the head, bend down so that the backs of the hands rest upon the ground and respire several times – a remedy for shortness of breath. With hands clasped in front of the breast, turn the head from side to side as many times as possible while holding the breath – to clear the head. With hands clasped and held below the waist, bend to left and right as many times as possible – to expel evil humours from the skin. Then grind the teeth in order to take command of your spirit, and swallow your breath to harmonise with the True.

Ingestion. Ingesting medicinal drugs is a practice long since discarded from the yogic regimen as having no part in true cultivation of the Way; nevertheless it once played an important role, for prolongation of youth and the attainment of longevity used to be regarded as secondary goals to be attained during the progress of the adept towards the ultimate goal. The matter is therefore of interest, if only as one of the many curiosities pertaining to the history of Taoist yoga. Among the exotic ingredients most favoured in the past were plants (or it may be fungi) of the *chih* family which may or may not be related to what are now called *chih* (plants of the sesame family), also podophylum, versipelle, pine kernels, calamus (sweet flag), *fu-ling* (china root), fungi found at the base of fir trees, jade, mercury, cinnabar, yellow sulphur, cloud-mother (mica) and something called cock-yellow. It used to be claimed for them that they would cause the body to shine with a holy light and make the four limbs feel light and comfortable. One interesting speculation remains in my mind. We know that poisonous substances used in small quantities have great medicinal value in certain cases. Is it possible that some yogins in the old days brought about physical changes within their bodies which made it possible for them to ingest with good effect substances which would in other circumstances have been harmful? If so, it would explain why so many believers, even emperors, died of the effects of Taoist elixirs; they would have seen those very elixirs taken with good effect by Taoist yogins and not realised that what had proved healthful in one very special set of circumstances might cause illness or death in most others. This speculation may seem far-fetched, but surely those emperors and noblemen would not have risked their lives by dosing themselves with medicines they had not seen tried out on the bodies of the persons who prescribed them?

The Yogic Alchemy of Eight Stages
The manner of refining and transmuting the Three Treasures in order to attain to true immortality is now set forth.

True Immortality. Subtle *ch'i* has first to be obtained or augmented by the interaction of *ching*, *ch'i* and *shên*. This must then be transmuted into *yang*-spirit (pure cosmic *shên*) wherewith physical limitations are transcended and the adept is empowered to merge with the limitless Source of Being.

> While life remains, his spirit can leave the body at will. At death, he will return to the Source, merge with it and thus live forever. If this state is not attained while life remains, though the twin souls may survive in spirit form for a period of time, they will ultimately fade into extinction. The golden leaves of autumn do not

survive separation from the parent tree for long, nor can the tree itself be expected to last for more than a few centuries.

The Basis. In nature there are two sequences. As stated in the *Tao Tê Ching*, 'The One gives birth to two [*yin* and *yang*], the two to three [*shên*, *ch'i*, *ching*], the three to all the myriad objects', in which process void is transformed to spirit, spirit to vitality, vitality to essence and essence to form. Conversely, the myriad objects return to the three, the three to the two, the two to One. When those who have grasped this method control their *shên* so as to guard well their physical body, nourish the body so as to transmute it into *ching*, accumulate *ching* in order to transmute it into *ch'i*, transmute the *ch'i* to bring forth *shên* and transmute *shên* that they may accomplish return to the Void (Tao), then is the golden elixir perfectly distilled. Therefore it is needful to possess these three energies in abundance. From the outset, both male and female adepts must conserve their sexual vitality by inhibiting emission, so that both coarse *ching* and its subtle counterpart will be replete; for then will *ch'i* be similarly robust and *shên* begin to glow. Thus will the body be strengthened and sickness held at bay, the five viscera [liver, heart, spleen, lungs and kidneys] will flourish, flesh and skin grow smooth and glossy, the face become radiant, hearing and vision grow sharp and even those who are advanced in years will become vigorous and robust.

Conservation is essential in that it ensures a rich abundance of *ching*, *ch'i* and *shên*.

Restoration is essential for making good deficiencies.

Transmutation is essential and occurs in three stages: (1) from coarse *ching*, *ch'i* and *shên* to their subtle counterparts; (2) thence to pure *yang-shên* (cosmic spirit); (3) and thence from pure *yang-shên* into void.

(Should a yogin chance to embark upon this yoga late in life at a time when his semen has been wastefully expended over a course of many years, this earlier depletion can still be repaired by the method known as restoration, provided he is prepared to husband and nurture his vital essence henceforth.)

The eight stages of the alchemy are: (1, 2 and 3) conservation, restoration and transmutation of the body's *ching*; (4 and 5) nourishment and transmutation of the *ch'i*; (6 and 7) nourishment and transmutation of the *shên*; (8) transmutation of voided *shên* to make it identical with the Void.

The Eight Stages

1 *Conservation of the Ching.* Essential to success is retention of the semen. Not only must lust be eradicated, but also desires in general must be continuously refined away. If semen is wastefully expended, failure is certain for 'when the oil is used up, the light goes out'. It is held that total exhaustion of *ching* (of which semen is the vehicle) inevitably results in death. Intercourse is not an evil in itself, but does great damage by leading to frequent seminal emission. It is set forth in the *Secret Instructions for Compounding the Golden Elixir* that:

> when people are tranquil and limit their desires, the *ching* and *ch'i* rise from the 'three receptacles' [in the region of brain, heart and kidneys] and run through the lustrous psychic channels; the sexual act, however, draws them down from thence so that they pass the 'gateway of life' (between the kidneys) and are emitted. Even though the arising of sexual desire be involuntary, the fire at the gateway of life stirs, the *ching* and *ch'i* overflow; unless they are channelled back whence they came, the loss is the same as if emission has occurred.

What is said about the *ching's* being drawn by sexual excitement down past the gateway of life in the neighbourhood of the kidneys makes it clear that coarse *ching*, though intimately related to semen, is not identical with it; even so, a clear warning is sounded to the effect that sexual intercourse, whether or not emission is withheld, is wasteful of the precious *ching*.

It is true that those initiated into the yoga of dual cultivation, for which a sexual partner is required, find in it a fruitful aid to progress. Besides having the strength of will to stop short of emission, they know how to cause the *ching*, now blended with the yogic partner's essence, to return and pass upwards, whereupon they experience great bliss. For them, 'life blazes'. However, the technique of returning the *ching* is very difficult to master and quite impossible without an experienced teacher. There is a text which states:

Only men of rare talent are suited to undertake the dangerous yoga of dual cultivation. Men of lesser talent end by exhausting their stock of *ching* and *ch'i*, thereby impairing their health and being compelled to abandon forever the sacred task of creating an immortal body. In the end, they become mere libertines, effete and doomed to final extinction – such is what they choose to call cultivation of the Way! It would be laughable if one did not feel saddened by their loss.

For the yogically uninitiated to try to make the best of both worlds by enjoying frequent sexual intercourse but withholding emission is entirely useless; the semen, once drawn towards the sexual organs, will (unless yogically precluded and turned back) pass from the body in another way and be wasted. Accordingly, most authorities on the yoga agree that chastity, or at least strictly limited indulgence, is for most adepts essential to success. (If Taoist yoga ever 'catches on' in the West to the extent of becoming an 'in thing', followers of the Way will need to be wary of so-called masters who, making a great parade of their pretended knowledge, will offer 'instruction in the dual yoga' as an excuse for libertinism. Even in China, where zeal for sexual enjoyment has generally been better controlled than in the modern West, such things have been known to happen.

In spite of what has just been said, Taoists have since ancient times disliked extremes of any kind. Recognising that perfect chastity is too much to expect of most young people, the philosopher Sun Szû-mo gives the following advice:

For people in their twenties, one emission in four days; in their thirties, one in eight days; in their forties, one in sixteen days; in their fifties, one in twenty-one days. From the age of 60 upwards emission should be avoided altogether; nevertheless, a 60-year-old who is still robust may permit himself one emission a month, though, by that age, his thoughts should have long been tranquil and total abstention should be easy.

Though chastity is held to be by far the best course for those intent upon achieving the yogic goal with a minimum of delay, progress will not be very seriously impaired if the limits laid down by Sun Szû-mo are never exceeded.

Just what all this implies for female adepts, I have no present means of learning. In certain contexts, the coarse *ching* of male and female are described as white and red respectively, but this is clearly not applicable (unless the colours are given only symbolic meaning) in the present context. However, since Taoists do not doubt that women as well as men are fully capable of attaining the Way, the absence in Chou Shao-hsien's work of special directions for women suggests that the same degree of abstinence according to age should be adhered to.

2 *Restoration or Reparation of the Ching.* To repair harmful expenditures of *ching* sustained prior to embarking upon the yoga, the adept continues to practise abstinence, eats nourishing foods in sufficient quantity but never to repletion, exercises his body healthfully but without strain, and allows nature to take its course. This is called 'collecting *ching*' and should not be confused with 'gathering' – a term used by exponents of dual cultivation with reference to the plundering of their partner's essence for blending with their own. For collection, what is needed is to avoid sexual intercourse and to curb every kind of desire, so as to ensure continuous tranquillity. Alcohol and strongly seasoned foods are to be avoided; for coarse *ching* (here meaning semen), being secreted from the blood, needs to be nourished by eschewing overstimulation of the senses and mind. Anger and similarly strong passions cause the fire *hsing* to preponderate in the liver and other viscera; and alcohol heats the blood; all these are harmful and should be eschewed. When care is taken in these matters, the blood is nourished and *ching* accumulates. Onions, leeks, garlic, chilli, pepper and other strong seasonings are best avoided or taken in very small quantities. Yogic breathing is of value, even at this stage, although it belongs in the main to a later stage; its importance lies in the close interrelationship between *ching* and *ch'i*, of which breath is the vehicle or conveyor. As to exercise, since it should be sufficiently strenuous and yet not lead to strain, there is nothing to equal the slow and graceful movements of *t'ai chi ch'üan*, on which a number of English works are now available. (Works by Chinese experts are likely to be preferable to others as, besides knowledge of the actual movements, a Chinese attitude of mind has to be inculcated.)

3 *Transmutation of the Ching.* Conservation and reparation of one's stock of *ching*, though healthful and indeed essential to the yoga, are

not ends in themselves, but preliminaries to the even more important task of transmutation. Transmuted *ching* is an important source of *ch'i*. By way of preparation, the adept cultivates serenity of mind, letting the existing stock of *ch'i* be still and causing the *shên* (mind, spirit) to grow limpid. A passage in the *Classic of Tranquillity* runs: 'Abstain from desire, then the mind of itself grows tranquil. When the mind is limpid, the *shên* is purified.' Vanquishing desire, the adept stills his thoughts, for only thus can the consciousness be fixed; so, too, with the *ch'i* and *shên*. Emptying the mind of thought causes *ch'i* to gather and *ching* is thus produced. With due preparation, it can easily be transmuted.

Whereas coarse *ching*, being intimately related to blood and to semen, is produced within the body, the subtle *ching* into which it has to be transmuted has a prior-to-heaven nature, for it is similar to the cosmic *ching* which existed prior to the birth of the universe; thus it has a special quality of holiness. Formless it dwells within subtle and cosmic *ch'i*, from which it never separates unless moved thereto by some external influence. The *ching* required to assist in the transmutation of the adept's *shên* into pure spirit is of the subtle kind, yet intimately bound up with coarse *ching*, hence the need to conserve its vehicle, the semen. When longings and sensations are stilled so that the mind, free from discursive thought, comes to resemble a placid lake, then *yang-ch'i* consolidates therein, nourishing subtle *ching*, the product of transmutation brought about by perfect stillness, perfect voidness; simultaneously must consolidation of the *shên* be brought about by contemplation of the light that shines within the place known as the 'precious square inch' lying at a point equidistant from and a little behind the eyes. No concepts! No thought at all! Stillness, perfect stillness! During this contemplation of the inner radiance, stillness assures the mind's quiescence; and, conversely, the radiance ensures that the stillness will endure long. When the mind is void, *shên* consolidates, whereupon cosmic *yang* energy (a property of the Tao itself, coming from without to aid the internal process) enters. So it is clear that stillness and remaining in a state of perfect spontaneity form the essential basis of this yoga.

So vital to success is stillness that, in the absence of all other components of the yoga, it would still be of value; whereas, in the absence of stillness, all the rest would be of no avail.

With naught to hold my thought without,
No dwelling-place for thought within,
The myriad causes come to rest
And all my being dissolves in void!

The third and fourth lines of this verse signify that by stillness the whole chain of causation binding the adept to finite existence is snapped and the components of his being are voided, leaving him in a state of pure spontaneity at one with the infinite shining voidness of the Tao.

According to Yuan Liao-fan, transmutation of the *ching* can be assisted by an esoteric practice that involves rising at midnight, sitting down on the bed, placing one hand round the scrotum and the other over the navel. 'Then *shên* will congeal in the inner channel of the scrotum and, with long practice, the *ch'i* can be made refulgent.' (The inner and outer psychic channels in the scrotum are known respectively as the 'sombre gate' and 'female gate'.) He adds that, provided no seminal emission has recently occurred, 'the *yang-ch'i* settling upon the outer part is at its peak between 11 p.m. and 1 a.m., when the *ch'i* of the human body and that of heaven [cosmic *ch'i*] are in accord. In case of recent emission, the peak period is retarded and fluctuates between 1 and 5 a.m. There may even be cases when it does not come at all, heaven and earth being out of accord.' Some yogic masters hold that the time of day or night makes no difference, that the cosmic *yang* energy can be drawn upon at any time by sitting quietly, emptying the mind and discarding all thoughts involving a dualistic distinction between the thinker and the object of his thought – thinker, thinking and object of thought being one in the seemless Tao.

Yuan's advice about handling the scrotum and navel in that manner must at first sight seem extraordinary. To understand it fully, one would need to receive the secret oral instruction that is so often required to round out the meaning of yogic texts. Subtle *ch'i*, especially in its cosmic and therefore purest form, can certainly pass through matter without the least difficulty, so it is hard to understand how it could be trapped in the body by closing the entrances to one or more psychic channels, since the human hand is no more of an obstacle to it than any other part of the body. However, the sequence of processes comprising the internal yogic alchemy is, as with Buddhist and Hindu yogas, guided from first to last by the adept's mind. From a study of Tibetan yoga, one knows the importance and effectiveness of visualisation accompanied by the use of ritual gestures. In certain breathing yogas, for example, the breath (or, rather, the *ch'i*) is guided to parts of the body at a distance from the respiratory system wholly by the power of visualisation. One may suppose this case to be similar. The cosmic *ch'i* is trapped because the mind wills that to be so, the part played by the hands being no more than ritual gestures used to support this activity of mind.

This section on transmutation of the *ching* is rather long; it may be summarised thus: Let the *ch'i* be stilled so that the *shên* becomes limpid; trap the *yang-shên* from without at a time when its flow has reached its peak; mentally discard the dualism of 'I' and 'other'; restrain the flow of coarse *ching* lest the subtle *ching* be diminished; achieve stillness of mind and contemplate the radiance within; then will the coarse *ching* be transmuted into subtle *ching* within the yogin's body and become identical with the cosmic *ching* without. Though these steps do not constitute the whole of what is involved, since a certain part of the process is taught only to initiates, enough is disclosed here to be of great assistance in achieving results both with the yoga of eight stages and most others.

4 *Nourishing the Ch'i.* Subtle *ch'i*, like subtle *ching* is of prior-to-heaven origin and thus a cosmic energy into which the coarse *ch'i* of the yogin must be transmuted. It has been described as 'wind that stirred within chaos preceding the universe's birth'. It, too, is immeasurably holy. Nourishing *ch'i* means accumulating a full store of subtle *ch'i*. As before, stillness is the basis; but for this the practice of stilling the mind must be alternated with the practice of yogic breathing. The latter may be highly complex or very simple. During the months or years spent in cultivation, the yogin guards against giving way to extremes of elation or depression, preferring unalterable equanimity. All powerful stirrings of the mind are harmful to the accumulation of *ch'i*. All emotions, whether violent, joyous or woeful must be kept within bounds. The mind must retain unwavering calm, the breathing must at all times be even, for even the coarse *ch'i* (very nearly identifiable with breath) must be preserved from being tainted by the *ch'i* of temper, the *ch'i* of vengefulness, the *ch'i* of cold rage and so on. (This last sentence may look rather odd in

English, but not in Chinese, for the names of such emotions even in
the common speech all contain the syllable *ch'i*, e.g. *p'i-ch'i* meaning
'anger'.) Both the coarse and subtle *ch'i* have to be carefully nourished, the former being the chief medium whereby the latter is conveyed within the body. Air of course is everywhere and breath enters
each living body; though they are not the same as subtle *ch'i*, that
holy substance could not stir without them. In the words of Ko
Hung, 'Man is within *ch'i*; *ch'i* is within man. From the great cosmos
down to each separate object, nothing can exist without it'.

The regimen to be followed when nourishing *ch'i* is set forth in a
work entitled *Record of the West Mountain Assembly*. It runs:

> Men of limited talent *force* their minds and thereby only do them-
> selves harm. When restraint in the use of one's powers is replaced
> by an emphasis on forced action, no good results. Sorrow and
> melancholy are harmful. Ready anger is harmful. Excessive affec-
> tion for loved ones is harmful. Spending time on idle gossip and
> pleasantries is harmful. Forever engaging in field sports[1] is harmful.
> Drinking copiously and eating oneself into a state of lethargy are
> harmful. Rushing about until one gasps for breath, doing some-
> thing with such zeal that serenity is lost, allowing resentment to
> get out of hand, laughing until tears come to the eyes – all these
> failures to balance the *yin* and the *yang* are harmful. Those who
> permit such harm to accumulate throughout the years die young.

This passage demonstrates the close relationship between coarse and
subtle *ch'i*; for whereas some of these implied prohibitions relate
directly to the breathing, others relate chiefly to states of mind.

It is taught that there are four principle kinds of breathing – *fine*,
which is so soft as to be inaudible to the breather; *long*, which signifies slow, placid, sustained breaths with no intervals between them;
deep, which is a technical term for bringing the breath down towards
the navel with the belly held in, to be pushed out only when the
breath is expelled; and *equal*, which means that each successive
inhalation and exhalation must be of equal length and in all ways as
nearly identical as possible with those which precede and follow it.
This so-called 'deep breathing' is what Lu K'uan-yü in his 'Taoist
Yoga' refers to as 'pot breathing'; that is, one inhales deeply with the

[1]   Literally, 'archery'.

stomach drawn in instead of being allowed to expand in the ordinary way; and then exhales while simultaneously pushing the belly outwards. The exact details of the various methods are communicated only to initiates; however, the following instructions would seem to be well suited to adepts not in a position to come upon an experienced teacher. The *Longevity Classic* recommends that adepts in the process of nourishing their *ch'i* should:

> Sit quietly for some time, letting the mind grow limpid as though preparing for Ch'an-style [Zen-style] meditation, eyes resting on the tip of the nose, nose aligned with the navel. Exhalations and inhalations should be calm, slow, equal in length and not at all like panting. While exhaling, the *ch'i* rises from below; while inhaling, it descends. There must be no intervals, no holding of the breath. One should give only slight attention to the breathing, amounting to no more than a calm awareness of air passing into and out of the nostrils; yet, even so, the sense of hearing must not be permitted to dwell on any other object.

These instructions are straightforward and easy to comply with, but what is said about the rising and descending of the *ch'i* may seem so obvious as to be surprising. The point is that, in yogic breathing, the adept is concerned with more than the passage of air (and *ch'i*) into and out of the lungs. It is understood that some part of it (part of the *ch'i* at any rate) penetrates more deeply than the base of the lungs; what passes down beyond them must also be caused to rise during exhalation.

Subtle and coarse *ch'i* are breathed in together. In nourishing them, one first sees to it that the coarse *ch'i* is inhaled and exhaled with a rhythmical movement, every breath being of equal length and pace; for thus are the inflow and outflow of subtle *ch'i* harmonised, even though it is not a material substance requiring the orifices of nose and mouth. Indeed, a store of subtle *ch'i* resides within the body; breathing is required merely to cause it to stir. Its coming and going are so soft that only experienced yogins can detect its passage. It was this form of *ch'i* that Chuang-tzû must have had in mind when he spoke of 'breathing through the heels'. Another reference to it is to be found in the passage where he says of the True Man (meaning the Perfect Sage) that his breath, being stored in the 'place of no-breath', can penetrate the whole body without the least obstruction.

A form of yogic breathing favoured by Ko Hung that derives its name from a passage in the *Tao Tê Ching* is described as 'breathing without using mouth or nose like a baby in the womb'. According to one text, this signifies that 'adepts inhale once through the nostrils and then change from normal breathing to breathing through the kidneys from six to a hundred and twenty times before exhaling so softly that the hairs within the nostrils do not stir'. The text goes on to say that 'breathing through the kidneys can be extended up to a thousand inhalations, the motion being so imperceptible as to cause onlookers to suppose that respiration has ceased'. However, another writer declares: 'Womb breathing does not really mean that ordinary respiration must be halted – a dangerous practice! It means that, when *ch'i* has been suitably nourished and transmuted, normal breathing becomes so spontaneous, soft and sustained as to give the impression of having ceased. Even so, in time, normal respiration does sometimes cease without causing death or even discomfort, a little breath being drawn in through the kidneys and pores.'

It is important to recognize that *ch'i*, besides being the vehicle of subtle *ching*, as pointed out in an earlier section, is also intimately connected with *shên*. It has been said: '*Shên* is our nature; *ch'i* is our life; morever, the former has a close relationship to breath control.' Speaking of these two, Heavenly Teacher Chang Hsü-ching declared; 'When *shên* goes forth, it can be brought back; as for *ch'i*, it returns of itself.' *Ch'i* returns through the mere act of breathing and can even enter through the pores, whereas *shên*, as the constituent of a yogic spirit-body, can be summoned to return at will. In any case, the very critical part played by *ch'i* in yogic alchemy is due to its being the subtle link between *ching* and *shên*. It is identical in all respects with the energy denoted by the Sanskrit term *prana* and plays the same role in Hindu and Tibetan Buddhist yogas as in Taoist yoga.

In brief, nourishing *ch'i* involves tranquillising the passions, stilling the mind and practising breathing yoga, not because the yogin's whole store of *ch'i* depends on inhalation, but because it is by breathing that the subtle *ch'i* residing in the body is stirred and thus enabled to play its part in the transmutation of both *ching* and *shên*.

5 *Transmutation of the Ch'i.* Initiates are taught how to arouse internal heat wherewith to bring about transmutation of the *ching*, *ch'i* and

shên in turn. This process involves both mental visualisation and certain muscular movements; but not all versions of the internal alchemy stress the need for arousing psychic heat; those who have no teacher should certainly not attempt it. In the absence of special instruction, the transmutation of coarse *ch'i* into subtle *ch'i* and of the latter into *shên* may be difficult, but not impossible. The difficulty need not be too discouraging as, according to some authorities, the stages of the yoga involving *shên* can be embarked upon when sufficient subtle *ch'i* has been accumulated by the method laid down for the fourth stage.

As a matter of interest, I offer the following poem to show the way in which the secret knowledge pertaining to the fifth stage of the yoga was in one case transmitted:

> The full moon shines within
> The stillness of the void.
> So when the wind disturbs
> The surface of the lake,
> Store a drop within your breast.
> The red sun's kin will know.

According to my understanding, the meaning is: 'The mind now shining with inner radiance is plunged within the stillness of the void. So, when the *ch'i* fanning the blazing furnace [in the vicinity of the solar plexus] causes the *ching* to rise, retain some of this transmuted *ching* in the upper storehouse [just beneath the crown of the head]; its presence will attract the cosmic *yang*-energy to assist in the transmutation of the *ch'i*.' I am by no means certain that this interpretation is correct, but the verse fully demonstrates the need for oral instruction to elucidate what written teaching there is on such secret matters as the transmutation of *ch'i*.

6 *Nourishing the Shên*. Shên being spirit is known as 'the lord of the body', 'the mother of the golden elixir' and by other exalted titles. One of the classics bearing the Yellow Emperor's name states that 'nourishing the *shên* is the highest task, nourishing the body – though certainly important – being secondary.' Subtle *shên*, also known as 'original *shên*' with reference to its 'prior-to-heaven' nature, is said to have stirred within the chaos from which the universe was born'. It is likened to a spark of spiritual radiance implanted in each man's mind, uniting it to that which lives beyond such transitory develop-

ments as the birth and destruction of a universe. This is reminiscent of such terms as the *istadeva* (in-dwelling deity) of the Hindus and the 'Christ within' of the Christian mystics, or even of the 'holy spirit' when conceived of as dwelling within the hearts of men.

Coarse *shên*, on the contrary, seems to equate better with mind than with spirit, for one encounters such terms as 'desire *shên*' or 'knowing *shên*', it being regarded as central to the faculties of observation, discrimination and desiring. Since it came into being after the birth of the universe and is therefore transitory, it has to be nourished and transmuted into subtle *shên*.

Properly nourished, *shên* can be concentrated within the adept's body. This causes *ch'i* to gather, which in turn gives nourishment to *ching*. The way to concentrate it is to fix the mind so that it becomes pure spirit unstirred by the movement of thought. 'Therefore must thought be eschewed and desire abandoned; then the mind will be righted and *shên* will consolidate.'

In one treatise of unknown authorship but ascribed to Hsi Wang Mu, a Taoist divinity credited with having attained immortality by the practice of dual cultivation with a thousand devoted youths as partners, the task of fixing the *shên* is surprisingly made to seem wholly a matter of attitude and of meditation, there being no complicated yogic steps such as first transmuting the *ch'i*. It runs:

The way to fix [the *shên*] and hold [it] is to know what is happiness, [namely,] being satisfied with what is enough, being beyond the power of cold and hunger to dismay, being free from the bondage of idle thoughts – for then arises *ch'i* wherewith the mind is nourished. Practise in the middle watches of the night, not troubling about special postures. Just fold your hands together, relax your limbs, banish idle thought, let your own body be the sole object of awareness. Then will the *shên* be fixed, the *ch'i* righted and your spirit impervious to aging and death.

One may ask why, if that is all there is to it, there is any necessity for the earlier stages of the yoga. I believe the answer is that the yogic stages are indeed not absolutely essential, but that, correctly carried out, they ensure very much more rapid progress for ordinarily gifted people .

This advanced stage, nourishing the *shên*, seems to involve no special requirements beyond stillness of mind – that is, 'blocking the outside, controlling the inside', or cutting off the attractions of sense objects and causing the mind to become limpid and still. However, many Taoist authorities – not all – take the view that, without the prior transmutation of *ching* and *ch'i*, attaining stillness and limpidity would be beyond one's powers. The yogic stages are intended to provide necessary supports.

7 *Transmutation of the Shên.* At this penultimate stage, coarse *shên* (pertaining to the knowing mind) is transmuted into pure spirit. By this time, 'cares have been banished, worries tossed away; there is not a thought to mar the stillness – everywhere just holy radiance'!

An adage written by T'ien Hsüan-tzû (Master of Heaven's Dark Mysteries) runs: 'When the *shên* of knowing ceases, great wisdom then takes birth.' Knowledge is a toy beloved of scholars. A mind cannot shine when stuffed with a myriad facts, for it then resembles a garden choked with weeds. Worldly wisdom is a barrier to the light of truth. Where subtle *shên* is not permitted to fix itself unhindered, the knowing *shên* pertaining to this transient universe is bound to take control; then will the mind be lost in pointless discrimination. All is confusion. Therefore must the knowing mind be transmuted to pure undifferentiated awareness; only then can coarse *shên* be transmuted to subtle *shên*, of an identical nature with the cosmic non-substance of the Tao:

> That your minds may be as the sun shining upon all, you must strive to put forth radiance like the Void's. For *yang-shên* is composed solely of prior-to-heaven *yang-ch'i*. In the beginning there was no thought, no activity, no infection of the senses. Take no heed of what you see; then will you rest spontaneously in the perfect stillness of undifferentiated being, with holy radiance shining everywhere and passing effortlessly into your being from the pure undifferentiated Source.

It is written in the *Book of the Elixir*: '*Yang-shên* transcends the triple world. [With it] your task will be complete, your practice done; and you will ascend to the shining canopy of heaven.'

The final transmutation process demands no special practice. As a result of all that has gone before, the knowing, discerning mind is ready to dissolve into the pure spirit of the void.

8 *Transmutation of Voided Shên to Make it One with the Void*. Having purged and transmuted one's stock of *shên* so that it is identical in nature with the void, the final stage is to transcend individual existence, to 'return to the Source'.

By now, if all the previous stages of the yoga have been completed, coarse *ching* has been transmuted into subtle *ching* to assist in transmuting first *ch'i*, then *shên*. Using subtle *ching*, coarse *ch'i* has been transmuted into subtle *ch'i*; by using both those substances in their subtle form, coarse *shên* has been transmuted into subtle *shên*, and this in turn transmuted into void. A 'spirit-child' has been created, a void entity which, with the dissolution of the body, will be able to unite with the Void. Thus will the adept's spirit return to its Source, the Tao. In alchemic terms, coarse *ching* has provided the initial substance for transmutation; using the body as furnace and cauldron, and with *ch'i* as the wind to fan the furnace, the ultimate product has been attained by a process of continual refinement – namely, subtle *shên* so refined as to be conceived of as a spirit-body ready to plunge back into the cosmic void; and, carrying the analogy further, the chemical reagents by which this has been achieved have been *ching*, *ch'i* and *shên*. Among the many versions of this alchemy, all are more or less agreed upon the nature of the processes and their sequence. Where they differ considerably is in the degree to which the alchemic terms are to be taken literally. At one extreme there are forms of the yoga with steps that correspond very closely indeed with those that would be needed to transmute base metals into pure gold; at the other extreme are versions which make scarcely any pretence of adhering to an alchemical sequence, except insofar as a continuous process of refinement and re-refinement is under way from first to last.

As to the name of this final stage, by 'voided *shên*' is meant mind or spirit so free from bondage to the senses and to such dualisms as 'I' and 'other' that individual existence has been transcended, except to the extent that the yogin still possesses individual bodily form (that will not be discarded until death). By 'the Void' is meant 'pure *yang*' not emptiness, but undifferentiated, wholly intangible fullness, or formless *yang-shên*. When some yogins speak of 'giving birth to an immortal child', they mean taking on or returning to the true and holy nature of original being; the womb in which this 'child' is formed is no other than 'original *yang-shên*'. Having achieved perfect stillness, the mind plunges into the lake, that is, into the radiance of concentrated *shên*. Now in full possesion of the pure and holy nature of original being, tranquil, self-existent, the yogin finds no barrier between himself and his glorious final goal.

By now, according to some schools of thought, the yogin has acquired what is called 'a body beyond a body', meaning that, even while his mortal body continues to encumber him with a lingering individuality that precludes total union with the Void, he is able to leave this fleshly envelope at will and, as it were, 'soar among the stars'. For this Chou Shao-hsien offers an interesting (though obviously incomplete) analogy, likening him to a film-goer who, carried away by emotion, forgets his physical existence, enters into the story portrayed on the screen and becomes part of what is going forward there. While this condition lasts, he is oblivious of other sights and sounds, forgetful of hunger and fatigue.

It is because ordinary people do not know how to transmute their *shên* that the *shên* 'does not congeal into a spirit-body' wherewith to journey forth from the fleshly body for a time and encounter glorious relaxation in the totality of being. Those who can do this are the true immortals; their 'flying' signifies floating off at times to merge with the primordial condition beyond the universe of form. This 'flying' is a state of consciousness in which all sense of self and other, of heaven and earth has vanished; there is naught but pure void, a limitless ocean of *ch'i* resembling a panorama of ever-changing cloud-forms. Chuang-tzû describes this as 'merging the voidness of one's own *yang-shên* with the voidness of the original Void'. His spirit shining, the yogin becomes one with all the myriad changes that comprise the universe. Thus heaven and earth are united. Beings described as 'alike mysterious in spirit and in form' have really attained the Tao. Original spirit, being indestructible, can never diminish. Through the final transmutation of personal *shên* into cosmic *shên*, one enters upon a state wherein he will live for as long as heaven and earth endure.

To sum up:

Fullness of *ching* wherewith to preserve our human body for as long as it takes to complete the yoga requires physical tranquillity; only when desires vanish will *ching* attain to fullness. Fullness of *ch'i* wherewith the body is well nourished requires that the mind be stilled; only when no thought arises will *ch'i* attain to fullness. Fullness of *shên* wherewith to return to the Source requires absolute dedication; only when body and mind are in perfect harmony will return to the Void be possible. Therefore are these three known as the 'three mysterious medicaments'. Body, heart and mind are essential to the production of these three.

The following verse, though less than adequate as a reminder of all that is involved, may serve that purpose more or less.

Stages
1   First let the vital seed be husbanded, enriched.
2   Next let the yogin nourish his frame abstemiously,
    Rule his wild passions, take healthful exercise
    And draw deep breaths, yet smooth and soft, inaudible.
3   Third let cosmic *ch'i* accumulate midst stillness.
4   Fourth let him cease to be too fond, too this or that,
    Needlessly rushing here or there, and *just be still!*
5   Fifth, should he know not how to stoke the body's fire,
    Let him accumulate fresh store of cosmic *ch'i*.
6   Sixth let his mind abide in calm serenity.
7   Next let him cultivate pure objectless awareness,
    Dwelling in undifferentiated emptiness.
8   Last let him cast away all thought of 'I' and 'other'
    And soar beyond the sun and moon to where the Way,
    Stretching out endlessly beyond the universe
    Waits to receive the wanderer returning.

The Case for a Spirit-Child
Mystics of other faiths are likely to concur with the ideas underlying this yoga, even if the alchemical analogy does not appeal to all of them; for, expressed in different terms, the whole process amounts to such a refinement of the adept's endowments that passion and delusion fall away and, leaping from the scattered debris, 'the god within' prepares for conscious union with That from which, in an important sense, there has never been separation. Yet, if *refining away* is the essence of the task, why do some Taoists speak of *creating* a 'spirit-child' or 'spirit-body'? Can digging out a sparkling jewel from a sea of mud and forging a new jewel be the same?

Logically they are not the same, but here the difference is not a real one; it results from the use of two different analogies for an ineffable experience which words of any kind are bound to distort. The 'spirit-child' analogy has the advantage of indicating a choice, for a child cannot live unless first conceived. Aldous Huxley, a writer deeply knowledgeable about mysticism both Eastern and Western, makes an interesting point in his *Devils of Loudun*. He affirms that the soul is a compound capable of disintegration which, 'though it probably survives after death', is doomed to ultimate dissolution, immortality being the property only of (impersonal, universal) spirit with which, however, the psyche *may* identify itself, *if it so desires*. Elsewhere in that work, in speaking of the fundamental identity taken on by a mind by virtue of its being incarnated in a body, he asserts that it is 'permitted by the Order of Things' to *choose between* unregeneracy and enlightenment. From this one may conclude that the individual psyche must choose to identify itself consciously with universal spirit in order to win to the goal. It is my understanding that those Taoists who speak of creating a 'spirit-child' or 'spirit-body' have this same choice in mind, a choice between disintegration at some time after death and forging a 'new entity', a vehicle in which to take the final leap into the Void. 'New' is perhaps not quite the right term for it; 'renewed' might fit the context better. If expressed in terms suited to what has just been said about Aldous Huxley's view, that vehicle or spirit-child could be described as 'the individual psyche now purged of dross and so interfused with universal spirit as to be ready for final union with the Void'. Just as 'child' means a potential man, so does spirit-child convey the idea of a potential immortal.

It is also held that the spirit-child or spirit-body can be employed at any time prior to physical death as a vehicle for travelling beyond the confines of the body; in this sense, it is to be equated with that much cruder concept, the astral body of Western Spiritism. This is a matter that takes us into a realm perhaps explorable, though not yet much explored, by science. Though of great interest, it has only peripheral importance in the present context; whether one does or does not believe in the possibility of this sort of astral exploration by a living person does not affect the main issue relating to what becomes of a fully realised adept after dissolution of the body.

Chapter 9

遂 Return to the
Source
元 (The Ultimate Attainment)

Though the various yogas pertaining to the internal alchemy, of which the yoga of eight stages is but one, are held to offer the swiftest means of arriving at the ultimate attainment, there is another way open to adepts endowed with a rare capacity for stillness and powers of mystical intuition. The name of this purely contemplative yoga is undoubtedly derived from two passages in the *Tao Tê Ching*. In the tenth section it is written: 'Can you embrace the One and not let go?' In the thirty-ninth section occur the words: 'Heaven owes its limpidity to the One. Earth owes its firmness to the One. Gods owe their holy powers to the One. Valleys owe their fullness to the One. The myriad objects owe their existence to the One. Princes and governors owe their ability to rectify to the One.' The One, needless to say, signifies the Tao, the fullness of the Void, that which existed before the universe was born.

The Contemplative Yoga of Guarding the One
Though man has fallen victim to the snares of passion and inordinate desire, the One remains within him like a mysterious pearl hidden beneath the dust of worldly things. When it is allowed to lose its radiance, man loses his inborn holiness; whereas he who guards this 'precious drop of spirit' flourishes. It is said of such a man that he 'sheds light upon the myriad laws of nature and his person becomes luminous. He is like a breath of pure spirit. Though heaven frown and earth darken, neither sun nor storm, lightning nor rain can

cause him to lose his way. Though his journey through life be full of danger and hardship, he stays safely on the middle path.'

Master Ko Hung spoke eloquently of what is wrought by guarding the One, declaring that he who guards it scrupulously will attain to exalted state; furthermore he declared: 'To know the One is easy; the difficulty lies in cherishing it to the end. He who manages to do so attains eternal life. Beasts, insects, reptiles, gods, devils, fire and sword are all powerless to harm him.' Chou Shao-hsien, in summing up quotations on this practice, declares: 'When inordinate desire is banished, no errant thoughts arise. The mind is stilled. The spirit becomes radiant and its brilliance illumines all the mysteries of the universe; then there is no limit to the marvellous powers attained.'

Guarding the One requires firm restraint both of body and of mind. In the *Book of Immortals* it is written: 'When the mind is taken up with worldly things, the spirit grows dull, man's essence is dissipated and the Way cannot be attained.' Ko Hung, speaking further of the matter, declared: 'Guarding the One and keeping the mind fixed upon it demands the utmost sincerity of purpose. The thoughts must be fixed on pure spirit – the One; then will the mind reach out to the mysterious Way and the longed-for state be attained.' It was this Taoist concept that led the early Ch'an (Zen) Buddhists to recognise that, in order to penetrate to the ultimate mystery, the mind must be cleared of dust and made to gleam like a polished mirror.

This doctrine, so easy to comprehend so difficult to practise, as Ko Hung pointed out, resembles that propounded by Wang Yang-ming, a Confucian philosopher closer in some ways to Taoism than to the teachings of Confucius. He taught that every man has within him a spark of unsullied mind or spirit uniting him with heaven and making him potentially the equal of gods and sages; but that, though pure in itself because no more capable of being marred than a mirror of being polluted by the images it reflects, it is so thickly overlaid by the mists of passion and desire, by the dust of the myriad objects, that ordinary people remain all their lives unaware of the existence of this, their most precious possession! It is bootless, then, to seek for some good lying outside one's own mind; what must be done is to rediscover the treasure hidden within the inmost recesses, wipe away the dust, polish it and live wholly by its light. This is a doctrine likewise proclaimed by the followers of Ch'an (Zen); it is what the Tibetans call the Doctrine of the Great Liberation; it forms the basis of the secret explanation given in Japan to followers of Pure Land Buddhism, which on the surface seems so different from the others. Every student of Eastern religions is familiar with this doctrine; but, of those who espouse it, how many succeed in keeping the bright mirror polished?

The doctrine that man is born with a precious jewel in his heart, a 'drop of spirit' that unites him to the Way, and yet is not his own possession but held in common by all, is not only widespread but also of great antiquity. None can say when the existence of this jewel was first proclaimed or, indeed, when and why it first came to be overlooked and forgotten. Almost all the great thinkers in China, prior to the coming of the modern age, were imbued with perception of the mystical unity between man and the cosmos. To this Confucius himself was no exception. Though the Taoists had reason to feel contemptuous of run-of-the-mill Confucian scholars with their tiresome pedantry and tendency to occupy themselves commenting upon commentaries written upon commentaries, the fact remains that the truly great Confucians – the sage Confucius, Mencius and, later, Ch'êng Yi, Chu Hsi, Wang Yang-ming, etc., were aware that man's greatness comes not from himself but from the Tao within. So has it been with the true mystics of other faiths, as evidenced by such terms as *istadeva* (the indwelling deity) and the 'Christ within'. Taoists, then, are not unique in holding this doctrine, but their contemplative techniques have characteristically Taoist features, and the thrilling audacity of their concept of the goal is probably unique even among accomplished mystics.

Certain highly gifted Taoist adepts rely wholly upon guarding the One to lead them to the ultimate goal, though it is much more usual to supplement it by having resource to other and more specific yogas. Taken by itself, this method may be called 'the way of attainment by direct mystical perception'. If this way is adopted, it generally consists in fact of two parts. Since guarding the One is a practice that must be continued during every moment of the day, it chiefly entails keeping a very strict watch upon the senses so that no stirrings of desire can displace consciousness of the One even for brief intervals now and then; and the negative task of keeping longings and passions always under control has to be accompanied by frequent recollection of and perception of the One, no matter what day-to-day affairs may happen to be engaging the periphery of the mind. Therefore, as a means of heightening that recollection and intuitive perception, the adept spends some hours a day in formal contemplative exercises centred always upon the presence within his being of the One. The meditation posture, except in some cases for position of the hands, is the same as for Buddhist meditation; but, Taoists, by and large, are much less strict than Rinzai Zen Buddhists, for example, with regard to posture; whatever happens, there must never be a sense of strain. During a meditation session, a technique widely favoured by Taoists is to direct the attention to the spot known as the 'precious square inch' lying midway between and slightly to the rear of the eyes. Light seen streaming from this spot, as clearly visible as would be a brilliant flame placed *in front of* the eyes, is taken as a sign of successful meditation; but it is not held to betoken *more* than that, for 'the radiance of the precious drop of spirit' is something else again, pertaining as it does to the realm of 'the seeing that is not seeing and the hearing that is not hearing'.

Approaching the Ultimate Goal
When Lao-tzû spoke of the teaching without words, he was entirely serious, not seeking to be witty. Moreover, his famous adage, 'those who know do not speak; those who speak do not know', is no more or less than truth. Recognising this, I feel hesitant to place myself among the speakers by trying to convey in words the highest goal ever conceived by the human mind! Words are so limiting; how can they be used to evoke more than a mere shadow of its splendour? One may sooner hope to capture in words the gleaming azure of a turquoise sky seen in autumn from a Himalayan peak soaring above the clouds than convey the majestic reality of the apotheosis known as 'return to the Source'. A Chinese friend of mine suggested that the final pages of this chapter should all be left blank with just an exclamation mark at the very end to indicate that nothing remains to be said. Wang Yang-ming seems to have been of much the same opinion. When questioned about Taoist immortality by his Confucian students, though he generally felt it his duty to disparage Taoism, his honesty compelled him to reply: 'How can I answer? If you really want to know, you must seclude yourselves in the wilds of mountain and forest for thirty years or so, perfect your hearing and

your seeing and, with whole-hearted determination, cleanse your hearts so that not a speck of dust remains – only then will you be able to speak knowledgeably of immortality. As things are now, you have far to go if you would tread the Way of Immortals.' Yet something must be attempted here if Taoism is to be seen in proper perspective. I hope I shall be forgiven for making the approach gradual, first very briefly summing up and evaluating all that has gone before and then selecting therefrom what seem to be the principle steps to be taken in cultivating the Way, thus coming by a natural route to the point of culmination.

We have seen that Taoism, like all great spiritual traditions handed down from high antiquity, has acquired its share of picturesque but spiritually unprofitable accretions. Were we to submit the whole body of Taoism to a process of refinement in approved alchemic style, the first 'dross' to be cast away would presumably be the rituals, priestly functions and hosts of divinities borrowed from the folk religion, at a time when recluses began seeking popular support, so as to have the means of earning a modest living that would provide them with a diet more satisfying than wind and dew. The next to go would be the external forms of alchemy and the long-moribund quest for flesh-and-blood immortality; for, though their contributions to medieval science, to Chinese art and to prolongation of life and youthful vigour made them worthwhile in themselves, they have little to do with mystical attainment. Four valuable components would then remain:

1 The philosophy of cheerful acceptance and of *wu wei* (non-interference and non-involvement), coupled with profound reverence for nature, knowledge of its workings and direct intuition of the holiness of every object in the universe as a manifestation of the Tao. All of these, though often cherished for their own sake without reference to a mystical goal, are of major importance to that goal's attainment.

2 The yogic alchemy for transmuting the endowments of mind and body into pure spirit. This is perhaps not quite essential to following the Way, but it provides a 'short path' leading to swift attainment.

3 The yogas of pure contemplation whereby passion and inordinate desire are vanquished, giving place to the equanimity and stillness needed for banishing ego-born delusion and entering into

the joyous state of spontaneity and freedom wherein the spirit goes forth to 'fly above the stars'.

4 The way of attainment by direct mystical perception. Full perception has been known to occur spontaneously to adepts with rare gifts of wisdom and stillness, and corresponds to the fourth and highest stage of Tibetan yoga, but there are very few adepts in whom it blossoms readily without assistance from some or all of the other three.

No matter what combination of these four components of cultivation is pursued, stillness is essential; only by stillness are the miasmas of passion and ignorance dispersed and that marvellous tranquillity gained whereby the adept becomes gloriously immune from whatever griefs and pains, whatever shocks and horrors life may have in store.

Cultivation of the Way

Bearing in mind all of the forgoing, it is possible to understand what is really involved in cultivation of the Way. Man's true nature (Mind as it is called in Ch'an (Zen) terminology) is not the personal possession of the individual; rather, individual existence is the prime illusion to be discarded. Belonging to none, the Tao is present in all. Therefore, as Mahayana Buddhists are also fond of pointing out, the only difference in this present life between realised immortals and ordinary men is that the former are aware of their underlying identity with the Tao, whereas the latter have not directly experienced that identity. Cultivation, then, is a matter of unveiling, of peeling off successive layers of delusion, each more subtle than the one before. It is a process of liberation. When the final delusion of personal separateness has been cast off, only the physical body (soon to be discarded) remains to be mistaken by the spiritually blind for a personal possession. By then, death has no meaning, except as a welcome release from bondage to an ageing carcass. The adept's *real* nature – the nature of all being – cannot possibly be diminished by the loss of an identity that has had no reality from the first. When clouds obscure the sun, its orb is not diminished; when they are blown away, its brightness is not augmented; the sun is always as it is, whether visible to the eye or not. Thus nothing starts with birth or ends with death; the real is there all the time. However, to understand this intellectually is not enough; it must become a direct perception. To this end, the would-be immortal (goal-winner) follows a regime set forth very simply some two thousand years ago in a work of the Han dynasty:

> Taking good care of his human body, perfecting within himself *his endowment of the Real*, cleansing will and thought, not straying into the paths of ordinary mortals, his mind and senses utterly serene, impervious to the effects of every sort of ill, welcoming life and death as parts of a seamless unity and therefore not clinging to the one or anxious about the other, free from every kind of anxiety and fear, roaming the world imperturbably at ease, he attains the Way.

How marvellous to wander through the world 'imperturbably at ease, no matter where one goes or what circumstances arise! No wonder the poems of the mountain-dwelling recluses are full of joy! With this philosophy they were able to welcome life's lovely scents and colours as gifts to be enjoyed from moment to moment, never regretting their transience or their passing, and with never a twinge of anxiety or fear. Where even the prospect of sudden, imminent death has no power to disturb, much less appal, one's feeling of security is as absolute as that of a child in its mother's arms! Yet all of these are but the first fruits of attainment!

The first step towards understanding the nature of the ultimate goal is to understand death, which has been termed life's only certainty. The Taoist view is that to feel regret on seeing the sands of life running out is to be like someone who, believing his purse contains a rope of priceless pearls, is horrified when the highwayman raises his pistol crying 'Your money or your life!' If only the poor fellow realised that his purse was empty, he could afford to hand it over with a laugh. That is exactly how it is – the purse contains nothing but a handful of yellow autumn leaves! The purse is the body; the autumn leaves with their *seeming* gold are the illusory individuality, the only *real* component of an individual being something more precious than pearls, but not his personal possession at all. That something did not begin, nor was it increased, when he was born; it will not cease, or be in any way diminished, when his body is discarded. To weep for a departed one is to shed tears for what has never been. Yet this is by no means the whole secret of immortality.

An immortal is one who, during his lifetime, has achieved the certainty of undergoing a glorious apotheosis unattainable by those who are overtaken by death while still lost in delusion. Some light on this difficult subject is shed by those professors of the internal alchemy who insist upon the absolute necessity of creating within themselves spirit-bodies into which to enter at the time of death. Stated thus baldly, this notion may strike us as only a degree less crude than belief in flesh-and-blood immortality. I mention it only because it presents immortality *in the light of a choice*. Alchemists of this kind hold that, should one fail to create a spirit-embryo prior to death, then his *hun* and *p'o* souls will linger in the upper and nether regions for some time, but finally disintegrate, the opportunity for winning immortality having been lost forever. Whereas, should he successfully create a spirit-embryo out of *shên* so refined as to be identical with cosmic *shên*, he will be able to reap the bliss of uniting with the Tao!

The Secret

Even at the highest level of understanding, that of true mysticism, the notion of a choice exists. Since Taoists, for the most part, do not accept the Buddhist doctrine of reincarnation, it is apparent that one must either attain immortality in this life or not at all, and that the penalty of failure is disintegration leading to extinction, which of course gives added significance to the term 'immortality' as a synonym for achievement of the goal. As to the nature of that goal, I cannot do better than repeat in slightly abridged form the words of the Taoist Master Tsêng, which appear in full in my earlier book on Taoism, *The Secret and Sublime*. This wonderful old man came nearer than anyone I have ever known, whether Buddhist, Taoist or otherwise, to expressing in words the exalted character of the apotheosis which those who have completed the necessary preparations may look for after death. Having heard from me of Sir Edwin Arnold's lovely expression for entering Nirvana, 'the dew-drop slips into the shining sea', he exclaimed with delight, but added:

'*And yet it does not capture the whole. Since the Tao is all and nothing lies outside it, since its multiplicity and unity are identical, when a finite being sheds the illusion of separate existence, he is not lost in the Tao. By casting off his imaginary limitations, he becomes immeasurable. Plunge the finite into the infinite and, though only one remains, the finite, far from being diminished, takes on the stature of infinity. Such perception will bring you face to face with the true secret cherished by all the accomplished sages. The mind of one who returns to the Source thereby BECOMES the Source. Your own mind is DESTINED TO BECOME THE UNIVERSE ITSELF!'*

Ah, in these words lay a splendour beyond all previous imaginings! To be a sage and live joyously drinking in the beauty of the sunshine and the rain, of thunder and lightning, of life and death, is a fine thing in itself. To know that at death nothing worthwhile is lost, since the only reality exists independently of your own existence is a satisfying philosophical reflection. But what are these in comparison to the knowledge that, since mind (spirit) is indistinguishable from Mind (Spirit), when wisdom has dissolved the shadowy barrier, the one is found to be coextensive with the other! In the light of this knowledge, you perceive yourself as a genie still confined within a sealed bottle, but now you have the power to melt the seal! Suddenly it is dissolved and your consciousness rushingly expands to the stature of a hundred feet, a thousand feet, a million – nay, a billion billion billion. You are now identical with the Tao, container and sole substance of the universe! Stars and suns innumerable are the atoms of your being; their whirling is the pulsing of your blood, their fiery brilliance the radiance of your person, the music of the spheres your voice!

This then is the secret! For years I had sat at the feet of Buddhist and Taoist masters, read the works of mystics of other faiths, and sometimes in my meditations made little advances towards intuitive perception of the Real. But it was Master Tsêng, or Tsêng Lao Weng (Grandfather Tsêng) as he liked to be called, who opened my eyes, more than any other sage encountered earlier or later, to what 'attainment', 'immortality', 'Enlightenment' really signify. Of course what his words conveyed, though he spoke from direct intuitive perception of the Nameless, can have been no more than a poor, poor shadow of the stupendous reality itself, so far is the Way beyond description. Even so, they endued life with a meaning far beyond what I have heard or seen expressed in other ways.

In the light of those words, I have often beheld in my mind's eye those ancient mountain-dwellers – immortals perhaps – living close to nature like the flowers, the winter-braving pines and the birds, poor in possessions yet richer in beauty than the Son of Heaven upon his

Dragon Throne, so inexhaustible and pregnant with meaning are the splendours of mountains, clouds and sky for them. Knowing themselves to be of the very substance of the rocks and streams, the windblown grasses and the wind itself – a substance infinitely holy, they had no fear. What enemies could blot existence out? In their piety they burnt fragrant herbs to the stellar divinities and made offerings to the genie of rocks and pools, seeing in everything the universal spirit that underlies and permeates the world of form. To them the entire universe was holy, awesome on account of its majesty and vastness, but never fearsome. On such unnatural notions as virtue and sin, they had turned their backs as being childish and sometimes mischievous delusions pertaining to the world of dust. Children of nature, what could tempt them to do harm? Who, having thrown away possessions as burdens too tiresome to be borne, prizing serenity and knowing passion for a foe, taking joy and seeing holiness in all that lives, would wish to steal or rape or kill? Above all, who, having through their yogas and contemplation attained to understanding of the secret I had heard, not by hearing it but by direct intuitive perception in a way beyond my power to emulate, would care to do more than live from day to day free from plans and speculations, just turning a hand to whatever needed doing, doing it well and putting it out of mind?

Though I arrived in China centuries too late to meet the original immortals who had lived as hermits, I found among their successors dwelling in small communities not a few who had inherited their naturalness, their ready smiles and laughter, their joy in things so simple that other people, unaware of the holiness of every leaf or puff of air, would have allowed to pass unnoticed. It may be that I enjoyed being in their company even more than if they had been the traditional hermits of ancient times; for, to the natural charms of their wild surroundings, had gradually been added the lovely dwellings and fanciful pavilions that, far from detracting from nature's beauty, had been expressly designed by an artistic people to embellish the cliffs and crags they adorned.

It is distressing to recall that those communities have been disbanded; that, even if the buildings stand as for centuries past, the recluses have been driven forth and that the ancient pattern of life maintained from the time of the Yellow Emperor has been broken off forever. Still, something of their peace entered my heart during my journeys among China's holy mountains many, many years ago. Certain combinations of things heard and seen, such as a flute being played in the open air when a full moon shines upon a vista of hills, or the music of the wind in the bamboo clump outside my window, can fill me with a rapture that owes much of its sweetness to memories, but something also to at least a faint perception of the inner beauty of the recluses' understanding.

Chapter 10

The Valley Spirit
(Living Taoism)

In the *Tao Tê Ching* occur the words: 'The valley spirit is undying; it is called the mysterious female, whose portal is known as the fundament of heaven and earth.' Valley spirit is a term exactly suited to the character of Taoist recluses. They did not seek to be known from afar like the peaks of lofty mountains, preferring to pass their lives unnoticed by the world like those hidden upland valleys known only to the local shepherds and their flocks. How well they succeeded! Book after book on China makes mention, usually unflattering, of those so-called Taoists, the priests of the folk religion, whereas accounts of recluses intent on cultivating the Way such as those I encountered towards the middle of this century are rare. Though warmly hospitable to all who sought them out, they liked on the whole to escape attention, dwelling for the most part in small inconspicuous hermitages, but sometimes as members of those larger communities wherein the presence of colourful magicians, exorcists and priests arrayed like themselves in Taoist garb made it easy for them to pursue the Way unnoticed by the world. Indeed, membership of a priestly community was a convenient manner of ensuring a supply of food, raiment and shelter without any necessity to engage in activities that would take up time needed for cultivation.

Perhaps in the present century, during the first half of which the Chinese were visited by disaster after disaster, there have not been very many of these true Taoists; nevertheless, prior to the red flood, the whole race was permeated by Taoist thought and Taoist attitudes. A feeling for nature amounting almost to worship was apparent to the traveller in any part of the country where traditional ways had not yet been supplanted. The onset of materialistic culture, though deadly, took time to blot out a way of life that had survived uninterruptedly for five thousand years, either unaffected by foreign influences or transforming them to harmonise with the Chinese ethos. The appreciation of nature so beautifully expressed in masterpieces of poetry and landscape painting was manifest throughout the Middle Kingdom – it was reflected in the cloud patterns on the robes of the imperial officials now no more, in the charming miniatures of landscapes, birds, animals and flowers ornamenting the eaves of traditional buildings, in the decorations on every kind of artefact from fans, wall-scrolls and vases to such humble utensils as rice bowls, wine cups, teapots and kettles.

Fondness for mountains, trees, streams, pools and flowers is, of course, not limited to the Chinese; other peoples also have recognised them as the abodes of gods and spirits, but some of the manifestations of this fondness are peculiarly Chinese. Take for example the extraordinary reverence for rocks, which certainly arose from a quality in stone that graphically suggests the interchangeability of all the myriad objects created by the Tao. No matter where one goes in China, it is rare to find a mountain ridge or rocky eminence of any sort that has not been likened to something alive. At the very gateway to the country, the mainland facing Hong Kong, one finds Nine Dragons (Kowloon), Lion Rock, Nurse-Carrying-Child Rock and so forth. South China, especially, teems with rock formations suggestive of the seemingly inanimate on the point of turning into living creatures – dragons, lions, tigers, buffaloes, turtles, frogs, herons, phoenixes or humans, but it takes a Chinese eye to detect the likeness without its being pointed out. *Then* one perceives how these rocks lend vividness to the concept of a single universal substance forever undergoing cloud-like transformations from form to form.

In the gardens and courtyards of hermitages situated in places devoid of picturesque rocks, the deficiency has generally been lovingly repaired. Rocks carried from afar will have been arranged in miniature landscapes, either beautiful or amusingly grotesque. On many a recluse's or Chinese scholar's writing desk one would see, ranged among writing implements of porcelain, bronze, ivory or jade, a lump of ordinary dark rock mounted like a precious curio on a chaste blackwood base. Ordinary in the sense of being of no greater intrinsic value than a large pebble picked up from a stream, it might prove to be the owner's greatest treasure – a word of praise for its shape and texture, its tiny cavities and involutions or contorted ridges would win his heart and more than redeem one from appearing a barbarian in his eyes.

Any number of different examples might be chosen to illustrate the Chinese feeling for natural beauty; but the most perfect expressions of that love were to be seen on the slopes of the holy mountains where Taoist hermitages clustered. Though generally remote and not very easily accessible on account of the distance from roads and railways, the hermitages were no longer simple cottages, most having been inhabited for centuries and gradually embellished to suit surroundings of majestic natural beauty. Invariably the sites had been determined in accordance with the sacred science of *fêng-shui* (wind and water, geomancy) to ensure their proximity to an uninterrupted flow of cosmic *ch'i*. In their vicinity, moon-viewing pavilions hung above tremendous gorges filled with irridescent clouds of spray and echoing the muted thunder of the torrent far below. As to the main buildings, these were likely to be invisible from afar, being sheltered from the mountain winds by groves of massive pines and cedars or natural rock formations. The steep and winding approach might lead through what in autumn became a tunnel of gold and scarlet foliage; or, in the warm south, there might be massed clumps of bamboo and tall flower-bearing shrubs such as pink and white oleander. Trees prized for their blossom – peach, pear, cherry, crab-apple or plum – rose from the midst of the little courtyards they shaded from the summer sun. The outer wall, following the contours of the ground with dragon-like undulations, might be pierced by occasional windows, one shaped like a bell, another like a vase, a maple-leaf or a moon seen at its fullness. The buildings, usually one-storeyed, had sweeping roofs, those of the larger and more famous edifices being sometimes covered with porcelain tiles of azure or jade-green; but the preference was for sombre hues that harmonised with earth and rock. Sumptuous temples with gleaming tiles, gates of scarlet lacquer and elaborately decorated eaves reflected Buddhist influence, being foreign to the Taoist spirit of simplicity. I preferred the smaller and more typical hermitages built of dark grey brick, roofed with earthenware tiles and guarded by lacquered gates, either black or austerely dark and plain.

A hermitage of middle size would consist of pleasingly unsymmetrical buildings ranged around a single grey-flagged, tree-shaded courtyard decked with earthenware pots of flowering shrubs or flowers appropriate to the season – hyacinth, peony, lotus, chrysanthemum or winter-plum. Or it might contain a rockery cunningly fashioned to resemble a mountainous landscape. The adjacent garden would be likely to have a wild look as though almost wholly the work of nature, man's handiwork being artfully concealed. Gnarled trees with picturesque curves to trunk or branches would seem to have chosen just that way to grow – were the curves perceived to be unnatural, the gardener recluses would have cause to feel ashamed of their inadequacy, though in fact the trees had received painstaking assistance in achieving their perfection. So, too, with rocks; they would seem to have lain just so for a million years, though their arrangement might in fact have been improved upon a hundred times. Vegetable gardens must have existed, though I cannot recall having seen more than one or two; perhaps they were hidden away, their appearance being too humdrum for the vicinity of immortals reputed to live on sups of wind and sips of dew, varied now and then by a meal of powdered pearl and moonbeam!

Within, each recluse inhabited a cell opening on to the courtyard. If these little rooms had a fault, it was that the light was poor, for the windows were shadowed by the great upward-curving eaves and the window-paper, though it shone with a pearly radiance, was less than perfectly translucent; on the other hand, the latticework was charming, there being many designs of which my favourite was the 'cracked ice pattern'. The furnishings were austere but handsome – a four-poster bed equipped with a wadded mattress, a pillow stuffed with grain or dried grasses and padded quilts; a massive wooden chest for storing clothes and possessions; a square or oblong table with one or two heavy wooden chairs, and some wall shelves. These did not vary much from place to place and always looked as though designed to last for centuries. Their stern simplicity and elegance of line were not marred by such frivolities as cushions or upholstery. Yet Taoists never carried frugality to extremes; usually there would be deft touches of refinement – a wall scroll brushed in bold free-hand calligraphy with characters lively enough to seem on the point of taking flight; a black and white brush drawing of some animal or bird, or perhaps of a laughing sage sporting with a bushy-tailed unicorn; or a softly coloured landscape with a vaguely outlined range of mountains fading into misty expanses of water and sky to suggest the underlying voidness and identity of the myriad forms. Here and there, one or two treasures might be displayed – a porcelain vase, a small bronze incense-burner, a miniature jade turtle, a statuette of Lao-tzû astride his famous ox, a handsome set of writing implements or tea things. The bookshelves possessed an austere beauty of their own, for the volumes of old wood-block prints, being flimsy, were housed in sets, each with its oblong box covered with dark blue cloth, a tiny ivory hasp and a long thin label bearing its name in elegant calligraphy.

Otherwise, luxuries were few – a portable tea-stove in summer that would be replaced by a large charcoal brazier when the days began to draw in; a pewter vessel for mulling wine, a padded basket in which a teapot nestled warmly. The refectory used for communal meals would, like the cells, have flagstones or a plain wooden floor, papered or plain walls and ceiling. It would be furnished with one or more large tables covered with shining black lacquer that could be made spotless by a quick rub with a damp cloth, so that no table-cloth was needed. Stools were commoner than chairs, perhaps because they could be pushed right under the table when not in use, leaving the refectory less cluttered. Here the window lattices were sometimes inset with thin layers of oyster shell instead of translucent paper; this was not an improvement from the point of view of lighting, but the light that did trickle through had the beauty of softly coloured jewels.

Not every hermitage boasted a shrine hall, nor was there any need in some of the smaller ones if the inhabitants had private means; but all had a statue or two, mostly of Lao-tzû and of the place's patron deity, for whom there was often a shrine in the refectory with no paraphernalia beyond an incense burner, two flower vases and two candlesticks. Whether one believed in divinities or not, it was held seemly to follow ancient traditions within moderation. On the other hand, in those hermitages which depended on lay support for their entire income, there was often a shrine hall, or at least a shrine room, lavishly adorned. Though the recluses might privately feel little enthusiasm for the gods, such places were of prime importance in that they were the major attraction for the pilgrims who came in crowds for the great festivals. Effigies of divinities and sages sat gazing down from carved and gilded cupboards upon elaborate altars piled with offerings.

As for the rest, most hermitages had a small library, a kitchen, storerooms, a bathroom and rudimentary lavatory. The kitchens of hermitages that attracted large numbers of pilgrims were a sight to see; there would be large cauldrons and gigantic pans in which rice could be boiled, vegetables cooked and water heated for several hundred people. In a hermitage bathroom, the usual arrangement was a sunken bath heated by underground flues in which several people could stand together in hot water that came up to their chins. A place to be feared was the lavatory; this was often a pit, roofed but otherwise unscreened against the mountain winds, over which one squatted precariously, feet upon slender planks that had certainly not been designed to bear the weight of a Western Ocean man! A hundred times I have thought that the planks were on the point of giving way; had this happened, I should have fallen into the accumulated waste of centuries to which all of us added our daily quota! Simplicity, though a beautiful ideal, has its drawbacks.

The recluses wore garments of antique cut that marked them out as Taoists, though in fact their costume was that worn by ordinary laymen prior to the time when the first of the Manchu emperors took his seat upon the Dragon Throne (1644) and instituted dress reform, including the wearing of the queue, from which Buddhist priests and Taoists were exempted. Over a short jacket and loose trousers fell a long and ample robe of plain but sometimes gaily coloured cloth, thin in summer, wadded with cotton wool in winter, the colours varying with the seasons. White cloth stockings confined the legs of the trousers; shoes were of black cloth with very thick soles made of layers of white felt stitched together. Headgear consisted of brimless hats through the crowns of which protruded luxuriant topknots secured by pegs of wood, bamboo, ivory or jade. These hair-pegs were sometimes curiously carved works of art; otherwise ornaments were rare, except now and then for a bangle or ring of thick green or white jade worn for a combination of magical and theraputic reasons rather than display.

In such communities old-world courtesy prevailed. By way of greeting the recluses would clasp their own hands and pump their arms up and down, either bowing or bobbing their heads repeatedly. Their conversation with strangers tended to be sprinkled with effusive compliments which, owing to the nature of the Chinese language, can be expressed in less time than it takes us to say 'How do you do' – for example, *Chiu yang* means all of the following: 'I have long heard your illustrious name, but have not until now had the pleasure of meeting you', *chiu* meaning 'long' and *yang* meaning 'looking up [respectfully towards you]'. Similarly, *shih sung* (literally 'lose send') means: 'With your esteemed permission, I shall refrain from accompanying you further towards the gate'! There was nothing especially Taoistic about such phrases, except that they tended to be going out of use elsewhere; the special character of the recluses was revealed by their conduct to a guest after the time for initial formalities had passed; for then they would treat him with the true politeness of doing all they could to make him feel happy and at ease so unobtrusively that he was never allowed to feel burdened by their attentions.

Truly they were lovable people and their company a rarely equalled pleasure. As to their attainments, these varied widely. Many were of humble origin and, having had little in the way of formal education even at the primary level, had nevertheless managed to acquire a sufficient knowledge of Chinese ideograms not to be baffled by the archaic texts they studied. Among them was a sprinkling of real scholars able to expound the subtleties of Taoist philosophy, metaphysics and yoga, not a few of whom turned out to be former bankers, generals and the like who had retired in disgust from the money-grubbing world of dust. Those writers who speak of Taoism in the twentieth century as having been a hotchpotch of superstition and charlatanism clearly have no first-hand knowledge beyond some acquaintance with the communities to be found in temples within easy reach of the cities, such as the new temple at Ch'ing Shan on the mainland opposite Hong Kong. How should one expect to meet real Taoists in close proximity with the world of dust? I do not know why scholars have poured scorn on Taoists for supporting themselves by fulfilling the popular demand for priestly services. Is it not the fate of the priests of other religions also to have to perform ritual functions only remotely connected with the life of the spirit? What of those Christian clergy who are obliged to affirm solemnly and in public before God's altar that they believe in the resurrection *of the body*? Are we to suppose them the less dedicated to fulfilling the demands of the spirit simply because the forms of their Church require affirmation of belief in something very similar to flesh-and-blood transmogrification? Conversely, is the popular Taoist belief in the necessity to create a spiritual body prior to death or else suffer extinction really more 'grossly superstitious' than the popular Christian belief that only those who are 'saved' will have the felicity of dwelling eternally in the presence of God, all others being 'cast into outer darkness'? Is it not more admirable and consonant with reason to suppose that immortality has to be won by cultivating and nurturing one's spiritual faculties rather than by a mere act of faith performed, perhaps, on one's death-bed?

The Taoists I had the good fortune to encounter were not over-superstitious. They included men both simple and urbane with a partly mystical partly humanistic philosophy. Though I do not re-member hearing any of them deny the existence of gods and spirits, I did not find them unduly concerned with rituals. Like Buddhists, they understood that spiritual development lies with oneself, that neither gods nor sacraments help or hinder in the gradual refining or coarsening of man's essential being. Given the likelihood of en-joying a lifespan of from sixty to seventy or more years, they set out to achieve within that space of time an inner development capable of negating the effects of man's departure from the ways of nature and enabling them to eradicate evil propensities – acquisitiveness, passion, inordinate desire – which lead to selfishness and callousness if not to deceit and downright cruelty. They longed to refine their spirits. What does it matter if their concept of the goal was in some cases naive? Doubtless that concept became more elevated as culti-vation of the Way proceeded. To me they proved charming com-panions who added to the joy of spending a few days or weeks in superb natural surroundings. They provided me with opportunities to glimpse facets of a venerable civilisation which they alone among the educated Chinese of my generation had preserved more or less intact. Besides an engaging kindness, simplicity and candour, they had an enchanting gaiety. The sound of their laughter echoed through courts where, had they been within the precincts of a Western monastery, joy would have been swallowed up in a sanctimonious hush. One of the great secrets of their charm was their philosophy of 'not too much of anything', which taught them to combine spiritual aspiration with warm humanity.

Their manner of life can be most satisfactorily conveyed by an account of a visit paid to one of the hermitages on Hua Shan; for, at the time, the ways of Taoists still had some novelty for me, so my senses were unusually alert to the impressions that came crowding in. To make the description more representative of the hermitages as a whole, I have woven into the narrative some details and characters encountered during subsequent visits to other holy mountains. The ex-general and ex-banker, both of whom belong to this category, may seem unusual and perhaps they were, but retired men of the world were by no means rareties in the smaller and more exclusive communities.

In the winter of 1935 I happened to be in the neighbourhood of Hua Shan and decided to explore it. A northern Chinese winter is not the best of times for such expeditions; ice lay upon the precipitous paths, glazing the flights of steps hewn from living rock, and a cutting wind howled about the exposed upper slopes. Here and there clumps of trees stood close to the shrines of deities or foxfairies, most of them looking as forlorn and in need of warm shelter as myself; otherwise the slopes were bare, having been denuded of their forests by generations of fuel gatherers from the teeming plains below. I never did succeed in reaching the temple that crowned the peak of what must be one of the most spectacular precipices in the world; as dusk approached, a chill mist blotted out the path and I sought refuge in a modest wayside hermitage, feeling hungry and miserably cold. All I could see of the place was a cluster of grey moss-encrusted roofs peeping above the high surrounding wall, also grey but showing less signs of poverty and neglect than many of the other hermitages. The ponderous lacquered leaves of the moon-gate were closed and unyielding. The young man I had met in the fields below and engaged as a guide, only to find that he had never set foot on the mountain in a life passed within a few bow-shots of its foot, suggested knocking as loudly as we could. So we pounded our fists against the smooth lacquer and shouted at the tops of our voices, but there came no answering voice. It was bitterly cold and, if no one heard us, darkness might fall before we had found refuge elsewhere. Dismally our voices echoed among the rocks.

Knuckles sore, arms aching, thoughts close to despair, we were about to give up when a voice, muffled by the thickness of the gate, cried: 'Pu yao chi. An-mên pu shih lung-tzû!' How comforting that sound, for all that we were being scolded for supposing the inmates deaf! Now a heavy leaf creaked open, but beyond the lintel stood a sturdy old greybeard, cudgel in hand, who yelled: 'Honest men don't come calling at *this* hour of an evening!'

Suddenly the old fellow's grim expression changed to one of vast astonishment. 'Old Father Heaven! A foreign dev–, er, er, a foreign guest!' Now he was all smiles and bows, pumping his clasped hands up and down in generous welcome, his eyes alight with smiling apology, his face aglow with human warmth. Taking the bag from my so-called guide and inviting him to go and sit by the kitchen fire, he led me across a modest courtyard to a room which appeared to be his own for, though no one was there, it was heated by a glowing brazier and rather stuffy. Motioning me to a couch, he hurried out and soon returned with a basin of hot water, soap and face-towel. Next he set about brewing tea and soon we were facing each other across the brazier chatting like long separated friends. Like many denizens of isolated places, he seemed glad of new company and brimming over with talk. Within an hour, besides having learnt something about their little community of five recluses and two serving lads scarcely in their teens, I had come to know most of the salient facts of his life.

The son of an impoverished ironmonger, he had had scarcely three years of schooling before being compelled to pad the streets of his native Sian vainly hoping to find someone in need of a barely literate clerk. In despair he had entered the service of a city priest who made such a poor living by divination and selecting sites for houses and tombs in the light of the science of *feng-shui* that he could afford to pay no wages, only to meet the bare cost of the boy's keep. Happily he had no objection to letting his new assistant make whatever use he liked of the books left behind by a more scholarly predecessor and gradually the latter became enthralled by works setting forth all aspects of cultivating the Way. Two or three years passed; then the youth set off for the mountains and, after wandering for several more years, settled on Mount Hua. At the time of our meeting, he had been doyen of the tiny community in that hermitage for at least a couple of decades.

'Your honourable abode must be lovely in summer,' I remarked, 'but are you never weary of it? Does time never lie heavily on your hands?'

'No, no, no!' he answered vehemently, his old face lighting up

with mirth. 'You talk as though this were a mansion crowded with
noisy womenfolk with never a thought in their heads beyond buying
clothes, dining off bird's nest and shark's fin, and playing mahjong
for heavy stakes. That sort of thing, I have heard, makes many a man
wish life were shorter. Here we have no time to be bored and, of
course, you can have no idea of the beauty of this place. Winter is
lovely on the whole. Had you come a day or two earlier, you would
have seen the sky from this level as an inverted bowl of flawless
turquoise. On most days, in the clear light of morning the peak
rises like an island from a sea of mist that blots out all the world
below. Bleak though it is today, if the fog lifts before tomorrow
morning, you may feel embarrassed to find yourself floating above the
clouds in what must surely be the court of the Jade Emperor, without
having changed your workaday clothes in his honour, let alone your
mortal skin! On clear nights both in winter and summer the moon is
enormous. As for the stars, you can almost brush them with your
hand. If you like plenty of company, come in spring or autumn when,
on festival days, the path to the summit is so thick with pilgrims
that it looks like a writhing serpent. Some bring flutes and jars of
wine to pay honour to our mountain deity. Ah, you prefer peace and
quiet? Then come back in summer when the lower slopes are so
densely carpeted with flowers that you might suppose someone had
brought a giant Mongolian carpet to make a collar for our mountain
god, from which his craggy neck rises not a hundred feet below
where we are here. Behind our hermitage there is a pool fed by a
hidden spring where the water is deep and crystal clear, the silence
so awe-inspiring that you are afraid to dive lest the splash disturb
the local genie. They say he is a dragon, by the way, but I cannot
be sure of that, for no one is known to have encountered him since –
when was it? – shortly before the fall of the Ming dynasty, I believe.
Even so, he might graciously manifest himself to *you*, a distinguished
foreign guest.'

'How lovely you make it sound, Your Immortality. You seem to
have no worries in this holy place. I suppose offerings made by the
pilgrims are sufficient for all your needs?'

'I would not wish to depend on them,' he replied. 'Ours is a
small hermitage and we seldom have people coming to pass the night
here, except during the great festivals when the temple at the peak
and larger hermitages are filled to overflowing; but we prefer not to

have *too* many visitors, though we should be sorry indeed to have none, for we enjoy the conversation of widely travelled and learned guests like yourself, if I may presume to say so. Without offerings, we could manage. Our needs are simple and two of our colleagues were once well off; though they abandoned their wealth when they left the world, you may be sure their families would help us if ever we were in dire need. For the most part we live off the proceeds of medicinal plants gathered on the mountainside. For example, we have . . .' He mentioned a dozen or more names of plants that meant nothing to me, adding that there was a steady demand for them from Chinese physicians and medicine shops. Though most varieties brought in no more than half a silver *yuan* (little more than three pence) per basketful, that sum was enough in those days to feed a community of seven for a couple of days or so.

'But how do you pass your time in winter when it is windy and cold like today?'

'Ah well, it is true that fog or heavy snowfalls sometimes isolate us for days at a time – but you see how snug we are. There is charcoal enough to last us. We have our books, some good tea, a mouthful or two of wine with evening rice to keep out the cold. Is all that not enough, do you think? Though we have two boys to help, household chores keep us on the move a good deal, especially in the mornings after we have warmed ourselves with hot tea and some vigorous *t'ai chi ch'üan* exercises. There is much to read and we have many books that repay rereading many, many times. We are fond of music, too, and have preserved some flute melodies so ancient that they may not have been heard elsewhere for centuries, as far as we know.'

'Do you write, Immortality, or paint perhaps?'

Blushing endearingly, the old man murmured 'No, no' in a tone that surely meant 'yes'. 'You cannot expect – well, you could say I like the fragrance of fine ink and the *sha-sha-sha* of a writing brush sweeping over paper made in the old way on this very mountain from barks and leaves that give it a pleasantly rough texture. My "writing" scarcely amounts to more than that, but two of my colleagues write fine verses. As to painting – ha-ha-ha – of course not. That is, I do sometimes just *try* my hand at it, brushing crude land-scapes with wavy strokes for mountains, mere dots and blobs to indicate clumps of trees or shadowed rocks. People? Animals? How could an illiterate old creature like me dare? Well, a long narrow blob perhaps with a suggestion of white upturned faces to suggest a line of pilgrims gazing up at the peak. Eh ? No, no, you cannot wish to see such trifles' – but he was already on his feet, a delighted expression giving something like youthful charm to his old face, and within a few minutes he had brought over quite a pile of unmounted ink paintings.

I knew little enough of Chinese art in those days, but it seemed to me that some of his paintings were really beautiful. Mostly they were impressions of mountain vistas seen at different times of the year, each with a couplet or four-line poem of his own composition in running grass-characters brushed on a corner of the page, relevant of course to the scene depicted. It may not have been great art, but it was certainly attractive. Years later I came to realise how lucky such recluses were to have escaped the kind of education available in government-run schools. Instead of having their minds corrupted by the usual second-hand versions of materialist ideas imported from the West, they had for their only models the masterly poems, essays and paintings in traditional style that one would expect to find in monastic libraries which had gradually been built up over the centuries. No wonder recluses who so often came from illiterate or barely literate families had, at least in some cases, accomplishments superior to those of a good many university students of the period!

Having expressed my admiration of his poems and paintings in glowing terms worthy of the occasion, I asked how he managed to find time amidst his manifold pursuits for self-cultivation.

'Where is the conflict, young sir ? *All* we do is part of cultivation. As to formal yogas and meditations, we perform them mostly during the first hour or two of the day and also late at night. We make no rules, so there are none to break and cause self-dissatisfaction. The secret is to *sense* when actions are timely and in accord with the Way or otherwise. It is a matter of learning to – to – how shall I say ? Of, of – ah, now I have it – of learning how to *be* !'

'Have you no worries, no anxieties at all ?'

'Young sir, you must be joking! We are humans. Ills happen. But we have learnt that calamities pass like all things. When we are sick or short of money to buy necessities, we naturally feel anxious; but, when this has happened many times, one learns to accept the bad with the good, to see them as they are – a part of being and not to be dispensed with without damage to the whole.'

'When you are *sick*, Immortality? It is hard to imagine an immortal with a cough or hiccups! I should have thought – '

He chuckled heartily. 'Worse than that, young sir. Immortals not only break wind or belch like other people, they *die*! Can it ever have been otherwise? Becoming immortal has little to do with physical changes, like the greying of a once glossy black beard; it means coming to know something, realising something – an experience that can happen in a flash! Ah, how precious is that knowledge! When it first strikes you, you want to sing and dance, or you nearly die of laughing! For suddenly you recognise that nothing in the world can ever hurt you. Though thunder roar and torrents boil, though serpents hiss and arrows rain – you meet them laughing! You see your body as a flower born to bloom, to give forth fragrance, to wither and to die. Who would care for a peony that stayed as it was for a lifetime, for a thousand or ten thousand years? A mere cabbage would be worthier of attention. It is well that things die when worn out, and no loss at all, for *life* is immortal and never grows with the birth of things or diminishes with their death. A worn-out object is discarded, life having ample materials to supply the loss. Now do you see? *You* cannot die, because you have never lived. Life cannot die, because it has no beginning or end. Becoming an immortal just means ceasing to identify yourself with shadows and recognising that the only "you" is everlasting life. Ah, what nonsense I am talking; they'll be waiting for us to join them at evening rice. Come.'

In those days my Chinese was less fluent than it afterwards became, so I cannot be sure I have reported the substance of his memorable words correctly, the more so as forty years have passed since then. Yet what he said was at once so striking and so simple that I am sure I got the hang of it and that not too much has been lost in the retelling. For the first time in my life I realised that a man may have no faith in *personal* survival and yet recognise that, in losing himself, he loses nothing. I saw that, to a man in his blissful state of mind, the loss of his spectacles would seem a greater inconvenience than merely dying! He had used the Chinese equivalent of 'want to sing and dance' with reference to a sudden perception of death's real nature! There was in him an abundance of joy not to be accounted for by anything within my understanding at that time; and it may be that this belated report of his conversation is more true to the spirit of his words than anything I could have written down on the spot. To see his smile was to sense his invulnerable serenity and I wonder now if the famed immortals of old attained to anything higher. *Is* there anything more, anywhere further to go than the direct intuitive perception that life holds no terrors, that death – like Cinderella's fairy godmother – holds out to us a new and shining garment, that the 'red slayer' never slays because there is no one to slay and no such thing as slaying? Clearly the old gentleman had long ago reached a point at which the word 'I' had no more than a convenient functional meaning like the word 'home' in a game of ludo. Yet, far from passing his days in a trancelike state waiting for death's liberation, far from being lethargic and withdrawn, as though his present life were of no importance, he was keenly alert, sipping his tea with evident enjoyment, revelling in the brazier's warmth, but also quick to see to practical matters, as when the charcoal embers needed stirring. Though clearly a holy man in the best sense, he had not a touch of the solemnity we in the West are apt to associate with the saintly. The strongest lines in his face were those that come from ready smiles and laughter. Even his little weakness, an innocent vanity in having made himself into something of a scholar and a painter, was lovable. His qualities, I was to discover, were typical of cultivators of the Way.

Evening rice, shared with the five recluses and with the two little boys who, having served us, sat at table and gobbled lion's shares, was a delightful meal. Though so very much junior to my five hosts, I was literally dragged into the seat of honour opposite the door. The food consisted mostly of vegetables and bean curd, but with slivers of ham and dried fish to give them flavour. Instead of rice, we had piping hot millet dumplings – coarse fare and cheap but tasty. From a pewter jug kept standing in hot water a delicious yellowish wine was poured into cups with about half the capacity of an egg-cup. Everyone drank several cupfuls, just enough to add to our conviviality.

It appeared that they had no abbot, but my friend was treated with special deference, probably because, though far below some of the others in social standing and scholarship and rather younger than at least one of them, he had long been the doyen of their community. Of the others, the Miraculous Moss Recluse, an octogenarian, had once been a farmer, but had sold his plot of land to buy food for his family during a famine. The Cloud Mother Recluse, a burly and rather handsome black-bearded man in his middle forties, had run away from home to enter a hermitage as serving boy while still in his teens. The Fragrant Sesame Recluse, now sixtyish, described himself as a poor soldierman, but turned out to be an ex-general risen from the ranks in the army of Marshal Wu Pei-fu. Finally, the Tranquil Wisdom Recluse, a pot-bellied, jolly fellow also in his sixties, had until about ten years previously been a silk merchant in Chengtu, but had tired of the quarrels among his ladies and, renouncing his wealth (except for a sum of money spent on restoring the hermitage and adding to its amenities), had joined the community on an impulse born of a two-day stay there during the festival of the Pole Star Deity. Naturally, not all these details were forthcoming at dinner and I owe most of them to the Moon Rabbit Recluse, their doyen; even so, they were cheerfully unreticent and most willing to answer whatever questions I chose to ask. (Had only one, rather than two, of the five once been a man of substance and standing, the proportion would have been more typical of such communities in general.)

Despite spiritually unpromising backgrounds, all were now devoted followers of the Way and could properly be described as adepts. Living in a place so remote from ordinary life and spending many hours a day in study or in contemplation with the mind turned in upon itself, they had been weaned from the world of dust and were as full of gaiety and laughter as a party of undergraduates, with something of an undergraduate's fondness for prankish humour. For over twenty years, three of the five had been living together in what, until the ex-silk merchant's arrival, had been a ruinous hermitage. The former general had been with them only for a year or so, having 'left the world' in his native Kiangsu province after the defeat of the scholarly Marshal Wu during the civil wars of the 1920s. The two little boys were the sons of local farmers who had welcomed the opportunity of placing them in service with people able to make scholars of them. None of the five recluses had received much of an education in the modern sense, the general having risen from the ranks and the silk merchant having inherited his father's business while still a high-school student. The lifelong Taoist had left the world as an illiterate teenager; my friend and the 80-year-old had neither of them completed their primary education. Now, all except the ex-general were scholars in the traditional sense, and even he had discovered a flair for witty extempore doggerel. This was a common state of affairs not often taken into account by the critics of Taoism, who seem to be under the misapprehension that to be without a high-school or university education was a grave disadvantage; that may be so generally, but not in circumstances such as these. Ignorant no doubt of matters outside their chosen field, the inmates were often erudite in the subjects that mattered for cultivation of the Way. All were steeped in the words of Lao and Chuang, in those of sages like Wei Po-yang and Ko Hung, and in the poems and essays of lovers of mountain solitudes. Their conversation, even when light and jovial, betrayed such learning. Their manners and attitudes were more redolent of what the Chinese mean by a background 'perfumed by books' than those of modern university students.

It was their custom to rise at dawn, summer and winter, there being no clock or watch within the walls. Breakfasting in their cells on tea and millet gruel with scones or fried twists of dough, they usually remained in seclusion for the greater part of the morning, each performing such meditations, yogas or studies as seemed best to him, except on the days appointed for visits to their current teacher, an elderly recluse who resided further up the mountain. The stocky Cloud Mother Recluse, being younger than the others, had taken on the tasks of overseeing the serving boys, attending to the housekeeping and to the tiny patch of garden. He could be said to run things, to the small extent that running was needed, and could count on help from his elderly colleagues, of whom all but one were capable of carrying and lifting, etc., when necessary. Several of them took it in turns to go down the mountain or even travel to the provincial capital, Si-an, when such journeys were needed for stocking up supplies or selling the herbs they had gathered. Lunch was a communal meal, eaten with a good appetite and plenty of conviviality. Weather permitting, the afternoons were spent out of doors, either in the garden and tending the shrubs in the courtyard, or going further afield in search of herbs, or just walking about in what, during most of the year, must have seemed like fairyland. Besides their yogic exercises, they practised *t'ai chi ch'üan* under the general's expert guidance; and the two boys received instruction in wrestling and swordsmanship from him. Around sunset, they returned to their rooms and continued the serious cultivation practised in the mornings. Some passed much of the night in meditation. When pilgrims came for the festivals, these pursuits were interrupted and various rituals performed, which the old gentlemen enjoyed because it gave them opportunities to indulge in stately dance movements and show off their expertise with flutes, *hu ch'in* viols, and all kinds of percussion instruments.

When the weather was inclement, they had amusements for whiling away the afternoons. Besides painting, calligraphy, composing poems and reading, they enjoyed preparing charms for the pilgrims (an additional source of income), employing the picturesque magic scripts which are so suggestive of nature's flow, of the passing of one thing into another. Also, the ex-general had grown very fond of the kind of chess known as *wei ch'i*, an exceedingly ancient game played with white and black stones, one hundred and sixty or more on each side. Popular among military and naval men in China and Japan, as well as among scholars, its 361-square board may be regarded as a battlefield, whether for a contest between two armies or between the opposing creative and destructive forces of nature. (It is said that in the cloud realms of immortals this game is played with the lives of human beings for stakes, each white gain saving a life, each black gain costing one.) *Wei ch'i* is Taoistic in character, for the skilful player learns to build up his strength wherever his opponent is weakest, thus emulating the action of water. Finding no worthy opponent among his colleagues, the general used to visit other hermitages in search of good players; for often the recluses would exchange visits and pass an afternoon sipping tea and nibbling melon seeds in hermitages at a comfortable distance from their own.

Summer pastimes included visits further afield, picnicking at various beauty spots, swimming in the clear mountain streams and pools, holding contests in extempore verse making at places specially noted for views of the rising or setting sun, the full moon and so on. Some of the neighbouring communities included skilled gardeners expert in helping nature to excel herself, although, as if to redress the balance, one of their pursuits was as artificial as could well be imagined, for they loved to train shrubs to resemble birds and animals, including dragons, unicorns and phoenixes. There were also experts in the growing of dwarf trees and I have seen cedars or pines less than a foot in height which showed signs of being between fifty and a hundred years old. In most hermitages could be found miniature landscape gardens complete with mountains, pools, caves, trees and little houses and men, each garden rising from an oblong earthenware container about two foot long and one foot wide, or even smaller.

When it was time for me to say farewell, collect my worthless 'guide' and go down the mountain back to Si-an and thence to Peking, the Moon Rabbit Recluse begged me to return one day. 'You must come in spring or autumn for one of our festivals, since you are fond of the sound of flutes by moonlight. You will hear some ancient melodies sacred to just one day of the year. In summer there are the wild flowers I spoke of and a pool so clear that you can peer down at a miniature forest of waving plants growing deeper down than a man can dive. Who knows but that its genie, the dragon I mentioned, will not emerge to make the acquaintance of a distinguished young foreign gentleman? At least you will see fish darting in and out of the "forest" like tigers stalking their prey. If you insist on coming again in winter, choose the First Moon (February); it will be even colder than now, your teeth will chatter, but imagine how splendid this great mountain looks when everything is blanketed by snow! That will inspire you to write poems filled with the spirit of the Way. The sky will be blue as sapphire, the sun red as persimmon. Seeing its light shining upon a universe of dazzling snow, you will understand what is meant by the "glistening void". Contemplating such a sight, you may well win suddenly to full attainment and thenceforth laugh your way through life, never having further cause for tears!'

I hope my picture of those honorable immortals is worthy of them. Men of shy elusive wisdom, too simple to hold their own in scholarly debate, they had intuitive perception of a world of tranquil, joyous beauty far beyond my, in some ways more sophisticated, understanding. Nothing extraordinary was likely to happen in their company; there was none of the atmosphere of awesome and perhaps dark mysteries that one senses in temples where the folk religion predominates, no talk of conjuring up or subduing demons, nothing exciting or dramatic, nothing that can easily be caught in words. Apart from the beauty of the mountain scenery (which on that occasion was lost in mist) and a manner of life belonging to an ancient world then rapidly vanishing, there were no marvels. And yet such a hermitage was a place of miracles – miracles unspectacular but profound and light-bestowing. Outwardly jovial and relaxed, often engaged in pursuits that seemed irrelevant to mighty spiritual endeavour, the recluses lived and had their being perpetually on holy ground (by which I do not mean merely that they inhabited a holy mountain). Some no doubt were close to or had already attained true immortality; they had passed safely beyond the realm of passions and desires; but such was their modesty that a traveller who came upon them knowing nothing of their inner life might have enjoyed their hospitality and returned to the plains below unaware of having done more than pass a day or two in the company of cheerful and amusing old men! It would not have occurred to them to speak, even to one another, of having attained anything at all. If one asked them such questions as whether they felt they still had far to go before reaching the end of the Way, their answers might lead one to suppose them idle creatures, pleasantly touched with madness. They would be sure to burst out laughing and protest that they had not thought of going anywhere at all, or do something unconventional such as mooing like a cow or dancing a few steps to indicate the folly of the question. They loved to refer to themselves as idlers or wanderers 'loafing about the world' and their eyes would twinkle if they found someone gullible enough to take them seriously.

As soon as one had an inkling of what cultivating the Way implies, it became easier to decide what lay behind their smiling disclaimers. The atmosphere in temples or hermitages where no real cultivation was taking place was very different; there, recluses stood on their dignity and one sometimes felt as though watching a charade. With men of true attainment, their sincerity could never be in doubt. Even if one knew too little of their language to be able to converse with them, their presence was sufficient to communicate feelings of tranquil joy and an incredible stillness. When one practised meditation in their company, results could be achieved of a very different order from those normally obtained. In their vicinity, sorrows and anxiety fell away and serenity spilled forth.

Beyond this, there is a dramatic means of identifying those rare beings who have reached the very highest attainment. During a conversation with such a being on some serious subject, an opportunity may occur to look, without making one's intention obvious, straight into his eyes, or, in special circumstances, he may himself choose to confer a revelation (as, on one unforgettable occasion, happened to me). In either case, it is as though for an ecstatic moment a curtain has been twitched aside revealing unimaginable immensities; for the space of a single flash of thought, one shares the vastness of a sage's inner vision! The bliss is indescribable, but not to be endured for more than a fraction of a second, its intensity being too great to be borne by ordinary mortals. Either he, knowing what is occurring, will lower his eyes, or one must tear away one's own. The fruit of such a momentous encounter is of inestimable worth, for never again will one's conviction of the reality of the supreme apotheosis waver.

I cannot say whether any of the five recluses just described would have been able to provide such evidence of the highest possible attainment. Knowing nothing of such things at the time, I did not think to look for it; but I do remember feeling a lovely stillness in their presence, which was all the more remarkable in that I had not learnt to expect anything of the kind.

Extraordinary signs of being far advanced along the Way are not peculiar to Taoists. I have occasionally met Chinese Buddhist monks and Tibetan lamas whose presence in itself communicates joy and stillness. Indeed, at the higher levels of yogic accomplishment or spiritual insight, great differences among devotees of different faiths are not to be expected. An accomplished mystic attains the same experiential insight into Reality, whatever path he follows. The one notable difference between Taoists and Buddhists, apart from their views on the subject of reincarnation, is that the latter tend to put more stress in their teaching on compassion, which together with wisdom forms the very core of Buddhist practice. At one time I used to think that this difference pointed to a defect in the teaching and practice of Taoism – now I am not so sure. From the earliest times, Taoists have been chary about speaking of the need for such virtues as benevolence, filial piety, righteousness, compassion; for, as Lao-tzû says: 'Cease this talk of benevolence and righteousness and the people will be benevolent and kind.' He goes on to point out that making much of these virtues is a sure sign of their absence. Why stress what should be as common as the air we breathe? A follower of the Way is by definition a stranger to anger, cupidity and selfishness. Aware that individuality is but a shadow, a delusion born of ignorance, he sees that 'I' and 'other' have no place in the seemless Tao, that causing harm to others is the very negation of *wu wei* and of the pure selflessness needed for attainment.

At most one could say that the Taoist attitude to compassion is more negative than the Buddhist, and even this may be an assumption based on no more than a difference in the way of putting things.

Writing this last chapter has caused me pain from which an accomplished Taoist would doubtless be immune. It is sad to recall that, even though the ancient hermitages still stand amidst the mountains, no smoke now rises above their roofs. Nothing remains but poems and memories, unless now and then some wayfarer surreptitiously thrusts a stick of lighted incense among the cold ashes in a tripod standing before a crumbling shrine. How gladly I would brave the coldest wind, the icy mountain paths and snow-drifts piled before the lacquer gates for the pleasure of once more sipping tea with an immortal, gazing upon his wise old face and hearing his merry laughter! It is good that I reached China in time to see many lingering traces of the beauty that, even in those days, was fast vanishing. The other day I came across a poem written by Li Po in the depths of his mountain solitude. Drunk with wine and beauty, he cries: 'I am three with the moon and my shadow!' In the China of today, living alone and cultivating stillness is a sheer impossibility. It is probably a crime to wish to do so!

Appendix

Tables Pertaining to the Wu Hsing Five Activities (Science)

A brief account of the science of *wu hsing* will be found in Chapter 1. The following tables are provided mainly for the convenience of users of the *I Ching* (*Book of Change*). With the help of Table 1, trigrams forming the lower and upper sections of a hexagram can be related to the appropriate *hsing* and these *hsing* will provide additional data on the hexagram's significance, which may be incorporated in the final reading or be taken into consideration during the process of interpreting the hexagram.

The science of *wu hsing* is often practised independently of the *I Ching*, but involves matters unfamiliar to most Westerners and not easy to deal with in a few pages. For what it is worth, therefore, I pass on the suggestion of a Vietnamese friend which, he claims, will obviate the need for special knowledge:

The *wu hsing* science enables mortals to understand, foresee and to some extent manipulate the unfolding of events. Normally, a professor of this science is called upon to identify the various *hsing* involved in a sequence of events, their relative strengths, mutual relationships and so on. In the absence of an expert, one may use coins or yarrow stalks to obtain *I Ching* trigrams, one for each component of the situation to be studied. These trigrams will indicate which *hsing* are involved. By studying the relationships among these *hsing* [from the tables] and giving more or less weight to each in accordance with the corresponding components of the situation, it is possible to discover how things are likely to turn out and what steps must be taken in order to alter the result in the manner desired. Thus, whereas the expert determines the *hsing* involved and their relative weight *vis à vis* one another by a hundred different means for which specialised wisdom and knowledge are required, the amateur can obtain the same results much more simply.

Table 1 *I Ching Trigram Correlations*

Trigram	Hsing	Flourishes or dominates in	Declines or oppresses in
1 Ch'ien — Heaven 2 Tui — lake	metal	autumn	summer
3 Li — fire	fire	summer	winter
4 Chên — thunder 5 Sun — wind	wood	spring	autumn
6 K'an — water	water	winter	turns of season
7 Kên — mountain 8 K'un — earth	earth	turns of season	spring

Table 2 *Wu Hsing Correspondences*

Activity	wood	fire	earth	metal	water
Direction	east	south	centre	west	north
Colour	blue/green	red	yellow	white	black
Numbers	8 and 3	2 and 7	10 and 5	4 and 9	6 and 1
Climate	windy	hot	wet	dry	cold
Planet	Jupiter	Mars	Saturn	Venus	Mercury
Sound	shouting	laughing	singing	weeping	groaning
Virtue	benevolence	propriety	faith	rectitude	wisdom
Emotion	anger	joy	sympathy	grief	fear
Hour	3–7 a.m.	9 a.m.–1 p.m.	{1–3, 7–9 a.m. {1–3, 7–9 p.m.	3–7 p.m.	9 p.m.–1 a.m.
Animal	dragon	phoenix	ox	tiger	snake, tortoise
Celestial Stem:					
(yin)	i	ting	chi	hsin	kuei
(yang)	chia	ping	wu	kêng	jên
Terrestrial Branches:	yin, mao	ssû, wu	ch'ou, wei, ch'ên, hsû	shên, yu	tzû, hai
Zodiac	{Gemini, {Cancer	{Virgo, {Libra	{Taurus, {Leo, {Scorpio, {Aquarius	{Sagittarius, {Capricorn	{Aries, {Pisces

Table 3 *Normal Wu Hsing Interrelationships*

(< symbolises 'gives birth to', 'produces', 'assists'; > symbolises 'checks', 'opposes', 'harms', 'destroys'; † symbolises 'is subjugated by'.)

metal < water < wood < fire < earth < metal
metal > wood > earth > water > fire > metal
metal † fire † water † earth † wood † metal

Table 4 *Metrical Verse Showing Correspondences between the Hsing and the Seasons.*

In spring, the trees are clad in dazzling green;	(wood)
In summer, blazing sunshine lights the scene;	(fire)
While melancholy autumn's tints are gold,	(metal)
And streams are frozen hard by winter's cold.	(water)
Through all the seasons, earth remains serene.	(earth)

Table 5   *Further Seasonal Correspondences*

In spring   wood burgeons, fire aids, water rests, metal's stopped, earth 'dies'.
In summer fire   „   , earth „ , , wood   „ , water   „   , metal   „ .
In autumn metal   „   , water , , , earth   „ , fire   „   , wood   „ .
In winter   water   „   , wood , , , metal   „ , earth   „   , fire   „ .

Note. This table makes it obvious that *hsing* ought not to be rendered 'element'. Elements do not die, but activities can do so. The meaning is that, during each season, one activity is dominant, a second helpful to it, a third neutral, a fourth temporarily blocked, a fifth ceases to act.

Table 6   *Further Interrelationships among the Hsing*

This will be found the most useful table of all, either for shedding additional light upon hexagrams received in answer to inquiries made during divination with the *I Ching*, always taking the lower trigram as representing the primary activity and the upper trigram, as subsidiary to it; or for divining the outcome of a situation in the light of the *hsing* alone. In the latter case, a trigram is obtained with yarrow stalks or coins to represent each person and each factor involved in the situation; the *hsing* should be weighed against one another in accordance with (a) their interrelationships and (b) the relative importance, sequence and relationships of the factors in the situation to which each pertains.

The data given in verse 1 reveals a favourable relationship between two *hsing* that may be seriously upset if the second of a pair is present in overwhelming strength. The data in verse 2 reveal the unfavourable consequences of activities good in themselves if they are carried to excess. Verse 3 reveals that there are circumstances in which the normal relationships between *hsing* may be reversed. Verse 4 indicates unfavourable circumstances for which there is no remedy. Verse 5 reveals that, where one *hsing* is present in very great strength, it is immune from the effects of one of the other four, except in the case of fire with earth.

1 a Metal relies on earth for birth; but where reath's aplenty metal 'dies'.
   b Earth   „   „ fire   „   „   „   „   fire   „   earth is
                                                              scorched.
   c Fire   „   „ wood „   „   „   „   wood   „   fire blazes.
   d Wood   „   „ water „   „   „   „   water   „   wood drifts.
   e Water   „   „ metal „   „   „   „   metal   „   water boils.
2 a Metal doth give birth to water; but where water's aplenty metal sinks.
   b Water   „   „   „   „ wood   „   „   wood   „   water
                                                              shrinks.
   c Wood   „   „   „   „ fire   „   „   fire   „   wood burns.
   d Fire   „   „   „   „ earth   „   „   earth   „   fire dies.
   e Earth   „   „   „   „ metal   „   „   metal   „   earth wanes.

3 a Metal overcometh wood; but where wood's aplenty metal fails.
   b Wood   „   earth   „   „   earth   „   woods' destroyed.
   c Earth   „   water   „   „   water   „   earth floats away.
   d Water   „   fire   „   „   fire   „   water gleams.
   e Fire   „   metal   „   „   metal   „   fire's put out.
4 a Metal hath not the strength of fire and therefore melts.
   b Fire   „   „   „   „   „ water „   „   'dies'.
   c Water   „   „   „   „   „ earth „   „   silts.
   d Earth   „   „   „   „   „ wood „   „   shifts.
   e Wood   „   „   „   „   „ metal „   „   falls.
5 a Metal, when powerful, if attacked by water can resist its fury.
   b Water,   „   „   „   „   „ wood dispels wood.s power.
   c Wood,   „   „   „   „   „ fire weakens the flames' voracity.
   d Fire,   „   „   „   „   „ earth just moves its flames else-
                                                  where.
   e Earth,   „   „   „   „   „ metal swallows the obstruction.

Example of Divination

As I am quite unskilled in this science, I shall not presume to offer examples based on my own experience; but I do recall an anecdote which indicates generally how to set about matters. In its original form, the story contained a lot more data on *hsing* than in the version that follows; the latter must be taken, therefore, only as a very general guide to the method.

Chin Hui, a district magistrate, once travelled all the way from Honan province to Mao Shan, a sacred mountain far to the south, to consult a certain Master of the Five Activities. 'My mother-in-law', he declared bluntly, 'is a tiresome hag forever interfering in my domestic affairs. My wife, though distressed on my behalf to the point of shedding tears, yields to the old harridan on every occasion, claiming that the laws of filial piety require her to put a good face on things and do what that wretch requires. As you may well imagine, my household is all at sixes and sevens. My own lictors laugh behind their sleeves whenever they hear our voices raised, which is often enough to affright the ghosts of the departed let alone all the living people within the vicinity of my *yamên* [official residence]. If things go on like this, the sacred authority vested in me by the Dragon Throne will be gone like a summer cloud or brought into contempt. Therefore have I come, and now beseech Your Immortality to pronounce a remedy.'

At this, the venerable immortal, who was having some difficulty in preserving his gravity, asked for the fullest possible details concerning His Honour's highly respected mother-in-law. It transpired that the old lady's maiden name was Li, a homonym of the *I Ching* trigram for fire, that the Celestial Stems and Terrestial Branches indicated by her hour and date of birth also pointed to a preponderance of fire, and that she had even managed to be born in a month of which part of the name was another homonym for fire. Naturally, varying proportions of the other *hsing* were woven into the whole, but it could not be disputed that the fire *hsing* was the main constituent of her personality and circumstances. Next to this, metal was present to a considerable extent and its proportion had been augmented somewhat by her marriage into the Chin family, since *chin* means gold, the metal of metals. As to Chin Hui's own affinities, earth predominated; metal came not far behind. The immortal, having given thought to the matter proclaimed that, since these two persons both had a secondary affinity with metal, this *hsing* could be discounted. The way to attack the problem was to concentrate upon the interrelationships between fire and earth, not altogether disregarding those between certain other *hsing* involved, but allocating to them a relatively minor importance.

'Your Honour,' he continued, 'the olding saying "where fire's aplenty, earth is scorched" is a telling description of your grave predicament. Since "earth relies on fire for birth", there is nothing surprising in the old lady's running your life for you. Nevertheless, it is also written "where earth's aplenty, fire dies". There should be no difficulty in strengthening your complement of the earth *hsing*. You could, for example, wear undergarments of yellow and avoid arguments with your respected mother-in-law except during the ox, dragon, sheep and dog hours [namely from 1 to 3 and 7 to 9, both a.m. and p.m.] at which times earth predominates.' Adding various further instructions for supplementing his store of earth *hsing*, the immortal advised his distinguished client not to hesitate to shout the old lady down, provided the proper hours of the day were chosen for the purpose. 'The hour of the dog is especially propitious to such an undertaking. That is a time when it might be appropriate to pretend to lose your temper and threaten her furiously with a hundred strokes of the thick bamboo your lictors wield upon the more vicious types of criminal when so commanded by the court. Your troubles arise from your being too good-natured. From now on be careful to hide your kind heart behind the face of a scowling demon.'

Chin Hui carried out these instructions to the letter, but with an unlooked for result; for the old lady was cowed by this new treatment only for as long as it took her to realise that her son-in-law would never go so far as to use actual violence upon the body of the woman who had given birth and suck to the wife on whom he doted. Coming to this conclusion, she subjected him to even fiercer torrents of invective and more thoroughgoing interference in his domestic arrangements than before. Finally things reached such a pitch that Magistrate

Chin flew into a rage that led to his losing consciousness; and within three days he had yielded up his twin souls to the celestial and nether regions.

On hearing the distressing news of his client's demise, the Master of the Five Activities grew thoughtful. That evening, when treating his disciples to a learned discourse, he remarked: 'When the fire element rages in its fury and the earth element lacks sufficient cohesion, unless one is possessed of unusual wisdom, there is very little to be done. A sage would have succeeded where Chin failed, simply because it was in his nature to fail, just as it is in the nature of a sage to succeed in everything by going along with things instead of trying to overcome them. Nature, you will find, takes her course whether men say yea or nay.'

'Then what', inquired one of the disciples, is the purpose of our learning the science of *wu hsing* ?'

'Ah well,' replied the Master, 'sometimes one can give nature a little push, if one knows the art of it; but it must be a push very nearly in the direction things were going any way. The late magistrate should have closed his ears and let the old lady talk herself to a standstill and then remarked quietly: "Do pray excuse my inattentiveness. Would you kindly go over all of that again." That is what is called "putting out the fire by exhausting the fuel".'

Printed in the United States
by Baker & Taylor Publisher Services